KURT KAISER

KURT KAISER

ICON AND CONSCIENCE OF CONTEMPORARY CHRISTIAN MUSIC

TERRY W. YORK

1845 BOOKS

© 2024 by 1845 Books, an imprint of Baylor University Press
Waco, Texas 76798

All Rights Reserved. No part of this publication may be reproduced, stored in a retrieval system, or transmitted, in any form or by any means, electronic, mechanical, photocopying, recording, or otherwise, without the prior permission in writing of Baylor University Press.

Cover and book design by Elyxandra Encarnación
Cover photograph by Alan Vandergriff

Library of Congress Cataloging-in-Publication Data

Names: York, Terry W., author.
Title: Kurt Kaiser : icon and conscience of contemporary Christian music / Terry W. York.
Description: Waco, TX : Baylor University Press, 2024. | Includes bibliographical references. | Summary: "Profiles the life, career, influence, and legacy of Contemporary Christian Music artist and composer Kurt Kaiser"-- Provided by publisher.
Identifiers: LCCN 2023050049 (print) | LCCN 2023050050 (ebook) | ISBN 9781481316729 (paperback) | ISBN 9781481322027 (adobe pdf) | ISBN 9781481322010 (epub)
Subjects: LCSH: Kaiser, Kurt. | Composers--United States--Biography. | Pianists--United States--Biography. | Contemporary Christian musicians--United States--Biography.
Classification: LCC ML420.K1215 Y67 2024 (print) | LCC ML420.K1215 (ebook) | DDC 782.25/164092 [B]--dc23/eng/20240213
LC record available at https://lccn.loc.gov/2023050049
LC ebook record available at https://lccn.loc.gov/2023050050

for Pat

"For me, sound has its beginnings in silence.
Music is an awakening from stillness."

—Kurt Kaiser, from the liner notes of *Kurt Kaiser: The Lost Art of Listening*, 1995

"There are some rules in music that are not to be tampered with, not to be broken. And I think, as I get older, people have a respect for that when they talk to me, when they deal with me, because they know, if we're going to talk to Kurt, Kurt knows what he's talking about, or whatever. So, I can't do things because he'll know that they're wrong. And I do think that that's true."

—Kurt Kaiser in an interview with his daughter, Kris Kaiser Olson, 2009

CONTENTS

Preface: On Biographies, and This One   ix

Acknowledgments   xv

Introduction   1

1   Owning the Gift   11

2   WORD Music and Kurt Kaiser Music   57

3   Icon and Conscience of Contemporary Christian Music   99

4   Adopted Son of Waco and Baylor University   127

5   A Church Musician   145

Conclusion   165

Appendix: Kurt Kaiser Memorial Service   169

Afterword   171

Notes   173

Bibliography   181

Index   191

PREFACE
On Biographies, and This One

Let it be known in these early pages that the backbone of this biography is an extensive recorded, and then transcribed, interview of Kurt by Kurt and Pat's daughter, Kris Kaiser Olson. The interview spanned several sessions in 2008–2009. We are in Kris' debt for her foresight. Long before the writing of this book she envisioned such a project and convinced her father that he should record the memories and insights of his life while he could still do so with some confidence. But a backbone must be fleshed out with additional skeletal structure, muscle, sinew, organs, blood, and a heartbeat. Toward that end, additional sources of information were sought and studied. Those sources included the following:

Recordings: a multitude of LPs, cassettes, CDs, and digital recordings of music, as well as videos and radio interviews;

Hard copy documents from Kurt's backyard office bungalow: letters, personal notes, contracts, and handwritten musical scores, as well as programs from performances, conferences, and award ceremonies;

Books, articles, and unpublished sources: published books, self-published books by family members, articles, and an unpublished thesis and dissertation;

Personal interviews: author interviews of Kurt's family, friends, colleagues, and fellow recording artists;

Personal recollections: this author's friendship with Kurt.

The simplest approach to this project would have been to take the transcription of Kris Kaiser Olson's interviews of her father and simply "connect the dots." A reliable timeline would have been established and reported. But, taken alone, without commentary or analysis, the result would have lacked a pulse, would have been offered without context. *Kurt Kaiser: Icon and Conscience of Contemporary Christian Music* was written with the intention of finding that pulse, uncovering what it was about Kurt that makes us want to listen to and learn from him once more. This book was written with the intention of understanding a bit more clearly what it is that pulls us into his music, even now. The pulse we seek is that of Kurt's "blood" coursing through the material at hand.

We write and read biographies with the hope that faith in humankind will still be rewarded and can still be renewed, even in our time, whenever that time might be. We hope that our lives, in comparison to the one studied, for whatever reason they are being studied, will show us to be at least average citizens, if not as notable as the one in the book. How are we doing? How is the world doing? Might there be in us and our world, good to which we have become blinded? We read.

This book is about a man who attracted attention, not from everyone, but from particular audiences at key moments. He was noticed because the work he did exposed his genius. His humility couldn't hide it. His work became a platform upon which he displayed God-given giftedness in front of Christian worshipers who knew that some of their praise and prayer could be most fully and properly expressed in song. These singers of worship lived the dynamic tension between the songs of long-ago Zion, and the singing of a New Song. Kurt Kaiser made timely contributions to this ushering from one expression to the other along the path of an ever developing and expanding repertory for the journey. His work was on display in front of people who first noticed his musicianship, then quickly and comfortably his Christian commitment.

We looked to him then, and we look to him now, with both gratitude and hope. Our gratitude is for his excellent stewardship of talent. Our hope is that we might catch a glimpse of ourselves also making a bit of a contribution.

In a sense, a biographer is a translator, an interpreter. The methodology is to translate life-to-life, rather than only asking what we can glean from one song, or one statement, or one isolated action of the individual being studied. In a life-to-life translation, we will seek to enrich our lives by studying Kurt Kaiser's life as a whole. We must hear the song "Pass It On" as something that emerged from his life, not merely from one of his youth musicals. We must see in his impeccable musicianship more than perfect pitch. We must see devoted stewardship of gift and life. The biographer is a translator, and at times an interpreter, of a life.

On the spectrum of written communication, biography is positioned somewhere between journalism and literature. This writer is neither reporter nor artist, claiming no title other than reliable commentator. Journalism contributes to biography the weight of being factual.

Literature makes its claim at the point of connecting and interpreting facts in engaging and relatable storytelling. Biographers must be humble and careful in their commentary, for a book is to be about the name in the title, not the name on the "by" line. Even so, authors possess an inescapable and personal worldview, a lens through which they observe human behavior and dare to suggest or assign value.

Biography is a means of seeing ourselves more clearly than we do when we gaze into a mirror. When we observe our weaknesses in others, we can face them without turning away; likewise, we can assess our strengths without self-centeredness. This is not *using* the subject of the biography but rather *learning from* the subject of the biography. Here, in these pages, Kurt Kaiser is once again our teacher. In looking through the eyes and the life of another person, someone who has drawn our attention for one reason or another, we can see more clearly our institutions and inclinations, our culture and society, our agendas and prejudices. Biography invites us to an out-of-body experience without risking death. It underscores the importance of understanding our vantage point's prejudices and uniqueness.

Kurt Kaiser sensed early on a certain responsibility to embrace and share the treasure of exciting and meaningful experiences that were coming his way in an ever-increasing flow. His faithful stewardship of experiences was held and nurtured humbly, and without any assurance that anyone would ever care. He saved documents of every sort, documents that were artifacts of both routine and special moments. He kept this treasure of observation tucked away in nondescript boxes, files, and, more securely so, letters to his beloved fiancé/wife across the years of his art and ministry. The chronicling that took place in his letters to Pat were the richest gifts that he had to share as he traveled, learned, and grew. In this way, the letters' value was liquidated in real time. Her treasured contribution in return was to keep it all in proper perspective.

Biography moves us toward healthy respect for ourselves and for others—perhaps, we might hope, moving us to extend grace to ourselves as well as to others.

There is poetry in biography. It is found in the meter and rhythm and rhyme of how the person lived their life. Every person's living bores a hole through life experience, a hole that lets in light and shapes that light; a hole that lets in air and freshens it. In these pages, we set out to explore the light-filled tunnel and fresh breezes that were Kurt Kaiser's life and work, the air we breathe as we sing his songs, and the light that glows when we listen.

It is no small thing to immerse oneself in someone else's story. To do so is to suppose that there are lessons to be learned in the life being studied and the risks that may accompany the dive. This immersion leads us to lessons similar to those learned in successful marriages and deep friendships, two sources of enriching life-energy. The challenge is one of integrity, to maintain your own story and identity while exploring the details and vast landscapes of someone else's life. When one writes or reads a worthy biography, two lives meet, and for a dedicated season live together in one "self." We cannot internalize the life of another without some sort of a "third thing" being born. That third thing is the vision of what our lives, now seasoned by another's, might grow to be.

We seek a simple transition into this third thing by embracing the hope of an enhanced self. But there is, in fact, much more that emerges with this third thing. It is the marriage itself. It is the friendship itself. In the case at hand, it is life itself. Biography results in something that is not exactly what the subject's life was and is not exactly what the reader's life might become. The writer's/reader's life combined with the subject's life produces the third thing: a conversation about living. As we have said, to write a biography must be, it would seem, akin to translating. In translating a poem from one language to another, something is lost, something is added, yet an essence is retained, honored, embraced, and communicated. We must have faith in the translator, but not the faith that we have in God. Neither the translator nor the biographer is all-knowing. The translator, the biographer, and their readers must be at home in an environment of lingering questions and vulnerable conclusions.

Indeed, to write a biography, one must allow something to die; not some*one*, but some*thing*. One must allow awe to die. One must allow hero-worship to die. If awe and heroics appear, they must be the result of facts—facts held at arms' length by the writer. The writer must allow wonder to dim, if it will. One must press through wonder to see both the sunshine and the clouds of everyday life, for greatness can only be detected and measured against a background of recognizable routine. The person being studied must first be one of "us" in one way or another, perhaps in a way yet to be discovered, if she is later to lift us up by means of her uniqueness. In these pages we sing of a near saint, without filling in the gap to complete the canonization. To fill the gap by means of hagiography, or even with tempered admiration, would be to discount the importance of unadorned life and work.

At the time of this writing, Kurt Kaiser is not a vague character from the distant past. Many who read this will have known him, loved him, worked with him. They will have been shaped by the spirituality of his music. His voice still echoes in the ears of many. They will listen as they read, to determine if the author knew him as well, as intimately, as they did, to see if this research revealed the essence of the man they knew. This fact is both encouragement and warning to the biographer. The book will not pass all the individual tests. Even so, I hope it will be obvious that I, too, knew him, admired him, and loved him as a brother in Christ.

A biographer should not set out to re-live his subject's life. Neither should a biographer approach his subject's life as if it were an eighty-year laboratory experiment, stilted and sterile. To do so would be to present a strained, mechanical, and cold story of a warm life. This book is about Kurt Kaiser's time within a time. The biographer pursues a spirit, knowing that in the end it is the reader's spirit that selects and opens the book in the first place. It is the connection of spirits that will ultimately determine if the book, eagerly or dutifully read to its conclusion, will be placed within easy reach on the bookshelf or will be tossed, with a disappointed sigh, into the donation box.

To write about Kurt is to write about a teacher, though he never held a faculty position. While it is true that good teachers are always and ever good learners, the maxim is underscored here in the reverse. Kurt Kaiser was a constant learner, therefore a teacher of the first order. Lifelong learners cannot help it. Teaching is the exhaling of one who is consistently inhaling new ideas, new possibilities, new relationships with people, the world, art, and creativity, and who is constantly processing what their surroundings are telling them. A degree in education is not a prerequisite for the native teacher. Even a classroom is unnecessary, for the world is their classroom. The world is where they learn and where they teach. To write about Kurt Kaiser is to write about a teacher of the natural sort, the inevitable and inexhaustible sort.

To write about Kurt Kaiser is to write about giftedness well-stewarded. The stewardship lesson to be learned here does not apply to music alone. It is a lesson applicable to any giftedness, to all talent, used for the good of humanity, applied directly or indirectly, one-on-one or en masse. Can anyone be such a teacher? Yes. Kurt was one of them and was taught by others of them. This is an important facet of what Kurt taught us: one person can.

To write about Kurt is to write about a musician—a composer, conductor, and performer—who understood music as a force with an inward and upward pull. Kurt understood music to be a spiritual force with a spiritual accountability attached. He made music in ways that exposed, as convincingly as anyone could, music as a force and freedom that calls out to all other freedoms. His personal jazz invited a vast array of music's forms and styles to "sit in" on his lifetime performance. Yet his musical call to freedom never broke the bonds of devotion to excellence, to authenticity, to truth, to the Church, or to art.

It has been said that biographers inescapably work from a predisposition either to lift up or to put down the subject of their work. Objectivity was the aim, but to the extent that the maxim is true, this biographer confesses a positive bias.

Kurt's story is best told in moments, conversations, and songs—encounters that hold important insights most surely and tell them most reliably. In this way, we shall proceed.

Terry W. York
Waco, Texas

ACKNOWLEDGMENTS

No one owns the story of Kurt Kaiser—not this author, not this publisher, not the wonderful Kaiser family—and, furthermore, they have no more claim than the remotest nonmusician who never knew Kurt but thoughtlessly hums "Oh, How He Loves You and Me" while at work. Every person who loved Kurt, knew Kurt, met Kurt, or simply encountered Kurt's music possesses a fragment of what made Kurt, Kurt, even if for a moment. The moment is a treasure that belongs to them. Like a jigsaw puzzle, each individual piece matters. Your puzzle piece matters, even if it is underrepresented here, even if the recounting of it after further research is not quite as you remember it, even if it is not present in writing at all. This book does not change the significance of your relationship with Kurt. To each and all who communicated with this author concerning Kurt, I treasure your input. It helped shape this book, and we thank you for sharing it.

As a rule, the names of those whose contacts with the author are acknowledged in the text or footnotes of this book will not be duplicated here. Risking inevitable oversight, other contributors are named in these acknowledgments:

Pat Kaiser must be acknowledged first and foremost. Her frequent trips from her house to the backyard office where much of this book was written provided welcome conversation. Further, those visits often resulted in valuable contributions of things remembered or discovered in a drawer or closet.

The author is indebted to the following for special access to archived radio programs featuring Kurt: Kevin Mungons, WMBI, Chicago, Illinois; Jeff McGarvin, KDUR, Durango, Colorado; Brodie Bashaw, KWBU, Waco, Texas. Further, he is indebted to Lanny Nye of Nye & Associates, Waco, Texas, for providing the turntable and related equipment that facilitated hours of listening to the LPs listed in this book's bibliography.

Between the lines lie conversations with, or correspondence from, Piers Bateman, Lois Bock, Tina English Davis, Ruth Dinwiddie, Benjamin Harlan, Dennis Hill, Nate Kaiser, Les Neugebauer, John Purifoy, Dr. Stephen P. Raley, Phil Shappard, Dr. Scott Smith, Don Wyrtzen, and others.

Retired minister of music and Baylor School of Music graduate David Bolin read the manuscript of this book before it was submitted to the publisher. Rev. Bolin's final place of ministry was the First Baptist Church of Waco, Texas. His experience, expertise, and friendship with Kurt made him a clear-eyed "outside" reader. Finally, my wife, Janna, with her remarkable proofreading skills, helped refine the entire manuscript before it was submitted. Even so, any mistakes and weaknesses in this book are the sole responsibility of the author.

The cover photograph of this book appears on the second inside panel of the case liner of Kurt Kaiser's CD *Legacy* (Kurt Kaiser Music, 5020/21 CD, Waco, Tex., 2013). There, it bears the caption "New Orleans." However, this photo, taken by Alan Vandergriff, appeared in the *Chattanooga News-Free Press* newspaper on Sunday, September 17, 1978. It was one of several photographs included in Richard S. Greene's article "George Beverly Shea Sings Out at 69."

INTRODUCTION

1959

1959 was a liminal year. It was a liminal moment for all that was established in the United States' culture of cultures. Something as new as television and something as old as music history, and everything in between, including the Church, stood at the brink. Everyone and everything was moving into the 1960s assuming only the calendar would change. A time of testing was coming.

In 1959, Rod Serling introduced the American public to *The Twilight Zone*. Americans were falling in love with television, giving that intrusive piece of furniture ever-increasing prominence and influence in their homes. Consumerism was becoming a recognized dynamic within the American culture, with television its seemingly limitless platform. Early, unmanned space exploration was exciting both fear and imagination. Rod Serling's weekly series stirred it all: fear, imagination, and the exploration of art's limits. TV would move from black and white to color, entwining art, entertainment, and real-time information along the way. The worldviews of growing numbers of viewers were expanded, challenged, and shaped by bold images and advancing communication technologies. Rod Serling took the energy of Orson Welles' decades-old radio play, "War of the Worlds," and embedded it more deeply into the cultural psyche week after week on screens in homes. Serling's work, and others like it, fed the new debate of what constituted acceptable and responsible television. Everyone knew that Serling's stories were not just entertainment, they were art. The stories were fiction, but there was truth to be seen in the scripts and the acting. What is the difference between art and fact, and what influence does mass entertainment have on both?

In 1959, Robert H. Young, a former Marine who spent his time during World War II guarding Pearl Harbor against a second attack, and who would become one of Baylor University's most beloved professors, earned a Doctor of Musical Arts degree from the University of Southern California.

Like many others who would become professors in Southern Baptist universities, colleges, and seminaries, he had studied under the watchful eye of legendary Professor Charles C. Hirt. Young's dissertation was entitled "The History of Baptist Hymnody in England from 1612–1800." This professor of music history had reached back in time to learn truths that could be handed forward to his young students, many of whom would become music ministers in churches—both Baptist and other—around the world. Dr. Young would become one of a small group of Baylor professors with whom Kurt would meet for lunch daily during the school week, contributing to Kurt's ongoing project of maintaining his reputation as a well-rounded musician. Baylor University's School of Music was becoming a center for both foundation and innovation in the music of the Church. There, traditional music became a launching pad for exploration and expansion of what music might become in new and informed combinations of past and future, orthodox and experimental, accepted and imagined sounds. How far forward could church music reach while still honoring its foundational past? Must the past always be present in the future?

Located in Waco, and launched upon his Baylor graduation, Jarrell McCracken's fledgling Christian publishing company, WORD, Inc., was established in 1951 to tell the Good News via entertaining and engaging audio recordings. With McCracken's vision and genius released, WORD would become an incubator for new music, keeping its traditional Christian foundation in place. The company had an unofficial "church": Seventh & James Baptist Church, located directly across the street from Baylor's School of Music.

In August 1959, Kurt Kaiser was driving from the 1950s into the 1960s. In a sense, he was driving from being grounded in what church music *should* be to being encouraged to imagine what it *could* be. Rod Serling was not the only creative person entering a "twilight zone." Kurt was moving his young family from Chicago, Illinois, to WORD's headquarters in Waco, Texas, which sits at the intersection of the Midwest, West, and South. Waco in 1959, because of Baylor University, was one of the capital cities of the Southern Baptist Convention. As far as the Southern Baptist Convention was concerned, Kurt was driving from the mission field to the homeland. There were, of course, Baptists of several sorts in Kurt's beloved Chicago, as well as Catholics, Anglicans, Presbyterians, Methodists, Evangelical Free, etc. But in Southern Baptist parlance and conviction, territory within the United States but outside of the borders of the earlier Confederacy was seen as pioneer missions, a field tended by their Home Mission Board, headquartered in Atlanta. No matter how many churches and denominations an outer region might have, if it had no Southern Baptist churches, or too few of them, the term "mission field" applied. Kurt may have known little about Baptists, but he was driving into a full immersion learning experience among *Southern* Baptists (pun unintended but accepted).

Robert Young was not the only advocate for foundational music bringing renewal to Baylor's academic environment. Kurt's musical skills and his formal music education of two degrees from Northwestern University put him in immediate good standing with the music faculty of Baylor University. Furthermore, his knowledge of and love for the Church and local congregations put him in good standing with the congregation at Seventh & James and the people of Waco and Texas.

Kurt's religious upbringing had taught him to be wary of mixing worship and entertainment, ministry and performance, innate skills and divine call, formal education and biblical faith. His "twilight zone" would be that wrinkle in time and space between a business with the warmth of ministry and ministry with the cool acumen of business. That same fearful region included music making with excellence that gives glory to God, rather than to self, and music making that entertains in the name of the Church, without breaching educational, liturgical, and evangelistic boundaries.

Kurt is driving, but he is not alone. He and Pat and their two young children, Kris and Kent,[1] were driving into a Southern Baptist environment and ethos. Kurt had grown up with a learned wariness about Catholic doctrine and worship. He would have a similar, but milder wariness about the doctrine and worship of Southern Baptists. That would soon change for the positive. Baptist doctrine was not as strict as that of his Plymouth Brethren formation and was a bit more open to exploring the leading edges of new expression in worship, especially in a congregation that was a "university-town church."

As Kurt drove from student to Christian publishing responsibilities, stirrings within the Catholic Church were building toward Vatican II, but it was of no concern to him, if he was even aware. Further, how could that matter to one so consciously "protestant"? Discontent among Catholics concerning worship and culture was billowing like an afternoon thunderstorm but was still just beyond the horizon of Kurt's new morning. In August 1959, Kurt was driving into a decade that would see Vatican II, in response to those concerns, leapfrog Catholics over Protestants in the mission of world evangelism by way of cultural assimilation. Kurt would show up on the scene in time to help protestants who were strategizing about how not to be outdone by Catholics, even if that meant embracing the contemporary culture. Kurt Kaiser would "get it." He would understand. He would recognize the concern and the opportunity. The year 1959 was a time for strategic positioning for Kurt, his energy, and his talents.

Rather than limiting Kurt, high standards and cultural awareness would free him. Vatican II's venture into embracing the "receiving culture" with respect, humility, and creativity challenged evangelistic-minded Protestants, and music was seen as its most likely hand to be extended toward the culture, the church's cutting edge. He would meet the challenge with the perfect combination of God-given talent, young passion for things new, and a solid church-oriented foundation.

PATRICIA ANDERSON

On May 18, 1955, young Northwestern University student Kurt Kaiser wrote a letter to Dr. and Mrs. L. S. Anderson of Worland, Wyoming, asking for their "approval" to give their daughter Pat an engagement ring on her rapidly approaching birthday. The beauty of their sixty-two-year marriage and life partnership shines a warm light back onto the contents of this letter. For that reason (and with Pat's permission) we include here the entire letter:

> Dear Folks—
>
> This is by far the most difficult letter I've ever attempted to write. I only hope that the attempt will meet with your approval. By now I'm sure you know what it is I'm driving at. Well, you're right!
>
> It's really a wonderful thing how that one thing leads to another. And those who know (by experience) tell how much more wonderful it grows as time passes. That thing of course, is love. I must admit that your daughter Pat is just becoming more and more wonderful to me day by day. I can't help but love her—and I don't want any help!
>
> Perhaps you already know of our plans from Pat or Sue [Pat's sister] through letters. (Probably Sue). Frankly, Pat's birthday is coming up soon, and I know of only one thing I'd like to get for her, and that—a ring. We have prayed much about this both privately and when we're together. I feel very definitely that she is the one for me, but only as you approve. I'm not sure, never thought of, what I would do if you said, "No." But, for strange reasons, I feel you'll not give me a rough time—(I hope!)
>
> Future plans we had made, though they may have to be altered a little, are to be married either in one year, or two years. Pretty big decision to make for us both. Humanly, I don't see how we could wait two years, it'll be rough waiting only one. But we have to do so. The reason for the wait

is my schooling. I wish so many times I were a senior instead of a half freshman-half sophomore.

I will be very much interested in your reply. In fact, everything that I've ever dreamed, will either become reality, or crumble.

For some reason, I can almost hear Doc laughing just as loud, and with Gusto, as he possibly can. All I can say is, I'd like to read the letter you wrote when you were in the same wonderful predicament I'm in.

Please give my best regards to Bucky[2]—tell him to write me a short note sometime soon. And folks, June 4 is coming soon, could you write back soon—real soon?

The letter's written, but oh, what a mess! All I can do now is hope and wait for your answer.

Much love—
   In Him,
   Kurt

P.S. I hope Pat <u>never</u> reads this letter!

In fact, Kurt had already proposed to Pat, in an elevator. Pat's parents were in Chicago visiting her and her sister, both of whom were in nursing school. In the elevator of the hotel where her parents were staying, Kurt kissed her and suggested that they "make this permanent." He confessed that he did not have a ring to give her at that time, so they agreed to be "engaged to be engaged."

Pat first remembers seeing Kurt from a distance at a big Youth for Christ gathering at The Church of the Air, a vibrant congregation in Billings, Montana. With the permission of his parents, Kurt was on staff at this church, transferring for a year from his Chicago high school. Pat, too, was still a high school student, in Worland, Wyoming. She commented to her mother, "That sure is a cute guy down there playing piano." Worland and Billings are some 160 miles apart. With Pat's observation, the distance would come to be calculated by a different metric. So, too, the distance between Worland and Chicago (1,200 miles).

During his summer and high school year in Billings, Kurt was not only playing piano for The Church of the Air, but also for the occasional Youth for Christ rally, and as accompanist for evangelistic singer Bill Carle. One of Bill Carle's tours included a week of meetings in Worland, Wyoming. Bill stayed in the hotel. But Kurt stayed in Doctor and Mrs. Anderson's house. It was Pat and Sue Anderson's house, too. Kurt took notice of the sisters. They took notice of him, as did their mother, who commented that Kurt's nose was too big. She did, however, concede

Kurt's High School senior picture (Chicago), 1952

that he would probably "grow into it." Kurt and Pat were in separate locations during their high school years, but after meeting they wrote to each other on a regular basis.

Pat's father was a deeply respected physician who had moved to Worland upon graduating from medical school in Denver during the Great Depression of the 1930s. The first hospital there was above a furniture store. He was also an involved layman in their church, but was, sadly, addicted to drugs and alcohol. Life at home for Pat was a constant swing between wonderful and difficult. It was not uncommon for Dr. Anderson to have his Sunday School class come to their house for dinner. It was a warm, loving, and happy place, when it wasn't a cold place of fear and disappointment.

Her father's condition set the current tone and the constant atmosphere of life in their home. To his credit, Pat's father admitted and regretted his addiction, leaving town at times for treatment. But the unsettling reality that the pendulum could at any time swing toward the addict's dark side was an ever-present part of the home environment Pat knew. Pat's mother, through strength, love, and devotion, kept home life on as even a keel as possible for her children. Her mother also traveled with Pat's father to his treatment sessions in California and Colorado. This was the shaping and strengthening that Pat would bring to her own marriage and motherhood.

When Pat graduated from high school in 1953, she immediately enrolled in the West Suburban School of Nursing in Wheaton, Illinois, affiliated with Wheaton College. Her sister followed her to West Suburban a year later. The two of them chose nursing, having watched their father deliver babies in the hospital above the furniture store, even helping him at times.

Now Pat and Kurt (who had graduated from high school in Chicago in 1952) could date because he, too, was in Chicago, though traveling extensively now with music evangelist Bill Carle. Kurt would leave the Bill Carle team and become a full-time student, enrolled at Northwestern University where he earned two degrees in music. He studied conducting with Northwestern's own Dr. Ewald Nolte and adjunct professor Thor Johnson, conductor of the Cincinnati Symphony.[3] Pat was a student in Wheaton, and Kurt was a student in Evanston, but at least they were geographically closer. They could date, but they couldn't marry while she was in nursing school.

Kurt and Pat married in August of 1956 in the Methodist Church in Worland, Wyoming. They returned to Chicago after the wedding.

Kurt and Pat Kaiser wedding. Worland, Wyoming, 1956

2018

On November 13, 2018, the *Waco Tribune-Herald* newspaper's front page, lead article had this headline: "Composer's Work Helped Shape Worship Music." The article announced to Waco that Kurt Kaiser had died just the day before. The editors knew the city would care. A great deal of music and church and community happened in Waco and in the Kaiser household between 1959 and 2018. Kurt's work with WORD Music, Inc. had been the arena, the stage on which the world would see his talent on display as gift, vocation, and devotion. Indeed, Kurt had driven from off-stage to center stage, from accompanist to maestro. Kurt Kaiser in Chicago, under the strict discipline of his family of origin, became Kurt Kaiser the composer in Waco, rising with the creative freedom of a Church becoming newly young, a Church that wanted to sing a new song. The "Waco Kurt Kaiser" never stopped being the "Chicago Kurt Kaiser" in that he continued to play to an audience of two, his Heavenly Father and his earthly father, but here on a bigger stage. The time was right for new things. Opportunity had taken on a new accent but still spoke in the familiar voice of the Spirit.

Opportunity's horizon had stretched before Kurt as Chicago's soaring skyline had transformed into wide Texas plains. But the same sun still rose and set on the horizon, and what constituted light and darkness for Kurt did not change. Early in Kurt's employment with WORD, he accompanied Paul Myer, WORD Music's "great salesman" in Kurt's memory, to a sales meeting in Miami Beach, Florida. In Kurt's words, "I had never been to Miami Beach, Florida. And it was really a very nice experience. And on a Sunday morning we were up on the beach having one of those really lovely breakfasts, and Paul said to me, 'Kaiser, where would you be now, if you weren't here?' And I looked at my watch, and I said, 'I'd be in Sunday School.'"[4]

WORD Music was not a Southern Baptist entity, but it was as Southern Baptist as Waco, and Texas, and Church "on a Sunday" along the Brazos River. Kurt had helped take Vatican II's cultural inertia and use it for the good of the Kingdom, denominations overlooked. Music in worship was elevated in an instant from fixed and taken for granted, to new arenas of cultural engagement, congregational growth, and youth involvement. Kurt had driven into that developing whirlwind of opportunity and challenge and had taken it on with confidence, encouraging all front-runners in the cause. Here, faith baptized ambition and adventure.

Kurt had driven into what was for him a new awareness of possibilities for the music of the Church, from a Sunday worship orientation to a Monday through Friday business orientation. Change hung in the air like the summer humidity of Chicago and Waco. But freshness, innovation, and opportunity rained down in Waco, and Kurt had been equipped for this journey into all things new by a disciplined yet enabling shaping by congregation, family, and audience.

Too often, the Church is concerned that its music not be embarrassing in the presence of the secular, or the popular. The Church does not want Jesus to be embarrassed by the music that proclaims his gospel. A closer look may reveal that it is we, the Church and its musicians, who do not want to be embarrassed. The motivation of saving face will not propel the gospel. Kurt knew that.

There is another motivation for keeping the Church's music up to date. It is the desire to give believers a voice that tells the truth in the language of the day, which is the language of their heart, their experience. The Church needs language that will, when embracing life and love, tell it like it is. Kurt knew that, as well.

To study a life is to learn about that person's moments. A person's minutes pale and fade, but their moments last, illuminating the trajectory and richness of their life. We learn to fully embrace moments in our lives, recognizing each one as liminal when they appear, by studying the moments in the lives of others. The mystic's eyes are open to the recognition and significance of the moments that enrich us, rather than the minutes that bully us. This is why mystics often seem to be out of touch with reality. In fact, though, it is the mystic who connects us to significance, calling us away from shallowness. Kurt was a mystic who communicated with clarity.

Making music was Kurt's life and breath and mother tongue. It was his "thing," whether it was the big things with world renowned artists on international stages or Wednesday night choir rehearsals with the small volunteer choir of DaySpring Baptist Church in Waco, Texas. With these pages we begin—but only begin—to hear what Kurt heard.

1
OWNING THE GIFT

To own a gift is to accept the responsibility of faithful stewardship of that gift. Otto and Elisabeth Kaiser knew this. Their gift was the chance to emigrate from Germany to the United States as Hitler was coming to power. The blessing was to live on the peaceful side of the Atlantic Ocean, even though they left family members on the other side. By example and instruction, they taught their children to live life to the fullest: work, play, worship, choosing commitments, freedom of movement and travel. Otto and Elisabeth embraced all of life with thankfulness, humility, and generosity. They owned the gift. They taught their children to own the gift into which they were born, and to own their individual giftedness. Their third child was Kurt Frederic Kaiser.

Kurt had a gift and a model for how to own it. Intuitively he understood that responsible ownership includes exploration of the gift. What are the possibilities and opportunities contained within the gift? Toward what end(s) shall the gift be directed? What might he learn from the gift? Certainty and risk must be seen as partners in responsible gift stewardship. Certainty and risk are not the type of partners that take turns coming to the forefront. They are, rather, partners that hold hands, side by side, walking forward in equal pace and prominence. Kurt owned his gift in this way, learning the nuances and intricacies, the art of ownership along the way, throughout his life.

FAMILY OF ORIGIN

Otto Kaiser, Kurt's father, was first and foremost a citizen of the Kingdom of God. Earthly citizenship was not so fixed. What strength and stability there was to be found in earthly citizenship was posited in the blessings of God: family, love, hope, and faith. Born in Hillesmuhle, Germany on February 27, 1905, Otto was still a child when World War I started in August of 1914. In 1926, when Otto, his mother, his six living siblings (his brother Fritz having been killed in combat), and his brother-in-law sailed for America, they were part of a group of thirty-two relatives who departed on the same ship. Germany was suffering in an extended postwar impoverishment. Relatives who had earlier emigrated from Germany to the United States served as sponsors for this latest wave of the hopeful. The terrible residuals of one war were beginning to mix with early unsettling rumors of another war. The economy of war was an economy of death. Otto invested his gifts of hope and faith in an economy of life, and for him that required a move to the United States, and a deep faith in God. Compared to war's economy of death, the disciplines of an economy of life were an easy yoke.

Otto Kaiser and Elisabeth Sumper were from different towns in Germany (she from Kierspe), but they had met and spent time together on a few occasions thanks to the mingling of friends and family. They had become interested in each other to the point that Otto's leaving for America was emotionally heavy for both. After a proposal and engagement (both by mail) survived separation across a couple of years and the Atlantic Ocean, they married in Hammond, Indiana on Saturday, June 15, 1929. Then, Otto recounts:

> On Sunday, we attended the service at the German Methodist Church. Uncle Emil Sumper preached the English sermon, and Uncle Emil Kaiser, the German. We wanted to enjoy the rest of the day in the dunes, but spent most of it on the over-crowded highway!
>
> Soon all guests had left and we moved into our new house which the bride turned into a cozy home, the culmination of a long dream. We continued what our parents had practiced, having family devotions, morning, noon and evening, praying together at the bedside, both praying audibly, thus sharing each other's inner life and also forgiving one another whenever needed.[1]

Otto and Elisabeth would later move to Rochester, New York, and then in October of 1933, they moved to Chicago. In Chicago, Otto worked in maintenance for Sears, Roebuck and Company, retiring from that company in February of 1968.

Kurt's story began in Chicago on December 17, 1934, at 4154 N. Kenneth Street. Three years later, Otto, Elisabeth, and their three children, Sigrid Friede (born in 1930), Helmuth Richard (Dik) (born in 1932), and Kurt Frederic, moved to 2165 W. Sunnyside Avenue in Chicago, Kurt's boyhood home. But the story is not as simple and straightforward as that. In August 1936, Elisabeth and the children sailed to Germany, fulfilling Otto's promise that she could return to Germany for a visit. The ship on which they sailed flew the Nazi flag. Otto didn't go on that trip because the United States was in the midst of the Great Depression; jobs were precious, and wages were low. Tante (Aunt) Emma Kaiser traveled along with Elisabeth to help with the children. It was while his family was away on this trip that Otto decided they could no longer afford to live in their own house. He and his absentee family moved in with the Gasts (his sister Herta and her husband and family) to share their house at 2165 W. Sunnyside Avenue. "When my family returned in January of 1937, they moved with me to a newly decorated 2nd floor apartment in the Gasts' home. The homecoming was muted, for the children returned sick with measles."[2]

The two youngest of Kurt's siblings would be born here, Martin Siegfried (born in 1937) and Gerhard Otto (born in 1940). Later, Kurt would refer to this house and those around it as "All in the Family" houses. The neighborhood was largely a community of families of German descent. Some of the neighbors were Catholic, and Kurt's family had little to do with Catholics, a distancing that young Kurt was taught.[3] Kurt did have a close encounter with a Catholic, despite the wariness. A Catholic girl who lived across the street from the Kaisers threw a snowball and hit Kurt. He ran across the street to chase her and, unfortunately, caught her. When he caught her, she rubbed his face in the snow.

Sigrid, Elisabeth, Otto, Kurt, Helmuth (Dik) (Chicago), c. 1935

Kurt was born into a world filled with God. Life's good things were blessings from God. Life's difficulties were tests from God. The Bible was a book of rules, answers, and promises that were foundational and reliable as both refuge for any current darkness, and illumination for the next step forward. Kurt grew up understanding life to be the constant bringing together of two realities into one awareness, into a singular experience. Two families in his house for years, one upstairs and one downstairs, equaled one extended family. Two languages spoken at home, German and English, equaled one linguistic environment. Two national identities, German and American, comprised one citizenship. Two places of belonging, church and home, constituted a unified sanctuary. These couplets blended into mutuality rather than duality, making it natural for Kurt to assume that two things moving in a similar direction, having similar purpose and function, could and should be embraced as one multifaceted entity. The assumption included the somewhat naive notion that all parties involved would, of course, want this unity, would welcome it as a normal processing of community and enriched existence.

For Kurt, mutuality made singularity of life possible. It protected life and identity against duality and exclusivity. Why, if approached with a bit of creativity and generosity, couldn't traditional and contemporary, business and ministry, worship and evangelism, even though seen by many as separate entities, work in tandem in one company, one composer, one church? After all, creativity is an engine that drives exploration and engenders courage.

In the context of music writing, recording, and publishing, Kurt's taken-for-granted openness (that older good music and newer good music were of equal value) would come to be seen variously as aloofness, entrenchment, or, more positively, freed creativity. In any case, Kurt's tempered openness, combined with his devotion to time-honored standards of music, church, and life, was known or sensed by those around him. He embodied a conscience that some would dismiss as quaint or impractical. Others, however, would come to rely upon this facet of Kurt's person as an external reminder of faded commitments within.

The readiest remembrances of Kurt's childhood, both his and those of his siblings, deal with Kurt's early pianistic talent and his fragile health due to asthma. Kurt's brother Marty remembered: "Many nights I saw my mother and father at Kurt's bedside on their knees, pleading with God to give Kurt relief and let him have a night's rest. Some nights when I could not sleep, I could hear mom and dad praying, not only for God to heal Kurt, but that they would dedicate his life to serving God and his Kingdom if he was healed."[4] Pianistic artistry and fragile health continued, becoming two thin places for Kurt throughout his life, internal holy places where the veil between heaven and earth was very thin indeed, thin enough for Kurt to see and hear the other side. But Kurt wasn't always ill. "Every evening we would all play outside games like 'It' or 'Hide and Seek.' Kurt would play, too. The unwritten rule was, when Kurt's lips began to turn white, the game was over for the night."[5]

Kurt's father eventually purchased the house they were sharing with the Gast family. The Gasts moved to a new street about a mile away, but not before Wally Gast and his brother, Paul, had collected many Kurt Kaiser memories. Even though the Gasts lived downstairs, and the Kaisers lived upstairs, Wally can remember hearing Kurt coughing during the night. Wally's mother would go upstairs to help Kurt's mother administer "medical fumes" for him to breathe. Wally remembered, "Prayer and home medicines were the cures at hand in those days. We did not have modern clinics or medicines."[6] But all was not sickness and fear. Wally could also hear the Kaisers' hymn singing after every meal:

> We also all benefited by a kind of musical heritage. It had been a custom of the Kaisers when they grew up in Germany to read the Bible and to pray and to sing hymns after each evening meal. This we did. Every evening, after the dessert dishes were put away, we'd sing German hymns: "Lobe den Herrn" (Praise to the Lord), "Danke den Herrn, Nein, Niemals Allein" (No Never Alone), and many others. I lived downstairs from the Kaisers, and when I heard them sing I was always jealous because I could hear that they were being accompanied in their singing by cousin Kurt on the piano. I was also jealous because they got done before us and would go out and play in the street while we were still sitting at the table.[7]

Indeed, the upstairs cousins had the advantage when it came to hymn singing. Kurt had been associated with the piano within the Kaiser family since he first picked out a tune on the keyboard at age four or five (accounts vary). Tune ("Jesus Loves Me") advanced to tunes, which advanced to piano lessons. An "elderly" German woman, Frau Helma Liesch, would go to 2165 W. Sunnyside Avenue every Saturday to give music lessons. There were eleven cousins in the house for a period of time, many of whom took either piano or violin lessons from her. A few continued and developed their skills, but, as Wally Gast recalled, "when recital time came, for Frau Liesch's students, it was Kurt Kaiser who was her star pupil." In addition to lesson fees, Frau Liesch was "paid" with a time of conversation, fresh baked kuchen, and coffee with Kurt's mother. Kurt's father would oversee his piano practice between Saturday lessons. After a few years, Kurt would go to Frau Liesch's house for piano lessons. She had studied with a student of Franz Liszt, placing Kurt a "third piano generation" away from Liszt. Knowing one's musical lineage is important for serious students in the world of voice and instrumental private lessons.

Kurt and his siblings knew the kids in the neighborhood, knew where the drunk lived, knew which house had a beauty salon in it, and knew which friend had the best collection of toy soldiers (a badge of honor during World War II). Kurt's awareness of his neighbors was a mosaic of details: who were Catholics, who mowed their lawn once a week, whether it needed it or not, who washed their car once a week even though they never drove it, who raised chickens, who was friendly, and who was grumpy.

Kurt's sister Sig's friend, Hazel May, came to their house every morning to walk to school with Sig. Hazel May always had orange juice around her mouth, and truncating time, he played for both of their weddings. Kids' lives happened, and life unfolded.

standing: Elisabeth, Helmuth (Dik), Sigrid; seated: Otto;
kneeling: Kurt, Martin, Gerhard (Chicago)

Kurt's family didn't own a car, so walking was the order of the day, every day. McPherson Grammar School was just a fifteen-minute walk from the house. But Sunday walks to church, both morning and evening, and walks to the Chicago River on Sunday afternoons, covered longer distances, at least a mile each direction to church and river. These were family walks, seen as routine. Happy memories of walking to their Plymouth Brethren Church, where the sign simply read, "Christian Assembly," inspired Kurt's song, "Sunday Mornin'" in the musical *God's People*. The first stanza recounts, "Walkin' to church on a Sunday morning, Walkin' an' hearing the church bells ring, Seeing the folks who mean everything to us, praising the Lord as we loudly sing!"[8]

On December 7th of 1941, the United States was pulled into war, and Kurt turned seven years old on December 17th. Kurt had two memories of the war. One was when "the police or somebody came into our house and took out the short wave [component of their] radio to prohibit us from tuning it in to Germany, I guess. We had this big clunky radio in the living room, and they took it out."[9] His other memory was their Saturday mornings being given to delivering food and clothing to the post office, to be sent to relatives still living in Germany. In other accounts, this weekly post office ritual did not begin until the war had ended, which sounds much more feasible. Throughout his life, Kurt would ponder from time to time the fact that Japanese Americans were placed in internment camps during World War II, but German American citizens were not. He approached the injustice from two angles: (1) What would it have been like if we had been interned? and (2) Why "them" and not "us"? On one occasion this pondering became a conversation with this author. The questions did not haunt him, but they did intrigue him and turn him inward from time to time.

A wartime story that Kurt learned only after the war involved his maternal grandfather. During the war, Kurt's family in Chicago and Elisabeth's father in Kierspe, Germany could not communicate with each other. After a wonderful six-month visit with Kurt's family in Chicago, his grandfather had returned to Germany just before war broke out. He caught "the last boat back to Germany," and all communication between the two families ceased. Kurt tells the story:

> And so one day he [Kurt's grandfather] left the basement of his house, they were relegated to the basement, and there were Americans [soldiers] living upstairs, where my mother used to live, but they were all pushed down into the basement. My grandfather dared to come upstairs one time and told all

these Americans how much he liked Chicago. And it turned out that the guy [the American soldier] to whom he was talking, lived two blocks away from where I was raised. So that's how he communicated with my family, because he lived on Matros [Street], and we lived on Sunnyside, which was two blocks away. And that's how we found out how they were, and they knew how we were.[10]

Kurt played the piano in grade school for programs and graduations. But when he got to Lane Tech High School, he didn't play piano. In fact, according to Kurt, the school didn't know he played piano, although there was a Christian student group who knew he played. He played cello in the high school orchestra, an instrument Kurt did not know how to play until then. He learned to play as a member of the orchestra and the string quartet, advancing quickly to the position of second chair in the orchestra. The traditional route would have been to start taking cello lessons at school in the fifth grade. Kurt didn't do that. His learning was more of the immediate on-the-job-training sort. Extraordinary. Kurt explained, "I didn't know how to play it. We got there, and they were like, 'Would you like to play cello?' So, I played the cello . . . it was fun."[11]

Before high school, during his most acute asthmatic years, at roughly ages nine and ten, Kurt contracted rheumatic fever and its accompanying St. Vitus Dance. The combination of asthma and rheumatic fever caused Kurt's attendance at school to be sporadic at best. At one point he had to drop out of school for six months. Even so, making use of summer school opportunities, he moved through the grades on schedule. But even with these setbacks and challenges, young Kurt was able to experience boyhood "learning experiences," including getting into trouble.

Once, ten-year-old Kurt distributed fliers promoting coming attractions at the Davis Theater. He went home to tell his mother about his good fortune of being paid fifteen cents for his efforts. In response, his mother promptly sent him to his bedroom closet to pray because he had sinned by encouraging people to go to the movies. On another occasion, while in summer school, Kurt stole a bicycle chain lock from a Sears store. The store detective caught him in the act, then called Kurt's mother. When Kurt's father came home that evening, he gave Kurt a spanking and then prayed with Kurt. The prayer was along these lines: Now Lord, You know that I love Kurt more than You do, or as much, and You said that one should reprove their children, and so, I'm simply doing what You said to do, Amen. Kurt remembered the prayer being more painful than the spanking.

At age seven, Kurt had listened to a broadcast of evangelist Wendell P. Lovelace over Moody Bible Institute's radio station WMBI. He and his siblings were not allowed to listen to other radio stations. Though only seven, when Kurt heard the sermon and then the evangelistic appeal at its conclusion, he knew that he needed to make the personal decision to receive Jesus Christ. He explained his spiritual restlessness to his mother, who was very happy to learn of his decision. Together they knelt by Kurt's bedside, and Kurt came to know Christ personally as they prayed.

When Kurt was age nine or ten, Chicago began to become aware of his piano talent. He participated in *Aunt Teresa's Know Your Bible Club*, a program on WMBI on Saturday mornings that showcased kids. He played the piano when the kids sang. This was Kurt's first encounter, but not his last, with the inner workings of this radio station. WMBI was becoming an incubator for preachers and Christian musicians whose ministries would spread to mass audiences around the world in print, in recordings, and in person. The list of evangelists and musicians who began at WMBI or who passed through there is long, impressive, and worthy of its own book. At a very young age, Kurt had joined this remarkable family of talent and Christian commitment. Kurt maintained a warm connection with WMBI throughout his lifetime, returning occasionally to be interviewed as his fame spread. It was as if WMBI was a part of the "village" that raised him, providing a family of sorts. Kurt became part of the WMBI universe that consisted of studio personnel and other future leaders in music publication whose early and basic radio experiences introduced them to life in front of vast, unseen audiences and congregations.

Kurt's older brother, Dik, rode with Kurt to the Moody Bible Institute's radio station on the Damen Avenue streetcar. When Kurt was about twelve years old the radio station asked him to play piano regularly for a radio program serial, again for kids. It was the ongoing story of a cowboy hero and his adventures and was a live broadcast. Before each broadcast, Kurt would meet with the writers, readers, and producers of the program for a run through of the story and its changing moods. One scene might call for a minor key, while others would call for a major key, fast or slow, loud or soft. This was all improvised. There was a script for the story, but there was no score for the music. Kurt had to make that up as the story moved along. Kurt would also play piano, sometimes the Hammond organ, as background for prayers and sermons . . . again, improvisations. He was learning that he could trust his creativity. He was learning that he could trust his instincts. He would come to see these as gifts equal to his piano talent.

As Kurt "aged" into his young teens, he also began playing piano for city-wide Youth for Christ Saturday night rallies at Moody Church and orchestra hall. His renown was growing among Christian audiences as a solo performer and congregational accompanist. Kurt's father accompanied him to one of the rallies. Kurt confided in his brother Dik the following account: at the end of a solo, Kurt turned immediately toward the wildly cheering audience of a couple thousand. He turned, smiled, and bowed. He was interviewed by the emcee for the evening, much to his delight and that of the audience. It was a great moment for the young teenager. However, the mood of the evening soon changed. During the streetcar ride home, Otto chastised his son for how he responded to the applause. Otto was concerned that Kurt was too quick to turn his face to the crowd, too delighted in accepting their applause. His father told Kurt that the look on his face in that moment was too full of pride. He reminded Kurt that all glory must go to God, that Kurt was to be a humble servant and steward of the gift. Dik shared with this author that from that moment on, when Kurt would finish playing a piano solo, he would, for a moment, stare straight ahead or fix his gaze on the keyboard. Only after a few grateful seconds had passed would he acknowledge the audience, and would do so humbly. Let the readers recall the times they saw Kurt perform.

It seems that Dik was the only other person who knew of that conversation, but many saw the results. In 1980, Kurt received a letter, dated September 20, from a woman in Palm Springs, Florida, underscoring how Kurt did, indeed, take his father's admonition to heart:

Dear Kurt,

Your contribution to the Music Congress in Dallas was very important to me in these ways: . . .

. . . 3) My favorite moment under your leadership was your piano improvisation on "My Jesus, I Love Thee." It was my highest moment of worship during the congress. I was very interested that in response to the standing ovation (which I interpreted as genuine recognition of your genius) you sat down at the piano and directed our thanks of you to praise God. (I also appreciated how you did that without sermonizing).[12]

When Kurt was sixteen, he spent the summer in a sort of missions/mentoring experience in Billings, Montana, traveling there from Chicago by bus. When his parents, driving Dik's car, came to take Kurt back to

Chicago, the head of the Montana Gospel Crusade persuaded them to allow Kurt to stay there for the following school year. He and others were quite impressed with Kurt's work at the piano and organ. The ministry included The Church of the Air congregation, and a radio ministry. It was live radio every day, affording Kurt opportunities for arranging and some on-air announcing. One pauses to ponder what it must have meant for Kurt's parents to allow him to stay in Montana for his junior year of high school. And how did his siblings react to such a turn of events? Older brother Dik summed it up this way, "If our parents had a peace about it, we kids were okay with it."[13]

Montana, a faraway place for a young man in Chicago, became for Kurt a place of life-accelerating awakenings and opportunity. It was a place to test his ability to live "on his own"; a safe place to stretch the wings of a teenager morphing into a young adult; a safe place to peer into the world outside of his family of origin and Chicago, comforted by the knowledge that he would return to that family. It was a safe place to experience the early steps of the inevitable maturing process. It was a place to discover whether his faith and beliefs were, in fact, his. In Billings, for the summer, and then for the extended stay through his junior year in high school, Kurt lived with different families within the congregation for a month at a time. During his time in Billings, Kurt took a course in German from Rocky Mountain College. The high school didn't have a college-preparation track, so the course from the college seemed to fill the requirement when he returned to Lane Tech High School in Chicago.

Kurt—Organist for the Montana Gospel Crusade (Billings, Montana), 1951

One Sunday in Billings, a young man stopped at the church, coming from Oregon on his way to Wheaton College in Chicago. He visited the Sunday School class of which Kurt was a member. One of his comments in class discussion was that while it is true that every day with Jesus is sweeter than the day before . . . it is also true that every day with Jesus is rougher than the day before. Kurt was intrigued by the person and the statement. The young man's name was Jim Elliot. The moment would sink even deeper into Kurt's memory and soul when in January 1956 Jim Elliot and four other missionaries were martyred by members of the Auca people group in Ecuador.

Perhaps going to Montana was nothing more than a unique summer job. Perhaps it was seen as an internship of sorts. Whatever the motivation to go, Kurt was afforded an early engagement with music ministry. The radio ministry opportunity at KGHL in Billings seemed a reasonable next step out, if not up, from his experiences at WMBI. In each of his endeavors and responsibilities, Kurt's talent was showcased and measured anew. His stay was extended because of his successes and the obvious value of new independence. It was in Montana that Kurt first met and teamed up with evangelistic soloist Bill Carle. Later, after high school graduation, Kurt would join Bill's team, touring as his pianist and working on occasion with Carle's organ accompanist, Jim Brewer. Kurt's earliest work as an arranger and music editor, and in recording, would come because of his work with these two men.[14] In addition, of course, Billings, Montana, provided the home base for ministry that allowed Kurt to meet Pat in Worland, Wyoming.

Appropriately, Kurt's continuing gratitude for the home in which he was raised is captured in a recording. And no recording that Kurt would do in his professional work would be more moving than the undated ("way back in 1970-something"), untitled, unpublished cassette recording that Kurt made of his father reading scripture, and his mother singing hymns in both English and German. Kurt recalled, "I remember one time . . . I was already down here [in Waco]. I went to pick them up at the airport at DFW and we went to a recording studio . . . I had my dad reading the scripture . . . and then I had my mother singing some songs."[15]

On the tape, Kurt can be heard giving his parents instructions about where to sit and when to begin, along with occasional loving encouragement. The cassette tape is old and fragile, a precious artifact of the environment in which Kurt was raised. His mother's singing is unaccompanied, her voice migrating across multiple keys in each song. Kurt never

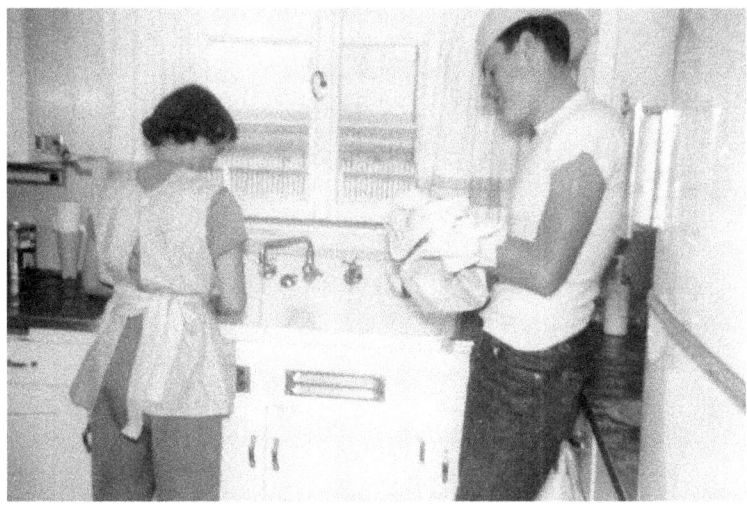

Patricia Anderson and Kurt (Worland, Wyoming), while Kurt accompanied Bill Carle in an evangelistic crusade, 1953

corrects her singing; rather, with love and respect that can be heard despite the crackling tape, he compliments her and calms her nervousness about her German accent. She sang "It Is Well with My Soul," "Oh, How He Loves You and Me," "Oh Love That Will Not Let Me Go," and "Gott Ist Die Liebe." Otto read 1 John 3:1, Isaiah 41:10 and 42:1, Psalm 23, and his favorite passage, Isaiah 43. Otto's and Elisabeth's voices are those of age and life experience. Kurt's voice is that of deepest gratitude and love.

Kurt with his siblings and mother: Martin, Kurt, Sigrid (Schultz), Elisabeth, Dik, Gerhard

CHILDREN AND HOME LIFE

As a reminder, Kurt and Pat were married in August 1956. Their children are Kris, born in Chicago in 1958, and her three brothers: Kent, born in Chicago in 1959; Craig, born in Waco in 1960; and Tim, born in Waco in 1963.

In 1958, between Kurt's undergraduate years and graduate school, Bob Pierce, President of World Vision, asked Kurt to go with him on an around-the-world crusade. The conversation took place at Winona Lake, Indiana, where Kurt was overseeing the music for the large Youth for Christ conference that Ralph Carmichael had overseen in years past.[16] The salary offered to Kurt would certainly help with the expense of graduate school, but there were family matters to consider. Kris was an infant, so Pat would need help for the two and a half months that Kurt would be away. Pat determined to move back to Worland, Wyoming during this time. Her mother could help with the baby, and Pat could help her father with his medical practice. This arrangement worked well for all practical matters, but the global tour led to fatigue and deep homesickness within Kurt. Even so, the cultural encounters Kurt experienced brought him to a deeper understanding of life, of Christianity in "non-Christian" nations, and of the importance of family. His letters to Pat spoke of poverty and "paganism" that he had not encountered before.

One of the key persons on the 1958 world tour was Dr. Dick Halverson, pastor of a major Presbyterian church in Hollywood, California, and later chaplain of the United States Senate. On the first leg of the trip, Halverson told Kurt, "You're very happy now because of all the things you're going to be seeing, but as we get into this thing, it's going to get really tough for you. And rather than say something that you'll be sorry for later on, take a nap." Kurt never forgot the advice.

After marrying, while Kurt was still at Northwestern University he and Pat lived in the upstairs portion of his sister Sig's and her husband's house in Chicago. Pat was employed as a nurse. When baby Kris came along, Sig would babysit her during the day. Kurt and Pat would leave early in the morning, so early that Sig would not yet be up and out of bed. Kurt would go downstairs and place the baby in bed beside Sig on his way out. Kurt was also the pianist at the Bethel Community (Evangelical Free) Church in Chicago, where he wrote for the church band and directed the choir. He would soon be given the title of Minister of Music. At the same time, Kurt led the men's glee club at Northwestern University and was a tutor for the university's basketball players when they enrolled in the mandatory music appreciation class.

From the very beginning, Kurt and Pat had devotionals after breakfast, which became harder to do after the kids got older but continued nonetheless. These moments of family worship consisted of Bible reading, questions, and singing. Pat led the devotionals when Kurt was away.

Another early established pattern was that Pat would take care of household finances. When the royalties from *Tell It Like It Is* started to come in, they made a significant impact on family income. Pat and Kurt, upon the recommendation of "someone in the Baylor business school," together decided to invest those royalties and use them to keep the house in good repair. That happy question settled, Kurt again, "didn't make a big thing about the money," and Pat was again in charge of household finances. She had left the nursing profession but incorporated those skills into the "toolbox" of her fulltime, multifaceted role at home.

Pat, Kurt; second row: Craig, Kent, Kris; front-center: Tim

Other family responsibilities and guidelines were established as needed and as growing children required. As the children got older, Kurt's busy travel schedule did occasion one other basic "policy" discussion. In just one conversation, Pat helped Kurt see that when he had been gone for an extended period, he needed to ease back into the role of disciplinarian with the children upon his return. Kurt understood, making the transition seamlessly in the eyes of the children—seamlessly, yes, but not without its moments. There was the one time when young Tim "made his father really mad." Tim was "being a jerk" outside. His father noticed and whistled for Tim to come to the door. When he did, Kurt pulled Tim's ear and kicked Tim "in the rear" with a firm but measured kick. "He was Dad, not my best friend."[17]

Not long after establishing themselves in Waco, Texas, Kurt and Pat were asked to help with the care of newborn babies who were up for adoption but not yet placed. The babies were in the Kaiser family for short periods of time, the longest instance being for a summer. This family project lasted for several years. When the babies were moved from the Kaiser home to their new family, Pat would write a long letter to the new mother about the child's habits.

In 1961, Kurt again agreed to be the crusade pianist for a World Vision tour that focused primarily on Japan and Korea. In the Tokyo crusade that took place in May of that year, Ralph Carmichael oversaw the music, leaning heavily on Kurt's availability and talent. Kurt even helped Ralph with the hiring of an orchestra, which turned out to be something of a cultural challenge.[18] One of the insider stories that helped cement the friendship between Kurt and Ralph happened in Tokyo. At dinner everyone around the table ordered water except for Ralph, who had discreetly ordered saki in a water glass. Ralph's antics in trying to disguise the heat of his drink, combined with the increasing cloudiness of his drink due to air conditioning, and the smell of his "water," caused laughter between the two men that could surface at any moment for the rest of their lives.

Bob Pierce, president of World Vision, continued to be impressed with Kurt's piano and travel capacities. The Tokyo crusade seemed to galvanize the friendship between Kurt and Ralph Carmichael. From that trip on, Ralph called Kurt "Kurt-san." The friendship deepened over the years and proved to be quite productive in terms of composing and recording. While Kurt was gone on this trip, Pat and their now three children stayed in Chicago. This made it possible for Kurt's parents and sister to help Pat with the children.

In 1963, Pat joined Kurt on an international tour that encompassed Kurt's work responsibilities at WORD and a visit with his family in Germany. The trip included recording in London and sightseeing in Europe and Asia. In Japan, Kurt worked with the Billy Graham Crusade across the country. Though not on stage with Billy Graham, Kurt helped Cliff Barrows by accompanying soloists in other venues and working with orchestras. On the way home, Pat and Kurt stopped to rest for awhile in Honolulu. While they were gone, their children stayed with family in Chicago: Kris primarily with Kurt's sister, Sig, and Kent and Craig primarily with Kurt's parents. Kurt and Pat flew back to Chicago, picked up the kids, and drove back to Waco. About two weeks later, Tim was born. Pat, "quite pregnant," was comfortable throughout the trip even though the timing was a bit close. Her doctor approved of the trip, quipping that "since she was a nurse, she could deliver the baby herself if she needed to." A physician whom Kurt and Pat met on the beach was on their flight back to the mainland and felt a bit more anxious. He offered his services should they be needed at an inopportune time or place.

As the children grew, so did Kurt's success and "celebrity." The children were proud of their father for different reasons at different times. Their awareness of Kurt's renown, and thus their pride, intensified as they enrolled at Baylor. For Kris, the name Kurt Kaiser came to mean something more than "Dad" when the musical *Tell It Like It Is*[19] released, bringing a great deal of attention with it, and then again when she became part of the Seventh & James Baptist Church youth group. In the youth group, she had to work at "just being me," but she couldn't be angry about her father's renown because "he was so humble about it." Home was stable but not always the "normal" that her friends would have recognized. When WORD signed the young singer Evie and Kurt began arranging music for her and producing her recordings, Evie was often in the Kaiser home. Although Evie was a few years older than Kris, the two had fun together. In Kris' eyes, Evie was "cut from the same cloth as Dad." It was not uncommon for Kris and Evie to be talking and hanging out together when Evie's attention would be requested by Kurt to discuss some aspect of a recording project. After the discussion, it was back to the conversation between young friends. Pat and Kurt also had parental sorts of conversations with Evie, whose mother was in New Jersey. It was as if Evie were the oldest of their kids. Kris also enjoyed meeting the "cool" people who came to Waco to work with her father, such as *Natural High*[20] choreographer Alex Plasschaert and his wife, Ellyn.

It was not uncommon for famous recording artists to be in the Kaiser house, but it was sometimes a surprise. Once, in the middle of a day that Pat had devoted to cleaning the oven, Kurt came home and announced that he had brought someone for Pat to meet. Wiping sweat and oven residue from her face, Pat rose to greet Dale Evans, of Roy Rogers and Dale Evans television fame. Pat still remembers that Dale looked like she had just stepped out of a magazine, while Pat had just emerged from the dirty oven.

From Kris' vantage point, there was no difference in the music of her father's work and his music in service of the church. She was moved by her father playing at church, and at home even while he was very ill. The piano soothed him. This is in keeping with an overall sense that the piano was an instrument of prayer for Kurt, and the cello an instrument of dreaming.

For a period of five years, Kurt was absent from his family on Thanksgiving, leaving Pat and the kids to have dinner by themselves or with the Weisingers, the family of a staff member at Seventh & James Baptist Church. Each of those years Kurt was with music evangelist Bill Mann, participating in a series of fundraising concerts for the Birmingham (Alabama) Symphony, sponsored by the *Birmingham News* paper. Bill and Kurt were joined by *The Lawrence Welk Show* celebrities Jimmy Roberts and Norma Zimmer. Pat and the kids used the Thanksgiving holidays to make decorations for Christmas.

In Kris' words, "Christmas was serious, then fun."[21] Continuing but refining a tradition from his childhood, Kurt would give assignments to the kids on Christmas Eve day, to be presented that night. The assignments ranged from memorizing portions of Luke 2 to memorizing a poem or reading a story. Sometimes they were to write on various subjects, creating works such as thirteen-year-old Craig's essay "What Christmas Means to Me" or ten-year-old Tim's poem "The Story of Christmas." The boys dreaded the assignments somewhat, especially as they advanced in their teens. They did see the custom as a challenge that gave meaning and "heft" to Christmas, but they also saw it as something that complicated Christmas. Sometimes the assignment was to prepare songs to sing or play on the piano or autoharp. The final products were shared the night of Christmas Eve in the den with candles lit. There were a few years in which the assignments were not as rigorous, such as the family taping cassette Christmas messages for grandparents. The ritual continued but lessened in intensity through the years as friends, and then spouses, were brought into the circle but not required to participate. There is still Christmas Eve

first grader Kris at the piano

singing at Pat's house, but only remnants of the original customs remain in the homes of the Kaiser children.

Each of the kids had to take piano lessons, which developed an appreciation within them for the piano but not much more. They were allowed to break away from piano lessons when other worthy interests drew them. For Kent and Craig, the other worthy interest was basketball. Kurt attended their practices whenever possible, something the coaches and the other kids noticed. But Kurt was not there to be a parent-coach from the stands. He was there to watch and learn. Kent was pleased to see his father in the stands during practice. Craig, however, was embarrassed, and at one point told his brother so. Kent helped Craig to see things differently. In a 1983 Fathers' Day note to Kurt, Craig confessed, "What Kent said and

[what] I have come to realize in the past few years is that we are so fortunate to have a father so interested in our lives."

Kent felt a deep sense of pride and gratitude when Kurt would bring the team to their house between games during junior high and high school tournaments "for hot dogs or something because the black kids couldn't get to their houses between games."[22] Basketball aside, the best times for Kent with his father were when Kurt was listening to music, perhaps a project he was working on. While listening, Kurt would be in "a trance," but he would come out of it to say, "Listen to _____, Kent," launching into a deep analysis of a particular moment in the music. Kent loved to hear his father talk about what he was hearing. When Kent would put some of his favorite music into the conversations, Kurt would often critique it.

Kurt wrote about one of his father/son experiences with Kent on the back liner of his album *Praise the Lord: 500 Mennonite Men*:[23]

> It was a cold, rainy April 7 that I took my fourteen-year-old son, Kent, with me to Hutchinson, Kansas, to record the album you're about to hear. It was to be a quick trip, flying up to Wichita, Kansas, and then driving west to Hutchinson, recording that night and returning home the next day. It's good for a dad and his son to spend time alone together and I wanted him to hear the sound 500 men make. They make a big sound! . . .
> . . . Oh, I should tell you that Kent and I stayed in a motel close by; and when we awoke the next morning it had snowed six inches! Not knowing our way around, we packed, ate breakfast, and took off on snowy, slippery roads toward Wichita and then Texas. We had a great time together.
>
> Kurt Kaiser

Years later, when Kent had his own family, he, Kurt, Kent's son Brett, and several Wyoming family members and friends went on a fishing trip to Alaska. Reflecting on that trip in a letter to Kent in July 2007, Kurt wrote, "For a dad to watch his son and grandson in Alaska was a grand experience. Your relationship with Brett is so easy, so relaxed."[24] Kurt's shoulder began to hurt soon after they arrived in Alaska, so Kurt spent most of the time observing instead of fishing. But he was not just pondering the scenery.

Kurt played sports with his kids, which would occasionally spread to the community, with Kurt organizing neighborhood games. Craig especially enjoyed these occasions. In high school, Craig's love for basketball and his skills improved to the point that his coach, "Poo" Welch, gave Craig a key to the gym so that he could practice at night. Later, Craig, playing for Baylor University, would see Kurt in the stands during practice, but not always just Kurt. Bev Shea, Larnell Harris, and other celebrities would go to Craig's practice with Kurt. At one point, Craig framed a picture of himself shooting the basketball in his Baylor uniform. He gave the picture to Kurt, along with a personal letter. Kurt cried upon receiving the gift.

Kent, Craig, Kurt

As the children grew older, their participation in church choirs and other activities was not required. But church (worship) attendance was not optional. Church was a family thing. Craig chuckled as he remembered: "Watching dad as a choir member was 'entertaining' at times. George Stokes would get him to laughing in choir."[25]

Tim's memories as the youngest of the Kaiser children reflect the consistency that Kurt and Pat managed to maintain in the home environment throughout the span of four children. Like his brothers and sister, Tim never resented his father's time away. "He was 'always' there for games and practice." It did seem to him, however, that his dad and mom's overseas trip was a bit long.

After a bicycle accident at six years old that was severe enough to warrant a trip to the hospital, Tim came home to find famed TV and recording star Carol Lawrence at the house. There was no evidence at home that Kurt himself was "famous," even when his songs would occasionally be on television. Realization of his father's fame did not occur to Tim until approximately age 8–10 years old, when he, his mother, and his siblings were sitting in the balcony of the auditorium at "Music Week" in Glorieta Baptist Assembly, the Southern Baptist Conference Center in New Mexico. The three-thousand-seat auditorium was full to overflowing, and his father was on stage playing. The fame was undeniable in that setting, but it never came home.

The Kaiser children's relationship to their grandparents was somewhat remote, but Kurt and Pat kept awareness alive by always talking to them about their grandparents. There were some visits to Chicago or to the Andersons' Wyoming cabin, but these were infrequent. Summers might also include a trip to the WORD company cabin in Colorado.

Kurt watched television with the kids, but he would change channels to PBS music shows during commercials.

RIVERSONG

Kurt and Pat owned property in Durango, Colorado, for ten years before building a vacation home there in 1990 and naming it "Riversong" in 1991. The inspiring setting resulted in the 1997 anthem "River Song." With lyrics by Burt Burleson and music by Kurt, the anthem was dedicated to the Baylor University Chamber Singers, then conducted by Donald Bailey. Friends and family continue to enjoy the peace, hospitality, and spirit of Kurt's special place.

Back door view of Kurt's and Pat's "Riversong" cottage near Durango, Colorado

CONTINUING HEALTH ISSUES

On July 31, 1975, Otto Kaiser wrote a letter to his son, Kurt. The first paragraph of the handwritten letter is copied here:

Dear Kurt,

> Mama and I did not notice that you were suffering when you and your dear family were visiting with us. You must be an accomplished stoic. Hearing of your trouble gave us quite a shock. So one will ask, "Why?" The answers one formulates are unsatisfactory. So one rather asks, "For what purpose?" Romans 8:28 comes to mind, "All things work together for good to them that love God, to them who are called to his purpose." From childhood on you have experienced sickness and pain and frustration. Isn't it that God has a purpose in it? Isn't it that the Psalms speak to the depth of our hearts, because of the often painful experiences endured by the writer? Perhaps this is the purpose in your suffering, that your verse and music express in a deeper measure the remedy for the wounded and sin-sick soul. Success tends to make one easily superficial. So God in His wisdom adds the needed weights. Dear Kurt, bear this without murmuring. I am so glad to notice that you have not lost your humor.

The specific pain referenced here was a result of surgery that Kurt had undergone in 1974, not one of Kurt's three heart surgeries (1970, 1999, and 2008). That surgery was less life-threatening, but Kurt suffered nearly unbearable pain from both the procedure and the follow-up treatments.

Reading Otto's 1975 letter of theological encouragement, we detect the echo of an event in Otto's teenage years. At age fourteen, in a confirmation class, Otto and the others were encouraged by Pastor Beck of the Reformed Church to memorize "many hymns, Bible portions, and much of the Heidelberg Catechism." Otto remembered:

> He wanted us to meet him on Sunday after church service. He became a real friend to me. Several times after work I walked from Waldbrol to Numbrecht to tell him my spiritual defeats. He encouraged me with Isaiah 42:3, "a bruised reed he will not break, and a dimly burning wick he will not extinguish." He gave me also this four liner:
>
>> Who always thinks on his misery
>> loses all pleasure and courage.
>> Who deeply meditates in Jesus,
>> despite his misery will flourish.[26]

Those words found a home deep within Otto's heart and mind. His 1975 letter to Kurt reveals the beauty in his mastery of the English language.

Kurt's parents, Otto and Elisabeth, on their 45th wedding anniversary, 1974

It also reveals a simple, if not simplistic, theology of pain and suffering, no doubt simpler than the actual living of that pain. Otto's handwritten paragraph is an example of his ongoing instruction to Kurt in matters of scripture and theology. He seemed to sense that Kurt would have increasing influence on the theology of the singers of his songs, and on that of the listeners. This expanding influence may well have made Otto's sense of responsibility to his son seem even more crucial—to know that Kurt could manage that influence and that Kurt understood the importance of writing the truth into his lyrics, even into the musical settings of those lyrics.

The lessons his father sought to teach were not lost on Kurt. He knew his father's theology and how openly he lived it and spoke of it. That was no surprise. What was emerging as something new, however, was Kurt's growing into and owning a learned-by-life, applied theology of his own experience and shaping. Kurt was always active in church attendance, a habit that kept his heart and mind in the Bible. He was learning the shaping and sharpening of theology that comes from life itself. Kurt was becoming more comfortable with his own developing lived theology, built on the foundation of his father's, and both his music and his day-to-day living worked together to sort things out. His father would notice this as he kept a close eye on the theology of Kurt's lyrics. Kurt would honor his father and the theological foundation of his own upbringing, which included a literal reading and understanding of scripture. But it was also true that the life and Southern Baptist preaching of a more generous orthodoxy (to use Brian McLaren's term) that he was experiencing in Waco was having its effect as well. Though perhaps a bit more cautious, his father was also a learner, even in matters of theology and scripture. Otto enjoyed, and was impressed with, the Sunday School lessons and sermons that he experienced when visiting the Waco Kaisers. Nonetheless, the father's watchful eye was ever vigilant toward the son with the ever-widening field of influence.

Perhaps in a sustained echo of the tenor of his father's July 1975 letter, but now in his own voice, Kurt held that artists work best from low places and times in their lives—not solely from that place, but *best* from that place. Thinking aloud in a recorded conversation with his daughter, Kurt confessed that even though low places, such as pain, may produce an artist's best work, he had not wanted to write for a year after his most painful surgery. Although he didn't want to write, he did still compose a wedding song for one of his granddaughters while he and Pat were at their cabin in Colorado. "I... finally did, but you know, it didn't taste good to me. Usually when I'm at the cabin, maybe the first couple of days, it doesn't taste good, about then it tastes good again, and I want to get into it. But not this time..."[27]

Perhaps this somewhat thorny analysis of pain as inspiration had come to Kurt and was being perfected in him over the years as he read biographies of famous composers, in school and beyond, and as he looked, thoughtfully, back over the years of his own composing. Kurt felt that this unhappy influence was seen most readily in his lyrics, but that careful analysis would reveal similar evidence in the music as well, acknowledging that life's struggles, and the theological wrestling with the related questions, could be heard in his playing.

Kurt pointed to two musical examples of this concept of pain-shaped creativity in his work. One was the song "I Am Willing, Lord" (WORD Music, 1976), which was a direct response to Otto's letter quoted above. The other is the entire album *Kurt Kaiser Piano: A Part of Me* (1981).[28]

Phil Shappard, who worked for WMBI radio in Chicago for many years, remembered...

> ... standing on the staircase between our offices and the on-air studios at that time and hearing Kurt tell the story behind the writing of 'I Am Willing.' His story of great physical suffering was quite real but was thankfully punctuated by either a call or letter from his father telling Kurt that

he must have been very special for God to have entrusted him with such pain and suffering. The lyrics of 'I Am Willing, Lord' have blessed and challenged many souls around the world. This had a profound impact on me at about the age of thirty at the time.[29]

"I Am Willing, Lord" is cut 3 on side 2 of that album. In this rare occurrence, he sings a duet with California Christian singer and actress Michele Pillar. The same performance is included as number 9 on the CD *Oh, How He Loves You and Me* (Kurt Kaiser Music, 2005). The sound is updated from the album to the CD, largely by improvements in recording technology over that fourteen-year period, but it is the same performance. Two other cuts are carried over from the 1981 recording to the 2005 recording: "He Careth for You," sung by Michele Pillar, and "Oh, How He Loves You and Me," sung by Diane Zagnoli in both recordings. For each of the songs on the 1981 album, words and music are by Kurt.

The arrangements on each of the songs of the 1981 album, and Kurt's playing of them, are exquisite, vulnerable, and honest, all other possible influences or agendas pushed away. Indeed, they make Kurt's point about writing from the struggles of life. The other songs on the album are "Early in the Morning," "His Will Our Own," "The Lord Is My Strength and My Song," "At the Name of Jesus," "To Know Love," and "This Is Why I Sing." The shared, connecting theme is obvious.

While the pain of a specific surgery would pass, two other struggles would continue for Kurt. One, his heart issues, was seen by the whole world. The other, just as formative but more private, was the work of embracing his own adult theology, somewhat different than his father's, shaped in actual daily living. This, of course, would be accompanied by the difficult effort of seeing his developing personal theology as "equal" with his father's. The direction and pace of Kurt's theological development can be seen in "I Am Willing, Lord."

The refrain, or chorus, of "I Am Willing, Lord" contains this line: "I am willing, Lord, to be just exactly what you want me to be." The key word "what" reflects an understanding of divine call that holds that God has made us for one specific vocation, one profession that God wants us to discover. In this understanding of vocation, one grows up hoping for correct discernment, and for the courage to commit to that one profession or vocation for an entire, productive life. It's as if the discovery of "what" God wants us to be is a sort of ultimate life game. "I am willing, Lord, to be just exactly *what* you want me to be."

Kurt was raised in a church and home environment in which the prevailing notion of "call" was a humble discernment of, and acceptance of, "what" God had designed one to be. This notion seems to be validated and underscored when one has gifts as obvious and unique as Kurt's. This theology was held and revered by many of the Evangelical Free Christians with whom Kurt worked in Chicago as Minister of Music, and by the Baptists whom Kurt encountered at church and at work in Waco. In Kurt's case, his remarkable piano skills were seen as evidence that "what" God wanted Kurt to be was a musician, and that the most devoted use of that gift would be to explore church music in one expression or another. Kurt should be a congregational minister of music or an evangelistic piano soloist, or accompanist. We could argue that "what" is not bad, it is simply secondary to the "who" of believers being transformed to Christlikeness.

Such an approach to the embracing and stewarding of skill and talent moved, in common understanding, from the high point of Church vocation (most noble being that of missionary) to Christian living in more commonly held but less church-related occupations such as medicine, law, education, or the trades. Pastors, Christian educators, and missionaries were seen as the apex of "what" one might be. With his personal, adult theology developing, Kurt wrote "what" in the song, but he lived "who" as an individual, a father, and an encourager of students. Here is the conflict point for his adult theology: he was living the who/what question rather than pushing it away as answered once and for all, even if unsatisfactorily so.

This conflict in writing and living a lyric should not be seen as an inconsistency but rather as a conflict over how to rank the two options. The struggle speaks of the importance of the transition from "what" to "who." The transition has implications for the work of a composer and shaper of new talent, one who is also a responsible administrator in a business. "To be just exactly *who* you want me to be" is the prayer of all believers, the number crunchers as well as the artists. Kurt knew this and lived this. But the line in the song could not be changed to "I am willing, Lord, to be just exactly *who* you want me to be." There is no indication that Kurt ever thought about changing it. By copyright, usage, and popular acceptance, "what" was the word, even if "who" was understood in the more mature spirituality of the writer and the Protestant Church. But Kurt's life clearly indicated that who he was mattered more to him than what he was. His work as a composer and producer spanned a time in which the Church matured, in large measure, from "what" to "who" in understanding the transformation toward Christlikeness that takes place in a believer's life and worldview. Indeed, in that period of history, all of American society and culture seemed to be involved in the difficult spiritual or mystical rethinking of the meaning of life, be it Christian thought or simply religious. Kurt's life and work provided comfort, challenge, and conscience on this matter to an industry that was providing the soundtrack for a Church in its own "who/what" transition, testing tradition against innovation. Kurt's life (home, church, and work) gave consistent evidence that he lived, "exactly who you want me to be," even as he was writing "exactly what you want me to be." For Kurt, "what" had been settled and refined, while "who" meant continuous refinement in spiritual formation. He did not have to choose one over the other.

Kurt didn't hide his struggles. They were real, and he was honest. He was a faithful steward of all of life. He published a summation of his journey for any who might recognize and relate, for any and all who might be wrestling, even as he was, concerning the processing of personal pain or balancing the "what/who" relationship to personal giftedness. From the *Kurt Kaiser: A Part of Me* back liner, the album that includes the song in question and its line ". . . what you want me to be," we read:

> A composer's music is at least a partial extension of who he is, his personality, his outlook on life, his relationship with others. This album is a part of who I am at this point in my life. Each song represents experiences . . . physical, spiritual, or emotional. Some stories are quite vivid to me. In some instances even the place where the melody came about is still a brilliant memory. A songwriter's dream is to share his experiences so that the listener might gain fresh perspective in his life. I want to keep telling the story in music.
>
> **Kurt**

A third piece of evidence upholding the pain-shaped creativity of Kurt's compositions is the song "Long Journey." The pain in this case is that of grief. In the CD case insert of *Hymns: Christopher Adkins, Cello, Stephen Nielson, Piano* (Kurt Kaiser Music, 2006), Kurt shares this bit of insight: "Long Journey–for Chad: When I heard the news that my nephew Chad had terminal cancer, I immediately sat down and wrote the melody for 'Long Journey.' The only 'program' is in the final three bars of music—an immediate transport from earth to heaven." To listen to this composition is to know that it needs no lyrics. The song and its composer could find no lyrics. It leaves the desire for lyrics behind because the bittersweetness of the melody fills all voids. Here the deepest prayer of the piano and the broken dreams of the cello combine in wordless lament. Here Kurt, the conscience of his compositional peers and anticipating audiences, bids them all, and us, to say nothing, for there are no words. No music of his was more severe, nor was any as gentle.

We cannot help but turn to Kurt's conversations with his father (see pp. 161–62) concerning the theological veracity of Kurt's hymn setting of "Bring Back the Springtime" in WORD's 1986 *Hymnal for Worship & Celebration*. Perhaps in 1970, the year of Kurt's first heart surgery, as well as the year this song was copyrighted, Kurt's theology did, in fact, cry from its depths in all authenticity and honesty when he wrote the questioned lines "of the streams that flowed from Calvary" and "return to me, sweet Holy Spirit." Should those expressions be corrected? Perhaps. But it is also compelling to think of daring to leave in print depths of grief that, at the time, were authentic prayer, even if they are questioned when grief has passed.

Kurt lived an active, vibrant theology as both a learner and a leader, characteristics of one who is both icon and conscience for a movement. Speaking at his father-in-law's funeral in 1975, Kurt included these comments:

> In 1970, the reality of major surgery loomed enormously on my horizon. Dad's ability of preparing me psychologically and emotionally for the trauma of the weeks and months ahead was invaluable to me and shortened the recovery period a great deal. Never was anyone better prepared than I. I lamely alluded to this in the last telephone conversation I had with him. I tried to tell him that it was my turn to prepare him for what lay ahead.[30]

KURT KAISER THE PIANIST

The discussion of the composer finding his most authentic creativity in the depths of pain and struggle presents an easy segue into similar thoughts about the performer. In her 2008–2009 interview with her father, Kris Kaiser Olson asked if his piano playing showed any of the marks or shaping that was evident in his writing after his recovery from difficult surgery. He responded:

> I find mine to be darker. While this has been true for the past several years, dissonance, unresolved dissonance, has become very important for me. And I'll play a ninth or a seventh in the right hand, where I used to always play an octave. But now I don't want to play an octave. That sounds too consonant. Let me lay a dissonance in there. And let it resolve in the

listeners' ears. So, I do a lot more of that than I used to do. And it makes playing a lot more meaningful.[31]

We return, for a moment, to an incident in Kurt's junior high school job, working for a local machinist/blacksmith, making eggbeaters and cheese slicers. His employer took Kurt to a room away from the busiest and noisiest work area where Kurt saw, for the first time, a player piano. This was fascinating technology but mildly troubling for a young piano student studying to become an artist. No matter how practiced and patterned they might be, worship and prayer were not to be mechanical. Therefore, by extension, he could easily surmise that piano playing, a gift used in the presence of God and for the glory of God, was not to be mechanical, even within the boundaries of proper historical performance practice. A purely mechanical approach to piano, by machine or human, could never convey the heights and depths of the human experience, could never be offered as authentic expression to a congregation, an audience, or God.

A player piano was inanimate, even though a human created the machine and the song rolls that held the prescribed performance like scrolls waiting to be unrolled and read. Much later in life, Kurt's long-harbored thoughts and questions about that player piano's limitations were rekindled when he observed a performance by Vladimir Horowitz. Kurt commented that Horowitz, the great classical pianist, could only play by the note on the page. "He can't improvise worth a lick . . . But [Horowitz] went to Moscow after having not been there for fifty years, and he played, and he recorded this thing played on CBS 'Sunday Morning.' And he played the simplest little melody. And I will always remember this, there was a guy in the audience with tears running down his eyes. It was the most beautiful thing . . . and it was so simple."[32] Authenticity, simplicity, familiarity, when passed through the human soul—in this case, that of a master at the piano—can move us.

Kurt Kaiser, the pianist, considered each note that he played, requiring each note to overcome any lifeless tendency that would fill the air but not the soul. Hovering over the keyboard, Kurt's hands cupped a chord just as one's hands might carefully cup a robin's egg. Then, when he approached the keyboard, several potential notes were dismissed and those few selected were held as gently as if holding a baby bird. Touching the keys, he let the fledgling fly. Here, Kurt prayed; words at first coursing through his head, heart, and fingers, then soon, wordless prayer sounded by the key-hammered strings, moans offered for the Holy Spirit to interpret at the heavenly throne, offered from depth to height.

Kurt may well have dreamed through the cello from high school on, but he prayed through the piano. The sixteen-year-old high school cellist, called into action because of the orchestra's need and Kurt's giftedness, must have, from time to time, dreamed of what his life might be if he focused on an instrument of his choice, rather than on the instrument that had seemingly chosen him, the instrument with which he had been identified since he was four. The cello reached deep into his inner being as it sang. What if he spread new wings, embarked on a bowed flight of his choosing rather than continuing the journey seemingly assigned to him? What might he have accomplished? Might there have been a Kurt Kaiser, cellist, out there, a new and different person with similar limitless horizons?

But dreaming and praying, while quite similar, are not synonymous. The heart must pray, even after dreaming.

Perhaps his prayers were refreshed by his dreams. God had, after all, created Kurt, who prayed, and dreamed, and created, and inspired. Perhaps the cello was the symbol, the instrument, of his submission, what he sacrificed to the will of God. But to do the will of God, to play the piano, was not punishment, nor was it secondary. The piano was both shelter and pathway for introspection and for growth. What is prayer's relationship to dreams? The question would be the source of dynamic and creative tension throughout his life. His life might well be described as a piano and cello duet. Prayer and dreams, production and reflection, practicality and creativity; the duets common to life, seen and heard in Kurt's work with keyboards and strings.

Indeed, Kurt the pianist would arrange for cello, orchestrate cellos to sing their wisdom out through the orchestra, out to the audience. The pianist would find and record the finest cellists, violinists, and guitarists and would simultaneously record their prayers, his prayers, and his dreams. Kurt could not stop dreaming any more than he could stop praying.

As in all good prayer, the pray-er listens to the God to whom they pray, knowing that prayer is a conversation. To listen to Kurt's piano playing is to eavesdrop. Quickly Kurt's Spirit-released prayer gathered up the prayers of the congregation, the audience, the listener, catching the breath of God, and then after the last note, the humble and motionless amen. His fingers are lifted from the keyboard. The grip on his prayer and the listeners' hearts is released. Exhaled breath is its own praise, and God seems to utter the "Amen." This was Kurt at the piano. This was the gift being owned and returned. This was holiness received, resurrected, returned, and sometimes recorded, even as some of the Psalmist's prayers are recorded. The God of David, the God of Kurt, and the God of the worshiping listener is the One and Same God. His introductions, played and composed, alerted angels ready to be deployed, messengers that carried the holy words of deepest conversation up and down, in and out.

An interesting 1977 recording, *Hymns: Anita Kerr, Kurt Kaiser*, features Kurt as a pianist, a co-piano artist, and "only" that. Anita Kerr, renowned leader of the "Anita Kerr Singers," is the arranger, conductor of vocals and orchestra, and producer for this album. Kurt plays one of the two pianos; she plays the other. She also sings in the vocal group. None of the recorded songs are Kurt's compositions. Kurt, the pianist, is but one of the pianists, an artist sharing the spotlight: humbling or at home for him? Kurt wrote on the back liner, "Several times during the recording sessions I looked across the strings of the twin grand pianos and mentally pinched myself. For I was involved in an album with someone whom I had greatly admired for a number of years." Anita wrote on her half of the back liner, "Every session was a joy. The reason for this was not only the joy of working with a good musician, but with a beautiful person as well."[33] Prayer and worship are interchangeable in the vocabulary of many Christians, as are joy and wonder.

In 1996, long after Kurt and WORD had parted ways, recording producer Richard Huggins called together four pianists whose artistry and varied ministries had stretched across the country and across decades. In overlapping fashion, they were competitors at times, coworkers at times, collaborators at times. Their styles differed, yet, without it having to be stated, a commonality among them rang true. This WORD Music project, *Keyboard Legends*,[34] includes the products one would expect, a CD and a keyboard book. Each pianist featured had a following that, no doubt, welcomed the release of the recording and the scores. But something more than projected sales seems to have motivated the gathering of these specific four men. As the subtitle declares, these were "four renowned pianists," but they were not the only pianists who were both excellent Christian artists and enjoyed large followings. Why these four? They were unquestionably acceptable representatives of their colleagues who, like them, in their professional work "soared to worlds unknown"[35] but never really left home.

Fred Bock, Kurt Kaiser, Max Lyall, and Don Wyrtzen held each other in high esteem, recognizing each other's artistry, integrity, and unique contributions to music ministry at a congregational level. Choirs sang their anthems. Congregations sang their hymns and choruses. Pianists and organists played their preludes, offertories, and postludes. Countless hours of studio, concert, and classroom experience notwithstanding, these four came together to record music of the pews, and not as a condescending gesture, but as personal testimony. At home among the celebrities and the academics of church music's "elite," their true home of rest and refuge was the congregation, and the foundational truth of the congregation's songs. The photo on the inside of the case insert shows a quartet that could just as easily be any congregation's deacons, ushers, or committee chairs. We speak not of physical appearance alone, but of their widely known dedication to the church, the "lower case" church, the congregation. Of course WORD would invite Kurt back into the studio for such a gathering as this. How could they, in good conscience, not invite him? They never forgot who he was.[36]

The 1960 album *Kurt Kaiser, Piano* is a collection of ten gospel songs that introduces Kurt to WORD's audience. Kurt had joined WORD only the year before. The back liner describes in some detail his travels with music evangelist Bill Carle, and then later, Dr. Bob Pierce, president of World Vision. Kurt's educational credentials are listed, as well as the note that he had served as minister of music at Bethel Community Church in Chicago. Mention of Pat and "their two children" assures listeners that young Kurt is a family man. This, too, is written on the back liner:

> The unusual and refreshing chord progressions indicate Mr. Kaiser's zest for the new and different. His honest interpretations of the composers reflect his true musicianship . . . and flowing through each note, each chord is a rich vein of Christianity that permeates the entire recording to make this a genuinely inspiring album.
>
> There you have a complete and accurate picture of Kurt Kaiser . . . young, adventuresome, a musician of enviable talents, and a man with a deep, abiding faith in his God and his fellow man.[37]

Another early album, *Hymns of Prayer: Inspiring Orchestral Arrangements by Kurt Kaiser*, is undated. However, the back liner includes a picture of Kurt that is somewhat "dated" by his youth. It appears that this album is also of early 1960s vintage, likely 1960 or 1961. Kurt's talent as an orchestral arranger seems to be introduced to the same WORD audience. It is significant, however, that Kurt is first presented as a piano artist. This was how he was known by those who already knew him. This is how the waiting, vast audience should come to know him. That identity established, WORD could now begin to boast of their new employee's additional gifts.

The undated album *Master Designer: Kurt Kaiser at the Piano with Orchestra*, was recorded in separate sessions in Sweden: orchestra first, then later, Kurt at the piano ... much later. Kurt had hoped to record the piano in sessions back in the United States, but he discovered that the orchestra in Sweden tuned to the note "A" at two vibrations per second higher than "A" in the U.S. His perfect pitch could not abide the difference, so he waited until a subsequent trip to Europe to finish the recording on a piano in Sweden. As interesting as that might be, the incident (recounted on the back liner of the album) is included here for another reason. Kurt recorded the piano parts in the studio in two evening sessions, with the lights off. Alone, except for the sound engineer, and in the darkness, except for the glow of a small floor lamp, Kurt created, thought, and played. Is that not prayer in the closet?

KURT KAISER THE ACCOMPANIST

In January 1979, composer Robert Sterling, having moved from Waco to Dallas, called his friend and mentor, Kurt, to ask if he would help him with a special birthday present for his mother. Robert's mother loved Kurt's music and had always dreamed of singing with Kurt accompanying her. So, Robert, his wife Cindy, their young son, Robert's mother Sarah, and Kurt met at First Baptist Church, Waco, to record Sarah singing with Kurt at the piano. The session lasted for a couple of hours inside a very cold sanctuary. Kurt wore a heavy jacket while playing the piano. He refused to accept any money for his time and work. He was moved by the idea of it all. Knowing this about Kurt, we can now consider his accompanying celebrities.

Kurt accompanied many artists in concert and recording session settings. Some of those occasions are reported in other sections of this book. Here we look at selected examples from across Kurt's life.

One would expect to find Kurt Kaiser on the stage of the Billy Graham Crusades that were so popular across the United States and around the world beginning in the 1950s. Kurt's work was not known to the masses, but it was known to Billy Graham's musicians, both staff and guests, both on stage and behind the scenes. Regular accompanists Tedd Smith, Paul Mickelson, and Don Hustad were well established on the Graham stage, and better known. Tom Bledsoe, of Dallas, Texas, became Director of

Music for the associate crusades in 1969. He also helped Cliff Barrows with the crusade choirs. Eventually Bledsoe added Director of Graham's School of Evangelism to his title. Tom, who first met Kurt at Baylor, was with the Billy Graham Association until 2020. He did not enlist Kurt to do any of the associate or main crusades, but he did call upon Kurt on a few special occasions, as did Cliff.

On one occasion, Cliff Barrows asked opera star Kathleen Battle to sing at a New York crusade. She said she would but only if Kurt Kaiser accompanied her (they had worked together before in other settings). Cliff readily agreed. However, the appearance never took place due to a disagreement between Barrows and Battle that did not involve Kurt.[38]

Not long after the success of *Tell It Like It Is*, Cliff Barrows made a recording with his friends Kurt Kaiser and Ralph Carmichael. Kurt pulled together a group of Baylor students and, for the occasion, called them the "Kurt Kaiser Singers."

In 1996, Paul Stilwell Enterprises and Brentwood Records combined to produce an LP/CD musical tribute to Billy Graham. On the back liner of the album, Kurt is given equal billing with Bev Shea, and is recognized as a "songwriter, arranger and producer, [who] has been accompanist to George Beverly Shea on countless occasions."[39] Kurt, as a ready accompanist, was never far away from the work of the Billy Graham Crusade musicians.

Before there was a Billy Graham Crusade "team," George Beverly Shea sang at Graham's first city-wide crusade, in 1947 in Charlotte, North Carolina. Bev Shea had been a staff announcer and singer for radio station WMBI since 1938 when young Billy Graham came by the studio to meet him. He had been listening to Shea on the radio and said that he wanted to "encourage" him. After their visit, Shea went for a year to help Graham where he was pastoring in Western Springs, Illinois. During those years, Bev Shea would often sing at conferences at the Winona Lake Conference Center. That's where Kurt first heard Shea in person. He had heard him on the radio. They would later work together in Graham-related crusades in Canada and Japan, and in numerous concerts on a regular basis in churches across the United States. The most important aspects of brotherhood fashioned their friendship. The many times Kurt recorded Bev across the span of five decades were as much about the joy of working together as they were "being about their Father's business." It is impossible to overstate the depth and breadth of the friendship between Kurt Kaiser and Bev Shea. Handwritten notes and letters between the two cover recording sessions, concerts, birthdays, illnesses, family, and visits, documenting a soulmate level of kinship.

Another early influence on Kurt was Bill Carle. As we have seen, Kurt first met Bill when he moved to Billings, Montana, in the summer before his junior year in high school. Kurt worked with Carle as his schedule would permit. His primary responsibilities during that year and a half were to the Church of the Air congregation and evangelistic meetings.

Later, in 1953, having graduated from high school in Chicago, Kurt would again join the well-established Bill Carle sacred music team, accompanying him on evangelistic singing tours throughout the United States. Touring with Bill Carle was an education for Kurt. Not only could they drive for miles in silence, true evidence of trust and friendship, but sometimes Kurt would read scripture aloud as Bill drove, initiating wonderful discussions about the things of God and life.

Their schedule was full of traveling from town to town, often for long distances to evangelistic meetings and recording sessions. In those sessions, Kurt accompanied Carle's singing. But at least once, they produced a solo recording of Kurt as well. Kurt may have tried his hand at producing during these recording sessions. He certainly watched and learned. He used his alone time on the tour to write to Pat, who was still living in Wyoming. Each letter was more relaxed in what he shared, especially regarding his affection for her. He ended his letter dated August 7, 1953, from Los Angeles in this way: "I guess I not only love your letters—I <u>know</u>, I love you. A little unexpected to say that. But I think I know what I'm talking about—Must close, Pat, Real much love, Kurt." It was the first time he told Pat that he loved her.

On July 27, 1953, still traveling with Bill Carle, Kurt wrote from Vancouver, Canada to Pat and included the account of an incident that had happened on a recent day off:

> The other day in Seattle, I had a speed boat ride I'll never forget as long as I live. This guy had his uncle's 16-foot speed boat with a 25-horsepower engine and we were three of us riding full speed ahead cutting waves from another boat's wake. We happened to hit one wave wrong and the boat tossed me out and this other guy after me. The driver didn't fall, fortunately enough! It happened so very fast—I just remember rolling in green water. I went down <u>real</u> deep, and it took me a real long time to come up again. We were fully dressed. I swam to the other guy that was thrown and tried to help him because he has cancer of the vertebrae and has to wear a brace

like a girdle all the time. Soon the boat came after us and we got in all soaked to the skin!

Less life-threatening than a boating accident, but equally etched in Kurt's memory were two spiritual experiences that he related, with some hesitancy, to Pat. On November 11, 1953, Kurt wrote of being in a chapel service at the Southwestern Bible Institute, a Pentecostal school south of Dallas where, for only the second time in his life, he heard people speak in tongues. What's more, all 700 students and faculty prayed aloud at the same time. He admitted to being frightened and to wondering about God being the God of order, not confusion. Two weeks later, from Omaha, Nebraska, Kurt wrote to Pat of witnessing the divine healing of Bill Carle by evangelist "Dr. Brown." Dr. Brown, Bill, and Kurt met in a private room. Bill and Kurt were instructed to kneel. Dr. Brown anointed Bill with oil, prayed for him, and ordered all evil to leave Bill in the name of the Holy Spirit. Then, Dr. Brown prayed for Kurt, after which both men were told to stand up. Kurt was frightened but had "a new look at the Lord," and Bill was healed of his throat ailment. Kurt opened the letter by writing, "Divine healing does work, Pat—I saw it with my own eyes!" After Kurt's account of the healing, he spent the rest of the letter asking Pat to "please don't think I've gone off my rocker."

In time, Kurt became more widely known than Bill. On the back liner of *Bill Carle: Songs from the Word with the Kurt Kaiser Orchestra* (LP, WORD, c. 1960), Kurt's growing credentials are touted:

> Kurt Kaiser, director of Artist and Repertoire for Word Records, conducts the orchestra accompanying Bill Carle. An accomplished musician in his own right, Mr. Kaiser did the arrangements in the album. He holds a Masters' Degree in music from Northwestern University, where he was in charge of the Men's Glee Club. He traveled around the world with Dr. Bob Pierce, president of World Vision, and was piano accompanist for Bill Carle on a nationwide tour.

Again, Winona Lake, Indiana, comes into the picture. It was at a Youth for Christ Conference at Winona Lake where young Chicagoan Kurt Kaiser accompanied established California musician Ralph Carmichael's choirs and soloists. Carmichael was instantly impressed. The names Kurt Kaiser and Ralph Carmichael would later come to be linked together in discussions of the development of "Contemporary Christian Music," spoken in a single breath as if they were one long name—this, of course, because of the youth musical *Tell It Like It Is* (to be considered in more detail later). From that point on, the two names and persons were, for a period of decades, in a dance of sorts, like the gravitational twirling of two galaxies in relative proximity to each other. Both became stars in their own right and at times, from a distance, would shine almost as one. Both were impressed with each other's musicianship at the Winona Lake, Indiana conference center where they first worked with each other.

Ralph was an up-and-coming composer of some renown; twenty-year-old Kurt was his accompanist for the summer gathering. Early on, Ralph was something of a mentor to Kurt. However, as the years passed, Kurt often played the role of mentor to Ralph. Mutual respect kept them close to each other as friends, confidants, and colleagues. In a letter dated July 4, 1955, from Winona Lake, Indiana, to Pat Anderson (not yet Pat Kaiser) who was working at West Suburban Hospital in Oak Park, Illinois, Kurt wrote, "Carmichael is really TREMENDOUS. You'll see when you come out." Just two days later, July 6, again in a letter from Kurt to Pat, Kurt continued to gush:

> Ralph is a genius! You should have heard how tremendous the choir sounded last night . . . Ralph just has it—and he's a really nice guy to be around. It's good for me to be with him because he's always a mental step ahead of me—I think you know what I mean. I like that, and he likes my being right up to him musically. You'll see what I mean when you come and can see him work. We get along like hand and glove.

From time to time, in later years, Kurt would try his hand at scoring movies, but that never became a primary outlet for him. It did, however, present yet another teaching opportunity for Ralph, the teacher, and Kurt, his student. Kurt had written the score for *The Addicts*, a film about a group of nine former drug addicts that Kurt had recorded.[40] The film was showing in Hollywood, and Ralph went with Kurt to the premiere. Kurt had not seen the finished product yet. "So we were surrounded by all these druggies, and this one cue [a particular moment in the soundtrack] that I knew was really great was way down, and I said, 'Oh, Ralph, that kills me.' He said to me, 'Don't worry about it, we'll talk about it later.'"[41] The later conversation was simply Ralph's telling Kurt to avoid writing for the scenes that don't need any help. Ralph reassured Kurt that his work was good, that Kurt was writing at a level which took him six films to attain. Other film score ventures for Kurt included some work for Gospel Films, Inc. of Muskegon, Michigan, a film about Bill Carle, and a film for the

United Fund in Waco, Texas. Kurt's song "That's for Me" was written as a part of the Waco film score. It was later incorporated into the musical *Tell It Like It Is*. It was the only prewritten song of Kurt's in the musical. Ralph put one prewritten song into the musical as well, at Kurt's suggestion. Ralph's song was "Love Is Surrender," made popular by the pop brother/sister artists *The Carpenters*. Kurt also accompanied, on occasion, renowned singer and movie star Ethel Waters; their friendship is discussed in the next chapter.

KURT KAISER THE COMPOSER AND ARRANGER

Personal pain and encountering life's difficulties, as shown earlier, may well be factors in shaping the artist's work, but they are only influences. They do not produce skill, talent, or giftedness. Non-artists can be creative in their processing of pain, but that does not equal artistry. Kurt was an artist, and a life-long learner. He had learned from Ralph Carmichael. He warmly credited composer William "Bill" Purcell for teaching him about how to write flowing passages for the orchestra. He inhaled great teaching and exhaled great art.

Kaiser, composer and arranger, did not demand of his listeners and performers that they experience his inspiration. Instead, he took them to the place of his inspiration, and gave them over to the movement of the Holy Spirit. For all its warmth, this approach to composing, and even performing, is what he would, on occasion, refer to as "serving it cold." Kurt did not manipulate his listeners in the name of the Holy Spirit. He embraced his gift of communicating the message of the gospel. He claimed his gift of revealing insights through the portal, or medium, of music. "Here is where I was inspired; here is what inspired me," is significantly different from "My experience of inspiration must be yours, swallow this." A fine line? Heightened nuance? Yes, but in the context of perfect pitch and humble acceptance of inspiration, fine lines and nuance are a way of life, a way of experiencing and processing the glimpses and whispers of the still, small voice. This understanding and approach matured and ripened over the years of Kurt's work. He found its authenticity to be the answer to accepting applause and accolades. He indeed heard such praise to be in response to his work as a shepherd, a steward, not as the source. Further, Kurt did not hesitate to admit that he experienced seasons of writer's block. During those times, even with due dates looming, he would turn away from his stalled writing to read the Bible and devotional books, opening himself to peaceful submission to new ideas that the Spirit would provide. Finally, Kurt would often say, "You just have to sit down and start writing." Often at that point, ideas would come "like an avalanche."

The most remarkable feat performed by Kurt (or any other composer/arranger) is the exploration, in arrangement or improvisation, of what he had birthed in original composition. This searching of his own music, as if it were new to him, is shared with the listener from time to time throughout the recordings of his career. Each instance is a new statement, a new insight. This can only take place when one has "let go" of the original work and then later revisited it as something fresh from outside oneself. Kurt's music spoke first to him, then to others, then back around as fresh to him. It is difficult to overstate how unique this is among artists. It can only happen to the humblest of them. The reader may here accuse the biographer of overextending, of reading into Kurt's work, rather than drawing from it. But there is a difference between eisegesis, imposing more than is there, and exegesis, discovering more than even the composer was aware of.

Let us consider the simple song "Oh, How He Loves You and Me." What we see in hymnals is the simple chorus. What Kurt saw in his revisiting of the song, now as arranger and performer, was the revisiting of a place of meeting with God, a thin place between heaven and earth. Kurt heard in this song, and in return visits to other of his compositions, the echoes of earlier prayer and the invitation to explore the further depths and reaches of a divine moment, a starting point for longer walks in the same direction with the Lord. Kurt may have put the song aside in a desk drawer at first. But then he revisited it and found a "thin place." He invited others to the thin place by publishing it. Then with each new arrangement or performance—new experiences. He returned to pray, again, and more deeply. In these second waves of arrangements, performances, and recordings of the simple song, Kurt serves as teacher. A teacher does more than merely transfer a body of knowledge or a fact. A teacher inspires the student to find truth beyond the teacher's knowledge.

Kurt's music mapped a terrain of thin places where encounters with the Spirit could be anticipated, not guaranteed. No clever formulaic manipulation here, only authentic moments where earlier encounters with God are marked like Ebenezers, notes stacked in chords like memorial stones, "hither by God's help we've come." We also saw Kurt return to these thin places in his live performances of his music at the piano. At the piano, Kurt returned to the thin places to pray to God "in front of God and everybody." The teacher led the students to the thin places and prayed. We returned with Kurt, not to revisit what he had done, but to be reminded of what the Spirit can do. Kurt was not playing or arranging what he wished he had done originally; he was not correcting an earlier mistake. He was reporting with each arrangement and performance what he had experienced since then, and recently. The studio was workshop; live performance was prayer. The studio was sanctuary; live performance was closet.

Kurt's return visit to his song "Oh, How He Loves You and Me," recorded on the album *Kurt Kaiser Piano: A Part of Me*, and later on the album *Oh, How He Loves You and Me*, is a return for new inspiration.[42] Indeed, we hear exploration as well as reminiscence in this solo voice, solo piano, chorus and orchestra arrangement. It leans forward. It is an introspective arrangement that knows there is more, eternally more, to his relationship with this song from the Source of Music. Kurt does not go back to hold on to the past, but rather, to embrace it as assurance of a compelling future.

Owning the gift for Kurt meant processing the results of his work in honest relief against the conviction and backdrop of a deeply held humility. One evening in 1972, Kurt made his way to his hotel room in Cincinnati, Ohio. He turned on the television and dropped down onto his bed without searching the channels. The scene on the TV was a gathering of some 80,000 students in the Cotton Bowl Stadium in Dallas, Texas. They were in town for Campus Crusade for Christ's Explo '72. It was the culminating evening of the event referred to by some reporters as the "Christian Woodstock." Others described Explo '72 as the most visible single event of the Christian cultural wave known as the Jesus Movement.

The stadium lights went down as the gathered high school and college students passed small flames, person to person, candle to candle, singing "Pass It On." The stadium filled with candlelight. Celebrities present included Bill Bright, Billy Graham, Johnny and June Cash, Kris Kristofferson, *Love Song*, and *Andre Crouch and the Disciples*.[43] Kurt's response was one of surprise, awe, excitement, humility, and thankfulness, all wrapped into one breathtaking moment. His overwhelming thought at the time was, "Look what God can do if we simply turn our gifts over to him." He never forgot the scene or the lesson.

If Kurt could have chosen another "life," another identity, it might well have been as a jazz composer and performer. Tucked away in a wall-mounted cassette storage rack, Kurt kept a roughly recorded tape. It is now brittle and "noisy," but still intriguing and compelling. It is a set of four improvisations on a jazz theme that he had imagined, captured, and explored. It is a deteriorating artifact of a Kurt Kaiser "what if?" moment.[44] Kurt admired the great jazz artists as he admired the great classical geniuses. This paragraph may be the height of his recognition as a jazz artist, but he did receive an acknowledgment of his talent from the acclaimed recording engineer Bruce Swedien, who once commented that Kurt Kaiser was the best improvisational pianist he had ever heard.[45] Improvisation for Kurt may have been his innate jazz instinct working its way through a staunch commitment to church music. However, he credited his improvisational skills to what was required of him as a twelve- or thirteen-year-old boy accompanying live radio broadcasts of a western (cowboy) serial for children on Moody Bible Institute's station WMBI.

Kurt taking hymn requests from the congregation to create a piano medley on the spot. FBC Norman, Oklahoma 1989.

In some ways, Kurt was Bruce Swedien's connection to the "Church" of his childhood, Bruce's priest of sorts. In actual practice, Kurt used Bruce as sound engineer on only a few of his productions. One of the more notable projects was the 1999 Kurt Kaiser Music recording, *Strength for Today . . . Bright Hope for Tomorrow*, in which Bill O'Brien was vocal soloist and Kurt was his accompanist.[46] This CD was not going to be a bestseller. All three men knew it, but by this time in each of their careers that didn't matter to them. There was nothing left to prove for Bruce Swedien, Kurt Kaiser, or Bill O'Brien. Bill had been a high-ranking administrator in the Southern

Baptist Convention's Foreign Mission Board. When he left that position, he joined the staff of Samford University in Birmingham, Alabama, where he created a vibrant center for the study and envisioning of world mission efforts. He ended his career as co-pastor/director, with Dr. Gary Cook, of the innovative Gaston Christian Center in Dallas, Texas. Three men, who had reached the heights of their callings, did a recording project simply "because." It is a prayer of thanks, an offering born of gratitude, a recognition of divine guidance. Two of the cuts on this CD, "Wings of the Morning" and "Musing," are Kurt's solo work in a smooth jazz/improvisation style. Perhaps those are the tunes that so impressed Swedien. This recording was done at Swedien's studio in Roxbury, Connecticut.

In 1977, Bruce Swedien had been the engineer of the album *Robert Hale & Dean Wilder: Break Forth and Sing*, for which Kurt was the producer. He was also the "Mixdown Engineer" for the recording of Kurt's 1979 young adult musical *Just for You*, for which Kurt was also the producer.[47] Bruce Swedien knew Kurt the man, the producer, the pianist, the composer, and the arranger. If Kurt was Bruce's connection to the Church, Bruce was, in turn, Kurt's connection to secular popular music.

Kurt's connection to jazz was kept fresh and alive by his friendship with composer, performer, and conductor Clare Fischer. Kurt listened not only for pleasure but also as a "student" to Fischer's albums such as *Free Fall*, 1985 and *. . . And Sometimes Instruments*, 2011. Kurt studied Fischer's instrumental bass lines and the intricate chords and voice leading of his vocal ensemble writing. Kurt was in awe, convinced that he was not capable of such intricacy.

Kurt's jazz and Church music "worlds" embraced each other when Clare Fischer recorded an album of organ arrangements of songs from *Tell It Like It Is* in 1972. Kurt and Ralph Carmichael's hit musical had impacted the vocal music of the Church from stage to dais to choir loft to congregation, accompanied by piano, guitars, and drums, but it had somehow missed the organ . . . until now. Ralph Carmichael confessed on the back liner of the album cover that an organ recording was "the farthest notion from anybody's mind." The 1972 album, *Organ Solos from Tell It Like It Is: Played by Clare Fischer*, brought fresh sounds to the musical and to the instrument. The best way to describe this recording is to say that it explains for organ purists, in sound rather than words, the changes that were pressing against traditional church music. Three of Kurt's songs from the musical are included in this recording: "What's God Like?" "MasterDesigner," and "Pass It On." Fischer's chord structure and harmonic progressions alerted organists, if they would accept the news, that what was coming was art, new but fully capable of engendering reverence.

Kurt's bent toward jazz was confirmed by his nephew Jeff McGarvin, the host of the radio program *Upbeat*. Jeff's program airs on Durango, Colorado's station KDUR, broadcast from the campus of Ft. Lewis College. During a period of some fifteen years, beginning in 1995, Kurt would be Jeff's guest once a summer. Jeff's program is focused on jazz, largely piano jazz. Jeff would air a piano jazz recording, and then he and his uncle Kurt would discuss it. In Jeff's opinion, Kurt "looked at music differently than anyone else, far above anyone else . . . His ear was unbelievable."[48] Kurt's favorite artists to discuss were Oscar Peterson and Count Basie. He would analyze a set and each piece within it according to key, something that Jeff was unaware of: "Oh, I see: A, D, F# minor, D, A." Kurt was expressive in his discussion of each piece, the music, and its performance. Jeff invited Kurt onto his radio program, not because of Kurt's Christian music compositions and recordings, or even because Kurt was his uncle, but because of how Kurt could talk about jazz.

2
WORD MUSIC AND KURT KAISER MUSIC

WORD MUSIC

Kurt's first job after earning his master's degree was a position that the admired composer, arranger, and conductor Paul Mickelson, working from California, had turned down. Paul chose to stay in Los Angeles rather than move to Waco, Texas and accept additional responsibilities. WORD was growing, and the work was becoming more demanding. Paul's decision created Kurt's opportunity. Paul stayed at WORD for a short time after Kurt came on board to help orient him. The position was a combination of recording producer and Artist and Repertory (A&R) development.

As early as 1957, Jarrell McCracken, President of WORD Records, saw glowing potential in Kurt as an arranger and recording producer.[1] Kurt had been recommended to McCracken by Cy Jackson and Bob Pierce. Jackson served as crusade coordinator for evangelist Merv Rosell, often calling on Kurt to play the piano at his crusades. Jackson was also in charge of public relations for Dr. Charles Fuller's radio programs and for Fuller Theological Seminary. Cy Jackson, who would later join WORD as Director of Public Relations, and Bob Pierce, president of World Vision, knew well Kurt's special talent and dedication to the work of the Church.

McCracken traveled to Chicago to watch Kurt in action as the producer of a recording and to have a conversation. The session turned out to be an audition that Kurt passed. Timing was crucial for McCracken's visit. Kurt was seriously considering a remarkable opportunity: a music faculty position at New Trier Township High School in Winnetka, Illinois. The school was known for its outstanding music program and faculty.

After a meal prepared by Kurt's mother, he and McCracken went outside and sat in the front porch swing of Kurt's childhood home on Sunnyside Avenue. In the ensuing conversation, Kurt's imagination was captured. McCracken described an opportunity that to Kurt was an invitation to explore the road "less traveled," and, as with the traveler in the poem, it "made all the difference."[2] Kurt joined WORD. "I recorded Bill Mann while I was still at Northwestern, although I was in the employ of WORD, but we hadn't moved down here [Waco] yet."[3]

Responsible for "A&R," Kurt's mind and emotions must have bounced between those of a kid in a candy store and those of a thief in a jewelry store: extraordinary opportunity, extraordinary risk. He would be the one to decide the focus, nature, and artists of future recording projects. Toward what end? Who would he enlist as artists? What would they sing or play? What would be the criteria? How many per year?

Kurt had been around microphones and studios, but he had never been the one in charge until this auditioning by McCracken. What exactly would be required of the "producer" in this new environment? He could choose an artist, launch an artist, become an artist. How do you approach a celebrity? How do you shape a celebrity in the making? How do you decide to become an artist? Could he think of making himself an artist without stepping over the boundaries of self-aggrandizement that his father had so firmly fixed in his conscience? After all, scripture was clear about "thinking more highly of oneself than we ought" (Romans 12:3).

What if he failed and brought the company down with him? What if the still fledgling company failed and brought him down with it? We might expect these questions of a young person in their first encounter with such breathtaking responsibility and opportunity. But this was not how Kurt saw it. Surely his boundaries and standards of musical excellence, biblical veracity, Church connectedness, and morale uprightness could be counted on as sufficient early goals and guidelines. He had what it would take; he simply had to trust it. He was just sure enough to say "yes" to God and to Jarrell McCracken.

For all his memorable and influential compositions that would come, for all his piano genius that would be on display, in the end, Kurt Kaiser's greatest industry-shaping influence would come through his work as a record producer. The recording of television and movie stars singing their Christian testimony was seen by many Christians as something of a victory for the cause of evangelism. It was seen as a door opening to take humble Christian testimony into the world of fame and entertainment, a door that was closed in the case of secular recording labels. Would anyone notice such work?

Where should he start? He could only start in the arena of his skill and experience, no matter how small that arena seemed. He would start with who and what he knew: connecting in new ways to existing ministries with which he was familiar and continuing with artists that Paul Mickelson had already signed. He began there, tapping into a fairly reliable source of immediate success and apparent aptitude.

Then, as confidence grew, he would record more far-reaching and more widely known persons and groups. Soon he could add the "creating" of celebrities. But he would always keep the mission and values of WORD Music in mind, staying within the trajectory of purpose and values set forth by Jarrell McCracken, and the focus that he, himself, held so deeply. That vision would have Kurt say in later years that he never had second thoughts or misgivings about passing up the opportunity to record Bob Dylan, and that he had made a mistake in not recording Cynthia Clawson. Such thoughts, taken together, might seem counterintuitive, even contradictory, but not to Kurt in his foundational consistency.

Bob Dylan approached WORD about doing a Christian recording after his conversion, but Kurt turned down the offer. He felt that Dylan was not sincere, and he didn't want WORD to be used in that way. In the article "Bob Dylan's Overlooked Christian Music," posted on the *Sojourners* online journal, Aaron E. Sanchez wrote that Dylan released three albums in 1979, 1980, and 1981, combining to form his Christian era. However, Sanchez also reported that "Dylan's Christian conversion didn't last."[4] To make too much of Kurt's encounter with Dylan would be to use Bob Dylan in the way that Kurt did not want WORD to be used. Yet, to pass over this intriguing moment would be to miss a glimpse into the depth of Kurt's spiritual awareness, a facet of the conscience that he brought to the Contemporary Christian Music industry.

Kurt didn't always make the right business decisions. He did record some new artists only once. But his criteria were consistent, a commitment to the highest standards of music, churchmanship, and biblical foundations. All three were ever present, even if, at times, in uneven measure.

RECORDING EXISTING MINISTRIES

The recording of existing ministries was a wise move for a novice producer. The "Christian Artist" had not yet been invented, surely not yet exploited, when Kurt began with WORD. The music evangelists of the time were the musical heroes, and they were still very much tethered to the local congregation and the city-wide rallies of well-known revivalistic preachers. These roving singers were something of a "safe bet" and a logical extension of Kurt's earliest ministry experience as pianist for radio programs and Youth for Christ assemblies, and as a minister of music.

There was a comforting humility attached to the recording of others' ministries. It was not uncommon for Kurt's name to be absent from the album covers and labels of his early recording projects. But success and its renown would call him out of the shadows and into a more proactive and entrepreneurial role as this medium grew into its adolescence, and his confidence grew into its adulthood. The people of the existing ministries were humble enough "heroes," not yet celebrities, of his early radio days. He was now meeting them with the opportunity to join them in their worlds as he recorded them.

Bill Mann was the first person that Kurt recorded for WORD, making him something of a guinea pig. But Bill was so impressed with young Kurt as a person and musician that he gladly continued to record for WORD with Kurt as his arranger, conductor, producer, and occasional co-artist. The early Mann recordings represented a learning curve for Kurt. The first Bill Mann recording, Kurt's audition in Chicago, not only impressed Mann and Jarrell McCracken but also launched a friendship with Mann. It was a friendship that brought warmth and confidence into Kurt's new professional world. Interestingly, Bill, who became a WORD recording artist not long before Kurt arrived on the scene, had served large Methodist congregations in Baton Rouge and Houston, not as minister of music but as director of youth activities. He would, however, go on to oversee evangelistic singing in the music ministry of the First Methodist Church of Dallas. While there, Mann frequently asked Kurt to drive up from Waco to accompany him in his Sunday Evening Concert series at First Methodist.[5]

Earlier, on the back liner of the first recording, *Bill Mann: Moments for Meditation*, bold letters near the top declare "Arrangements by Kurt Kaiser." This 1957 project seems to have been the Kaiser "audition" recording that so impressed Jarrell McCracken. The final paragraph of the back liner notes elaborates:

> The musical arrangements on this album are by Kurt Kaiser, a student in the Northwestern University School of Music, Evanston, Illinois, and one of the bright young Christian musicians in the country. Mr. Kaiser is also heard on the piano on several of the numbers, and conducted both choir and orchestra in the recording sessions at the RCA Chicago studios. In addition to his studies, Mr. Kaiser is Minister of Music at Bethel Free Church in Chicago.[6]

The album was to have twelve songs, but it only has eleven. Correspondence between Mann, McCracken, and Kurt indicates that Bill was concerned about three of Kurt's hymn choices for the album. "All Your Anxiety" and "In Heavenly Love Abiding" were songs that Bill had never sung. The third song in question was "Blessed Assurance," the hymn that Bill considered his "theme song." It turned out to be the twelfth, the "omitted," song. Jarrell let Bill and Kurt work out the disagreement, whatever it was. Bill was disappointed but was willing to move forward in order to complete the project.

Some time had passed, and Kurt's family had moved to Waco, when a new album, this one simply titled *Bill Mann*, was recorded (c. 1960) in Capitol Studios in Hollywood, California. This time the back liner notes give evidence of the continuing upward trajectory of Kurt's reputation:

> A talented musician, Kurt is well known for his piano interpretations and techniques, as well as his arranging and directing abilities . . . abilities evident in his arranging, directing and producing of this entire album. Kurt had extensive training at the Northwestern University School of Music and served as Minister of Music at the Bethel Free Church in Chicago. He is now a member of the executive staff of WORD RECORDS, serving as Director of Artists and Repertoire . . .
>
> My friend, Kurt . . . wrote all of the arrangements, conducted the orchestra, the woodwind and guitar sessions and produced this unusual collection of sacred songs. Kurt is not only one of the finest musicians I know, but more than this, he is a fine Christian gentleman. Much will be heard of this great talent.[7]

Kurt's experience as a student and a minister of music at Bethel Free Church was enriched with his position at WORD, but it was still very early in Kurt's career. Mann blessed Kurt by predicting, "Much will be heard of this great talent."

Now, back to "Blessed Assurance." Kurt did all of the arrangements of the songs on the (c. 1965) album *Go Tell It On the Mountain: Bill Mann with the Concert Orchestra of Stockholm*. The album includes, interestingly, an entirely new setting, not just an arrangement, of "Blessed Assurance." Did Kurt want to use this setting in the 1957 "audition" album? Was it composed back then for Bill Mann's voice but held in reserve until Bill Mann was willing to record it? Had Bill Mann refused to record a new setting of the beloved hymn, his signature song? Was the song's omission from the earlier album the resolution that Jarrell had let happen? It appears so. Kurt often wrote music for specific artists. Did he have the confidence and understanding to do that as a student in 1957, standing up as producer to the (nearly as novice) soloist Bill Mann? It was no secret that Kurt's confidence and negotiation skills as a producer impressed Jarrell McCracken from the very beginning as much as did his musical skills.

This new setting shows either a remarkably strong early self-confidence on Kurt's part, or the developing, even blossoming, of an initial careful confidence. Probably both. Whatever the answer, the "Blessed Assurance" issue also reveals Bill Mann's grace and his admiration for Kurt's gifts. To dare write a new setting for an old favorite like "Blessed Assurance," and to do so for a well-known soloist who considered the traditional setting to be his signature song was risky. Whatever other words might apply, "risky" is appropriate.

Kurt's setting is a courageous, creative work that is soloistic, beyond congregational accessibility. It was not meant to replace the beloved hymn tune. The setting is an insightful exploration of the text. It fits the tenor voice of Bill Mann and the confident testimony of Kurt Kaiser. Though some eight years separate the two recordings, Kurt's setting is at home in either environment. Starting here, Kurt moved ever deeper into the giving of himself to his work, the opportunities it afforded, and the freedom it awakened. Pat Kaiser received a request for a copy of the score of Kurt's "Blessed Assurance" during the writing of this book.

Significant connections in Kurt's life and work are represented in the recording *Just for You: Song Stylings by Dick Baker*, produced by Kurt Kaiser (c. 1962).[8] Dick Baker was a well-known composer and served as music director for large youth services across the Texas Baptist Convention, the national Southern Baptist Convention, and at international Christian conferences. It was not unusual for the young Billy Graham to be the speaker at these events. As a Baylor University student (class of 1950), Dick Baker founded the Baylor Religious Hour Choir (BRH), a group that Kurt would later lead. Kurt included two of Dick Baker's best-known songs on this album: "Longing for Jesus" and "So Many Valleys." In recording Dick Baker, Kurt showed that he knew the Baptist, Texas, and youth rally worlds and their music.

Kurt reached back to his Chicago roots in recording and producing the undated WORD record *Ladies of Song: The Soul of Gospel Music*. This Chicago trio, comprised of Margaret Aikens and two sisters, Celeste Scott and Robbie Preston, began their gospel singing ministry in 1961, performing in churches, on television, and in concert with Mahalia Jackson, who was an inspiring encourager for them. Kurt's Chicago ties may well have brought this group to his attention, even though he left there in 1959. Billy Lee Preston, son of Robbie Preston, was one of the most accomplished jazz organists of this time. The Chicago connection, Kurt's knowledge of jazz, and the Mahalia Jackson recognition no doubt attracted the young producer. The risk was low, the experience was priceless, and notice was spreading. Even so, Kurt thought his recording of the group would be more widely received than it was. He was surprised but not discouraged.

In 1963, "Pop" and "Mom" Rosado, pastors of Damascus Christian Church in the Bronx, New York, decided to write and produce the play "The Addict," a dramatization of the life of junkies. It is a real-life drama performed by former drug addicts. They performed the play in churches, schools, and community auditoriums across the country, and Kurt produced the recording, *The Addicts Sing*. Quoting from the back liner:

> In speaking of the album Kurt Kaiser says: "The record has about it a crudeness that cannot be described, but that you must hear. It has a haunting kind of strength to it, and a very intimate kind of beauty, particularly in some of the solo spots. This is a record that I can highly recommend because it depicts musically, not finesse, but strength; not nuance, but intimate beauty; not greatness (musically), but a reality in a new-found joy that few records we have can equal."

We must not miss the insight that this recording, and Kurt's comments, provide concerning Kurt's "ear." The young producer with perfect pitch and high musical standards released an album that "has about it a crudeness." Music was not Kurt's god. The authenticity of engagement and expression by nine untrained singers produced a sound that rose higher in Kurt's soul than perfection did in his ear. Kurt's future unofficial role as conscience of the Contemporary Christian Music industry is starting to emerge. With Kurt, authenticity of soul and sound had a chance to be recognized, respected, and honored, even in the sophisticated arena of musical excellence.

Kurt's overseas journeys did not make him a global citizen, but they did make him a seasoned traveler who was at home wherever music was being made. He kept in his heart a place for the ministry of World Vision International, especially their Korean Children's Choir. Kurt recorded that group across a span of years, from when they were known as the "Korean Orphan Choir" into the years after 1968 when their name was changed to the "Korean Children's Choir." Time had widened the focus from only children orphaned by the Korean War. Four albums are listed in the recordings section at the end of this book. In them, Kurt ranges from producer to arranger. Of special interest are Kurt's arrangements of the

German hymn "Voglein Im Hohen Baum" (Now Shines the Sun on High) and a "Hymn Medley" on the 1972 album, *The Korean Children's Choir: To the World with Love*. In the German hymn, Kurt relates to the children and their international, multilingual experience with church music. The hymn medley is a delicate and contemplative treatment of four evangelistic gospel songs. "Delicate" and "contemplative" are words seldom used to describe that genre. "Pass It On" serves as the opening and closing of the medley, as well as an angelic descant in "Hark the Voice of Jesus Calling"; the set is quite moving.

"Dana" (Rosemary Brown Scallon) was an Irish recording artist well known in the Christian music scene in Great Britain. On a trip to London, Kurt and Pat were able to meet with Dana at a hotel. Their meeting was warm and friendly. Kurt and Pat ended up visiting Dana and her family in Ireland just a few days later. Three weeks later, Dana and her husband found themselves in Waco, Texas, having dinner at the Kaiser residence. Jarrell McCracken and other WORD executives were also present. After dinner, Dana sang for the dinner party and a record agreement was struck. Dana was quite surprised because she was Catholic, and she thought the Christian market in America was controlled by the Southern Baptists. She was also convinced "that WORD was definitely not the company for me, as they already had a very big star called Evie, and there was little hope of their taking on another girl of similar type."[9]

Dana recorded two of Kurt's songs on her first WORD album *Totally Yours* (1981); "Sing for Me," written for her, and "He Careth for You." Both were arranged by Bill Purcell. On her 1984 WORD album *Let There Be Love*, she recorded "Portrait of Jesus" written by Kurt and Claire Cloninger. Kurt was the pianist for her recording of the song "Christ Is My Light."

RECORDING CELEBRITIES

On one occasion while addressing a group of ministers of music in Missouri, Kurt shared the insight that a record producer's goal is to get the finest performance possible from artists, and that even though many artists enjoy excellent reputations, you cannot overlook the fact that a phrase that is sung flat must be corrected. Kurt enjoyed the challenge of having the artist improve without "bruising" their egos.

Burl Ives, Ernie Ford, Carol Lawrence, Ethel Waters, Anita Bryant, Pat Boone, Dale Evans, Ray Price, Anita Kerr, Robert Hale, Dean Wilder,

Roy Rogers, Jerome Hines, and Wayne Newton are some of the television, movie, and recording celebrities with whom Kurt worked.

As mentioned earlier in this chapter, Bob Dylan came to Kurt at WORD, inquiring about a possible recording project. Kurt said, "No." When asked later if he regretted not signing Dylan, Kurt replied, "No, what he wanted to do was not in keeping with what we were doing." To "drop" yet another name, the renowned jazz pianist Herbie Hancock was, at one point, in conversation with Kurt concerning a recording project. Even though Kurt had deep admiration for Hancock's genius and genre, a project never materialized. The reason remains a mystery. Perhaps it was similar to the Bob Dylan situation.

Enlisting celebrities and producing their next exposure to the record-buying public was no small task. The relationship was not one of Kurt "riding the coattails" of celebrities. The dynamic was more of celebrities taking a chance on his production skills in the early days, and then seeking him out as successful years rolled by. They came to the studio and the projects with their standards in hand, even as Kurt did. His job included combining the standards in mutual agreement. It is also true that Kurt had to have the confidence to step into the celebrity's world as an expert worthy of their trust and reputation. The projects also needed to make it obvious to the WORD public that Kurt was about the music and the message, not the name recognition of the "stars." Kurt helped those known for their stardom to experience a moment of sharing their Christian testimony with their established fans; the work of a minister of music who thought of the studio as a sanctuary. Kurt shepherded the message and the high-profile messengers in a unique ministry setting, turning the studio, an arena of soundproof pride, into a chapel of reverent humility.

The move from singer and actor Burl Ives' folk song persona into that of hymn singer was a short journey. Hymns are folk songs, and they were Burl's "testimony." Kurt was not Burl's only hymn arranger or producer, but the two developed a deep friendship, holding in common an understanding of Christianity as something uniquely intimate. Two albums, *Burl Ives: Shall We Gather at the River?* and *Burl Ives: How Great Thou Art*, were arranged and conducted by Kurt. Both albums are all hymns.

It was Kurt who introduced Burl to the Korean Children's Choir. The album, *Burl Ives and the World Vision Korean Orphan Choir Sing of Faith and Joy*, produced by Kurt, combines several of Kurt's "worlds." The relationships with World Vision and its president, Dr. Bob Pierce, the Korean

Orphan Choir, WORD, celebrity, and friendship unite in a vision first imagined by Kurt.

Another "star" whose voice and persona captured Kurt's attention was Carol Lawrence. Kurt produced the album *Carol Lawrence: New Friends* in 1975. He said of Carol, "She probably dances even better than she sings . . . I wrote an arrangement of the Shaker tune, 'Simple Gifts,' with thirty-two measures of music in the middle that she could dance to in concert [the album arrangement of "Simple Gifts" is attributed to Ron Harris]. I saw her sing and dance it. Turning to Don Hustad at my side, I asked him the question, 'What do you think of that?' He said to me, 'Kurt, we may never see anything more beautiful this side of Heaven.'"[10] Don Hustad was Professor of Church Music at the Southern Baptist Theological Seminary in Louisville, Kentucky. He was also the organist for the Billy Graham Crusades. Kurt's question was voiced in conversation with Dr. Hustad, but was addressed, in concept, to all those whom Hustad represented in Chicago's Christian circles, in academia, and in Southern Baptist higher education.

The back liner of *Carol Lawrence: Tell All the World about Love* (WORD, 1977), contains this statement written by Carol: "My heart is full of joy and thanks for the chance to record this new album with (now my old friend) Kurt Kaiser." Insider jokes are born of out-of-the-spotlight experiences and friendships, which is why they are often seen as somewhat rude to those not in the know. Yet Carol risks that in front of her established audience. This is authentic friendship, not shallow gushing.

A note attached to a bouquet sent to Kurt after one of his surgeries reads, "Dear Kurt, just a few of the Lord's spring blossoms to remind you that you are constantly in my thoughts and prayers. I only wish I could lift some of the burden from you. Love Always, Carol Lawrence." She was a well-known TV personality and popular recording artist. But the studio, under Kurt's leadership, was sanctuary from all that.

Ethel Waters, movie and recording star, was buried at Forest Lawn Memorial Park in Glendale, California, on September 6, 1977. Kurt was there. He had been one of her preferred accompanists and a close friend, close enough that she called him "Kurty-Wurty." Sometime in the late 1960s, Kurt produced the recording, *Ethel Waters Reminisces: With Reginald Beane at the Piano*. Then, in 1977, that recording's music became the basis for the album *Just a Little Talk with Ethel*, produced by Kurt, with Cy Jackson listed as Executive Producer. Cy and Kurt traveled to Ethel's home in Chatsworth, California, where they recorded a conversation between

Kurt and Ethel. Segments of the conversation and songs from the earlier recording (with two exceptions) are interspersed like a patchwork quilt. Ethel tells the story of her life and work, obviously prompted by questions from Kurt. We hear a bit of his questions and short responses in the conversationally edited songs and story. Ethel was eighty years old at the time, just months before her death. The conversation has all the tone and depth of genuine friendship and trust. Kurt came to her. He knew the importance of what she had experienced and what she had to say. This was a life lesson, not a commercial strategy.

The undated album *Jim Roberts: How Great Thou Art*, with the Stockholm Concert Orchestra conducted by Kurt Kaiser, includes Kurt's song, "Where Shall I Run?" The commentary on the back liner of the record jacket is by TV personality Lawrence Welk. Jim Roberts was a regular tenor soloist on the Lawrence Welk Show. Equally as prominent on the show was soprano soloist Norma Zimmer, so Kurt recorded them together on the undated album *Jim Roberts and Norma Zimmer: Whispering Hope*. Kurt was the arranger of each song and orchestra conductor on this album. The television show studio audience was always dressed as if sitting in church. They were the people who would listen to the recording. It was age specific, not reaching out to young people. Soloists were revered on the show and in the sanctuary. To have two of them singing hymns in duet was not a novel idea; the two sang hymns separately and in duet from time to time on the TV show. But the album is much more than a move from TV screen to record album; it is both rich and enriching. The orchestra scores are far beyond simple realizations of a piano accompaniment; they have a life and an integrity all their own. The album is not simply a collection; it is an event. Kurt's reach on behalf of WORD was wide and authentic.

The album *Myrtle Hall: Thank You, Lord* (WORD Records, 1977) grounds its extraordinary quality in the Juilliard-trained voice of concert artist and King's College New York Artist-in-Residence Myrtle Hall. Maintaining that quality on all fronts, the producer/conductor of the album was Kurt, the engineer was Bruce Swedien, and the arranger was Bill Pursell. The back liner notes by Cliff Barrows, of the Billy Graham Evangelistic Team, are accompanied by a photo of Myrtle Hall and Billy Graham standing together. For Christian listeners, the aura of the Billy Graham team and crusades adds a balancing legitimacy and gravitas to the album's classical gospel feel.

Myrtle Hall's voice is enhanced by the expertise of renowned composer and arranger Bill Pursell, professor at Belmont University in Nashville, and recording engineer Bruce Swedien, whose work with the biggest names in popular music made him a celebrity in his own right. Several songs on the *Thank You, Lord* album stand out. These include one of Kurt's most artistic songs, "His Will Our Own," as well as "Come See a Man" (Lyricist: Ed Seabough; Composer: Buryl Red), "Lord, Listen to Your Children Praying" (Composer: Ken Medema), "Grace to You" (Composer: Mark Blankenship), and Aaron Copland's "Zion's Walls" (Adapted and Arranged: Bill Pursell). These songs broadened the scope and spread of this album across Christian music's many musical styles and denominational arenas. The quality of this project sets it apart, even among the best examples of Kurt's work as producer, composer, and conductor.

CREATING CELEBRITIES THROUGH RECORDING

Here, the tensile strength of the biblical concept of being "in" the world but not "of" it is put to one of its most rigorous tests: the nature of celebrity and a Christian worldview of all persons. Further, recordings must *sell* for any recording company to stay in business, whether secular or sacred. For records to sell, the music must be well written, arranged, and performed. The music must also be something that an identified audience will relate to and like. One of Kurt's moments of candor captured in Kris' interview was when Kurt talked about his taste in music—not his musical standards, but his taste. There is a difference. In the interview, Kurt said:

> Whereas if it had been too heavy duty for my tastes, I don't think WORD would be nearly as successful as they are . . . my tendency is to go for things that are really good as opposed to things that are going to sell. You know. That's why I responded to Billy Crockett because Billy Crockett writes music that's really very good, but he was too good for WORD. And that often happens. Artists are way too good for the masses.[11]

"Too good for WORD"; what does that mean? It means that Kurt had an admiration for Billy Crockett's art that rose above any inclination to capture it commercially. It may be difficult for nonmusicians to grasp the concept that Kurt is addressing. Artistic standards are always present and always important, but they are not always the determining factors in terms of mass appeal. Crockett's music was beyond WORD's recognized market.

There are additional criteria in the successful sales formula. It is important that the person who would become a recording artist possess a compelling stage presence for purposes of live performance of their music, which results in sales of their recordings. The classical concert artist and the pop singer must be at home in the spotlight, both figuratively and theatrically. Physical appearance is also a factor. As with other characteristics already considered in this chapter, all must be considered, even if they are not present in equal measure. It must also be stated here that musicians are trained to be critics, which leads very quickly and very easily to being crit*ical* of the musical skill, talent, and knowledge of other musicians. There is no course titled "How to Be Critical." It happens automatically in the study of applied (individual voice and instrumental performance) music, in the progression from one applied teacher to another, in the study of historical periods of composition and the study of composers. The music student is a de facto student of the art of critique.

As an Artist and Repertory developer, critique was a part of Kurt's professional reality and responsibility: did artists sound good, did they come across well, did they look good? How much is this to be discussed? In whose company and what circumstances are such things to be discussed? By what standards and evaluation shall an artist's or a potential artist's contribution to the art be measured?

A Christian is not, by definition, deaf to musical quality or blind to physical attractiveness. Grace can have more than one definition, especially on stage. Let us look clearly at the difficult dynamic tension of Kurt's competing (conflicting?) responsibilities: his commitment to the principles and standards of musical excellence, church-connectedness, and biblical truth, and the industry's demands for sound, performance, and looks. Now let us add to this complexity one's own experience, upbringing, preferences, business savvy, sensitivity, kindness, and Christian grace. In this environment, essential and crucial business conversation can sound shrill and cold, even when tempered by a warm Christian heart. The boundaries and filters of personal thought, private conversation, business meetings, musical critique, and discretion can shift, overlap, or, at times, disappear.

Kurt did not always get it right. His comments could be short, direct, unsheathed, politically incorrect. Even so, when the words with rough business edges made it past the tempering of Christian heart softness, how he lived his life was the corrective to what he may have said in the moment. Perhaps we can call upon the adage, "To the pure, everything is pure." His life was of a whole cloth. There were no divides separating his home, business, work, play, and church. His unity of "self" exposed and, at the same time, confessed his own occasional shrill evaluations and comments. He was the conscience of his industry, an authentic conscience because of his authentic humanity. The characteristics of principle, preference, and bias are separated by little more than mist. The mist is intent and perception. Those who would have Kurt coach them toward careers and ministries as recording artists would have to step into this world of specific conflicts. Kurt would be their usher and their conscience.

In a tug-of-war between his head and his heart, his head would most often win, citing the reality that you can't record all the great talent that exists out in the churches; that the Artist and Repertory person has to be very selective. That was often a tough decision to make. But some decisions were easier than others.

Songwriter and concert artist Ken Medema first met Kurt when two singers, Ron and Patricia Owens (well known to Kurt), insisted that Ken go with them to the offices of WORD Records in Waco, Texas. Ron and Patricia had heard Ken sing at a women's convention in Waco. They were certain that he would love Kurt and that Kurt would love him. After a bit of introduction and small talk about Christian music, Kurt invited Ken to sing some of his songs.

Ken sang what was to become the first of his songs that he ever recorded, the title song on his first WORD album. Ken sang "Fork in the Road."[12] Ken finished singing; Kurt said nothing. Long seconds passed. Ken was concerned that Kurt might not have liked the song. As Ken began to ask, Kurt answered, "Shut up, I'm crying." Kurt then called in some other officials at WORD, and Ken sang the song again. It should be noted here that no one in the Kaiser family can believe that Kurt would say, "Shut up." But Ken insists that it's true. This writer is inclined to side with Ken, hearing "Shut up" as a "left-handed" compliment but bows to those who knew Kurt best. The song, based on Judas' decision to betray Jesus, focuses on the importance of following Jesus, no matter the cost. It ends by incorporating the hymn "Beneath the Cross of Jesus." One wonders if Kurt was remembering the Sunday School class in Billings, Montana, visited by the eventual martyr Jim Elliot. Perhaps, as Ken sang, Kurt remembered his conversation with Jarrell McCracken in the Chicago porch swing where he decided to forgo the chance to teach at a prestigious Chicago high school, known for its music faculty, in order to join a small, start-up recording company in Waco. Either way, or neither way, Kurt wept.

That's how Ken became a WORD Records artist. It was also the beginning of a friendship that lasted throughout Kurt's life, as they discovered that they had many things in common, such as the music of Brahms, speaking in German, and telling jokes, among them. There were many happy recording sessions in the years that followed. Ken remembers that Kurt's patient but disciplined way of running a recording session was respected by many and matched by few. By Ken's own admission, Kurt was one of a very few heroes in his life.

At age seventeen, Evie Tornquist of Scandinavian descent, living in New Jersey, received a phone call from Kurt Kaiser. She had been singing in Scandinavia and had done some custom recordings there. "Custom recordings" means recordings not made as a signed artist for a recording company. In fact, she borrowed money from her dad to make her first recording in Norway. Evangelistic singers Phil and Louie Palermo got one of Evie's records from Sweden. The brothers were involved in the Youth for Christ world and began recording on the Sacred Records label in the early 1950s. They became friends of Kurt's. He had known them since his early Youth for Christ days. He recorded them along the way as their ministry stretched well into the 1970s.

When the Palermo brothers heard Evie's record they contacted Kurt at WORD, encouraging him to consider recording her. Kurt was hesitant at first because Evie was so young, but he obliged by listening to some recordings that Evie's mother sent to him. When he listened, he was impressed and called Evie's mother, who was also her "agent." Evie and her mother were quite excited when Kurt said that he would like Evie to do a record for WORD. When Evie graduated from high school, she flew to Waco by herself and had dinner with the Kaisers. Evie signed with WORD Records in 1974 and continued as one of their recording artists for the next decade. Kurt didn't produce any of her recordings but stayed close to her as songwriter and friend. Kurt and Pat became her mentors. Evie was single when she first met Kurt. She was dating different guys, and Pat and Kurt were always there to "bounce things off of." They were like an aunt and uncle to her, and a source of wisdom.

WORD artists such as B. J. Thomas, Amy Grant, and Ken Medema became like family to her. Others, including Bev Shea, the Palermo Brothers, Ralph Carmichael, Andrea Crouch, the Imperials, and the band LOVE SONG, were impactful in Evie's life as well.

Kurt didn't push his own material when songs were selected for her recordings. But she did record "Sunday Mornin'" and "Oh, How He Loves You and Me" on her 1975 album *Evie Again*, and then "Pass It On" on her 1976 album *Evie: Gentle Moments*. "Oh, How He Loves You and Me" now has a place in her family lore: her grandkids call it the "Oh How Song." "With Kurt we were a team. There was never any friction, only enjoyment." Evie loved Kurt's stories about friends and family and learned from him the importance of the integrity of the message and the integrity of personal life, including commitment to Christ and family, and precision in music making.[13]

When Evie and Pelle Karlsson were married in New Jersey, in February 1979, Pat and Kurt attended. Kurt played the music for the wedding, including accompanying Evie's mom when she sang. Cliff Barrows of the Billy Graham team "tied the knot."

In 1979, The Billy Graham Association produced a movie and a book about the life and ministry of Joni Eareckson Tada. A diving accident at age 17 paralyzed her from the shoulders down, casting a blanket of tragedy over her future. But through determination and faith she created a different future, a ministry of recording, writing, and speaking. The book and the movie *Joni* got WORD's attention. She sang the closing song in the movie, but that was the extent of her singing experience. She had no vocal training at all. Kurt signed her as a WORD recording artist in 1980, and she stayed with the company until 1994. The four-year overlap in Evie's and Joni's recording career with WORD was the beginning of a lifelong friendship for them. Both were nurtured by Kurt and Pat during their time with WORD and continue to stay in touch with Pat at the time of this writing.

Joni's first album was *Joni Eareckson: Joni's Song* in 1981. Kurt set up a recording session in Burbank, California, that included full orchestra. Joni was completely surprised when she entered the studio. She was not expecting anything on that scale. After only four measures into the session, Kurt stopped the proceedings, suggesting that everyone take a break. He made a couple of minor, perhaps even superficial, adjustments in the orchestra, and then worked with Joni as a vocal coach. He suggested that she relax and think about each note, remembering that she wasn't performing for people, but for the Lord. He helped her with breathing as a singer. Kurt was not only the producer for most of her albums, he continued as her vocal coach as well. Joni absorbed lessons from Kurt in gentleness, sweetness, kindness, and professionalism.

In a conversation with this writer about Kurt, Joni recounted an event at which Kurt was not present. When Joni's father died, she traveled to the top of Pike's Peak to scatter his ashes. As she arrived, on the far side of the parking lot Joni heard a girl singing the song "Spirit Wings" along with Joni's recording. "Spirit Wings" was the title song on an album that

Kurt had produced and conducted.[14] Joni made her way to where the girl was and sang with her. Place yourself in the girl's shoes at that rich, now surprisingly enriched, spiritual moment. Kurt was not the composer of the song. He was not the performer on the album. He was not present in the parking lot. But he was the one who had brought song and singer together in a recording studio before God brought singer and seeker together on a mountain top.

On Joni's fiftieth birthday, celebrated by some 200 guests in Los Angeles, Kurt played piano at the party. This was in keeping with the personal investment that Kurt and Pat had poured into Joni all along. The friendship continued even after the musical popularity had faded.

RECORDING IN ENGLAND

Kurt went to London to do much of his orchestra recording. Factors that sent him across the Atlantic included scheduling availability and more reasonable costs related to players and studio time. He made so many trips to England for this purpose that he joined "The Savage Club" (named in honor of eighteenth century poet Richard Savage) located in Berkeley Square, London. "One of the leading Bohemian Gentleman's Clubs in London," the club was founded in 1857 to facilitate "a meeting of gentlemen connected with literature and the fine arts, and warmly interested in the promotion of Christian knowledge, and the sale of excisable liquors."[15] The membership focus seems to have widened a bit in the following century: ". . . instituted for the association of gentlemen connected professionally with Literature, Art, Music, Drama, Science or Law in their creative or interpretative aspects, or who are distinguished members of the Legal Profession."[16] Be that as it may, Kurt's main attraction to The Savage Club was its quality as a dining destination.

The qualification under which he entered the club was music. On September 14, 1979, he was informed that his qualifications for membership had been approved by the committee and that he would probably be elected within a month. He was informed that membership privileges were his during that month if he would sign the attendance book and add a "C (for Candidate)" after his signature. Indeed, Kurt Kaiser, Esq. was finally elected with "Compliments and warmest wishes for a long and happy membership." Kurt took his membership seriously, but most of his subsequent personal correspondence with the officers of the club related to requests that late dues be paid.

One entirely British reason for recording in England was the 1977 WORD Records project *Hallelujah Jubilee: The London Emmanuel Choir*. Kurt arranged all the songs on this album and composed the title chorus. The final paragraph of the back liner reads:

> Rejoice in the blessings of the Hallelujah Jubilee Gospel as the London Emmanuel Choir ministers its truths to you so magnificently enhanced by the Westminster Sinfonia Orchestra under the guiding genius of producer and arranger Kurt Kaiser.

Paul Davis (UK)

THE MEDALLION SERIES (WORD MUSIC)

What does it mean to spread a series of "classical," or "traditional" recordings across the decade in which several Christian recording companies, including WORD, are trying to be the most contemporary? Was it an act of defiance? Was it an exercise in leadership? Perhaps Kurt launched the Medallion Series out of pure ego, holding high the banner of "good" music as its last champion. Or might it have been conscience at work? There is a difference between ego and conscience. Ego will soon be seen as lacking nobility. Conscience, on the other hand, is nobility, undemanding and unrelenting.

Kurt was an insightful observer and interpreter of changes in music styles, both inside and outside of the Church. Born of calculation, not of surprise, Kurt was concerned that the rise of new styles of music, in the minds of many, meant the demise of music that had passed the test of time and excellence. He felt that together, "established" and "innovative" could enrich the Church's diverse worship, and WORD's diverse audience. With the Medallion Series, Kurt Kaiser made his case tangible, recording examples of Christian classical's best, even while working to help shape the best of what was coming.

The following notice appears on each Medallion Series back liner:

> A collector's treasury of historic moments and milestone recordings in great music. Albums in this series are selected for their unique concert qualities and significance among the great music of the ages.

Kurt felt that, in part, Christian recording companies were leaving this arena because of low sales. However, he was convinced that new technology could boost sales strategies, especially within a company that had long boasted multiple style labels. He thought it was a responsibility as much as an opportunity.[17] The following are some of the recordings in the Medallion Series. Forgive the listing, but through it, Kurt's point is made, and the point is not about him.

Music from a Royal Wedding: Diane Bish at the Ruffatti Organ. 1981.
No attribution to Kurt Kaiser.
These are organ arrangements of the music played at the wedding of England's Prince Charles and Lady Diana Spencer. Nothing could have been more current in news around the world.

Diane Bish was organist at Coral Ridge Presbyterian Church and a concert artist for many years. She was the hostess and performer on the TV series *The Joy of Music*. Kurt was her guest on that program twice, in 1981 and 1983. In the 1981 episode, Kurt accompanied "Dana," the artist he signed at WORD.

How Sweet the Sound: The Baylor University Chamber Singers. 1981.
No attribution to Kurt Kaiser.
Dr. Robert H. Young, Professor of Music at Baylor University, established this elite group in 1962. Part of the "sweetness" of this "sound" is that of college students finding meaning, beyond course requirements, in classic hymns and art songs. Baylor University students found that they could do traditional music and still be recorded on the WORD label.

In His Love: Robert Hale and Dean Wilder. 1982.
Produced by Kurt Kaiser.
In the duets of opera star Robert Hale and voice professor Dean Wilder, there is art and worship, sanctuary and concert hall, the masters and the hymnists. Kurt was often the arranger and producer for "Hale and Wilder," and sometimes their accompanist. All but two of the pieces are accompanied by concert pianist Stephen Nielson. The remaining two are accompanied by Ovid Young. Kurt is the composer of three songs on this album, including the title song "In His Love and in His Pity" from his musical *Just for You*. Fame is not limited to contemporary recording artists. Concert hall excellence is not limited to academia. WORD is not bound to fad nor trend.

Music for Brass and Organ: Diane Bish at the Ruffatti Organ. 1983.
Produced and conducted by Kurt Kaiser.

Here, world-renowned concert artist and church organist Diane Bish is joined by a brass ensemble in classical works from the seventeenth to the twentieth centuries. This recording represents a valid and present niche within the Church's worship diversity. It should not be ignored.

Handel's Messiah: Recorded by Eastman Chorale and Philharmonia. 1984. Eastman School of Music, University of Rochester, Alfred Mann edition.

Conductor: Donald Neuen. Executive Producer: Kurt Kaiser
This was the first recording of Mann's edition of the original performance parts. Kurt brought this honor to WORD, but more importantly, he demonstrated that old branches could still produce green sprouts. The project elicited these handwritten responses from Mann and Neuen:

> October 6, 1984
>
> Dear Kurt,
>
> It was a wonderful day when the Messiah album arrived. None of the various publications have ever made me quite so happy. And how beautifully everything has been done! . . . What a happy and perfect collaboration it has been! . . .
>
> Sincerely, Alfred
>
> 12-16-84
>
> Dear Kurt,
>
> . . . If I thanked you for the rest of my life, I could never thank you enough for doing that recording—It means more than I'll ever be able to express! Have a super '85.
> Don

Parkening Plays Bach: Christopher Parkening. 1984.

No attribution to Kurt Kaiser.
All of the selections in this album had been previously released. But Kurt and world-renowned guitarist Christopher Parkening together chose the music to be included. Guitars were growing in acceptance in mainline Protestant and Baptist congregations via youth musicals, yet they remained somewhat controversial. Here that same instrument sounds from the classical repertory, without losing its voice in the contemporary. Kurt is subtly playing the role of "mediator" on behalf of the guitar. It is

not solely a "rock" instrument. It spans diverse performance venues. It can be an instrument of unity, rather than division, in the church. Listen to the instrument rather than the rhetoric. Learn from brothers and sisters in "other" social, and ethnic, cultures. The conscience pleads again in music and example, not in words.

The Cambridge Singers Directed by John Rutter: Volume II, The Heritage of English Church Music. 1985.

No attribution to Kurt.
At the time, John Rutter was as new and popular, and as much a "star" in the traditional music world, as was any contemporary Christian artist in that genre. This wasn't traditional Kurt/WORD in competition with contemporary Kurt/WORD, it was an appeal for excellence in two worlds by one company, one Church. Naivete? Stubbornness? Call and conscience. The champion of Evie and Joni was at the same time, the friend of John.

Canticles for Brass: King's Brass. 1985.

Producer: Kurt Kaiser.
Of the twelve pieces recorded on this album (hymn tunes and classical repertory), ten are arranged by Robert Nagel, and nine of those arrangements are copyrighted by WORD Music. Robert Nagel was one of the two trumpet players in the King's Brass. He was a graduate of Juilliard School of Music and the founder and director of The King's Brass and the New York Brass Quintet. He was also a faculty member of the Yale School of Music, New England Conservatory of Music, and the Manhattan School of Music. Kurt moved in and out of such circles with full welcome and brought their musicians to the WORD label, family, and reputation.

In Heavenly Love Abiding. 1985.

Hymn Settings and Producer: Kurt Kaiser. Cello: Anne Martindale Williams. Pianist: Stephen Nielson.
This album is discussed in some detail in the "Transitional Soundtrack" section later in this chapter.

Fairest Lord Jesus: The Baylor University A Cappella Choir. 1986.

Producer: Kurt Kaiser. Conductor: Hugh Sanders. Piano: Stephen Nielson. Hymn settings: Fred Bock, Tom Fettke, Clare Fischer, Kurt Kaiser, and Neil Richardson.

Again, Kurt widens the WORD tent, this time by bringing some of the more challenging choral composers of the day, both veterans and newcomers, to the label and to a remarkable Baylor choir. Jazz composer Clare Fischer's settings of *Fairest Lord Jesus*, and *Eternal Father, Strong to Save* are the most challenging. Kurt considered them nearly inaccessible. On this recording, popular anthem composer and hymn arranger Tom Fettke is given permission by producer Kurt Kaiser to move beyond the style expected by Tom's many admirers. Tom shows the art that undergirds his reliable masterpieces for the volunteer church choir. This is especially apparent in his setting of *O Love That Wilt Not Let Me Go*.

Neil Richardson, conductor of the BBC Radio orchestra in London, demonstrates the close relationship between jazz and symphonic music. Kurt knew the relationship but here allows Richardson to make the case. Richardson's arrangements of *Be Thou My Vision* and *The Lord's My Shepherd* take the human voice to the edge of its instrumentality, and then, take that same voice to the place where jazz and classical music meet in admiration of each other.

Fred Bock, composer, arranger, and publisher of choral music for the Church, brings two settings—*Come Ye Faithful, Raise the Strain* (accompanied) and *The King of Love My Shepherd Is* (a cappella)—that embrace the choir as those who rejoice, and those who have a message to share.

And then there is Kurt Kaiser the choral arranger, stepping away from his role as producer. His arrangement of *O Word of God Incarnate* lifts high the completeness of a cappella, giving the instrumentalists the opportunity to sit and listen and be enriched. Yet his arrangement of *Thy Word Is Like a Garden, Lord*, brings Kurt's piano prowess to the project. Stephen Nielson has the artistry to play the producer's arrangement on a largely unaccompanied album.

Kurt, the energy, heart, and visionary of the Medallion Series, put a truth on exhibit, trusting that it could tell its own story. He demonstrated that worship is a dynamic tension that stretches from the comfortable to the challenging, from the close-at-hand to the just-out-of-reach. He is voicing the conscience of all worshipers: worship should cost us something, the stretching of talent, the humbling of pride, the focus on God.

CAREER ARC AND APEX

It is here that Kurt Kaiser's story, for some, reaches its apex: Kurt *came* to WORD (1959), Kurt *"became"* WORD, Kurt *separated* from WORD (1991).

It's an old story often told: one gives their full and best energy to a concept, a vision, and that complete commitment works. It inspires, fashions, and energizes growth, identity, and place in a particular arena of endeavor. This extraordinary influence braids business and belief and life. The person becomes the company, or at least an icon of it, and the company becomes an extension of the person, and all is well until someone else, an insider or an external observer, sees a new vision emerging from within the glow of success. This happens to many people in many fields and disciplines. It happened to Kurt. He left WORD, in part because he could no longer contribute to the company's agenda with good conscience and authentic enthusiasm. For Kurt to be present in body but absent in spirit, because of new twists and turns, made him something of a ghost, a haunting reminder of earlier standards in music, biblical reflection, church connection, and perceived ethics.

For many, Kurt's artistic life is traced by the "came, became, and separated from" arc. WORD afforded Kurt a vast and invigorating field of opportunity and exploration, but the field was not without its boundaries. In fact, he brought the boundaries with him, encased deep within his soul. At WORD he would measure the width and generosity of those innate boundaries. The boundaries of high musical standard, obvious connection to the work of the Church, biblical veracity of lyrics, and high moral standards gave shape to opportunity. This new and inviting vastness engendered freedom and permission for innovation. Company President Jarrell McCracken encouraged Kurt to stretch his imagination, but he also added a boundary to Kurt's pre-existing set. After the success of *Tell It Like It Is*, which was distributed by WORD but not published by WORD, the boundary was first refusal rights: in other words, WORD would get first choice of all of Kurt's compositions. Kurt saw this as an understandable addition.

Kurt *came* to WORD and looked forward to going to work nearly every day. "One of the nice things about my work, I didn't have to be there at 8:00 in the morning, nor did I have to leave at 5:00. I could be there longer, and I liked that pretty much. I liked the openness of it, the open-endedness of it. I thought that was really great. And I liked the idea of being my own boss. Jarrell never asked me what I was working on, not one time."[18] Kurt had neither an operating budget nor a travel budget. McCracken gave him (as far as Kurt knew) free rein.

Over the course of transition from "coming to WORD" to "becoming WORD," Kurt had several positions of responsibility. Each title change, at this point "promotions," attracted the attention of the recording industry. This spotlight afforded Kurt the platform on which, over time, he would become seen as the conscience and the icon of Contemporary Christian Music (CCM). On that platform he wrote two of CCM's iconic songs, *Pass It On* and *Oh, How He Loves You and Me*. Welcomed or shunned, his personification of the highest standards helped shape the entire Christian music industry. It also brought an ever-deepening reputation for quality to WORD. His formative influence on the industry and movement began in the 1960s and continued strong until his death. Kurt and Pat's home in Waco became a destination of pilgrimage for those who sought to "pay homage" to the mentor.

Kurt's work and reputation hovered over the Christian music industry and across its landscape of companies and denominational departments. One didn't have to work with Kurt to be aware of his high standards. Whatever facet of the "industry" in which the people of the industry might have excelled, their excellence was measured, directly or indirectly, by how Kurt Kaiser did it, or might have done it, or would have expected it to be done. Ragan Courtney, poet, lyricist, and playwright of *Celebrate Life*[19] fame, never worked with Kurt. Even so, he was always aware that Kurt might encounter his work, and he wanted Kurt to be impressed with it.

Kurt's name sits near the top of any list of composers of Contemporary Christian Music whose work is still known and sung. Were "Pass It On," and "Oh, How He Loves You and Me" Contemporary Christian Music's best songs, or even Kurt's best songs? The questions are irrelevant. Whether in praise or in critique, these two songs have come to represent that time and genre. Further, there is no composer from this movement whose face is more recognizable than Kurt's. His face and work are iconic. That one could be considered the conscience and icon of a movement is a recognition far more admirable than that of "first," "best," or "most."

Even so, institutions of every sort experience change along the trajectory of their existence. As that happens, it is sadly common for the founders and shapers of the early days to be left behind in a dimming past by new employees, administrators, and owners. This was true of Kurt Kaiser's relationship to the new, green edges of WORD's stretch into its future. But it would be a lazy understatement of the changing status of Kurt at WORD simply to say, "This sort of thing happens to many, and quite often." Sales of WORD to the American Broadcasting Company (ABC), then to Gaylord Entertainment, and then to the Thomas Nelson Publishing Company stretched the cords of loyalty and vision between WORD and Kurt. Something of the original ethos was lost in each administrative and corporate transition.

Transition, forever present, is also forever difficult. In every major or significant transition, some of those involved will rush to the new vision, some will move with caution toward the new vision, and others will hold on to the old vision as if they are the last guard standing. Kurt was seen as a guardian. If he was a guardian, it was of lifelong commitments that he considered to be foundational, not of an earlier WORD status quo. Within himself, he was in the second category of transition, moving forward, but with caution. Not everyone shared his concern that these essential values were at risk, but he could only act on his own convictions, and within the arena of his responsibilities. The foundational values remained at the core of his being, even as they were perhaps secondary or tertiary in the thinking of others within the business called WORD, or the movement called Contemporary Christian Music.

Kurt's foundational principle that new music should never forget the Church as its home, and the accompanying responsibilities, were at times frustrating to those who wanted to stretch toward evangelism as an enterprise that could live untethered from all other concerns of the "steeple." Business success is not always a sign of God's blessing. Kurt's care that new music meet the demands of excellent performance, with entertainment being weighed in the context of engagement, but not of showmanship, was seen as unnecessary baggage from an earlier, simpler era. When conscience and icons are seen as relics rather than guidelines, heritage is seen as a hindrance to innovation.

Kurt's transition from source of new ideas and energy to perceived source of old ideas and stagnation within the WORD organization seems traceable in artifacts from four WORD milestones: the company's 10th, 25th, 30th, and 60th anniversaries.

An LP recording was produced in 1961, proclaiming on the front of its jacket, "10th Anniversary Album, *A Decade of Dedication*." The back liner, touting "A Decade of Dedication to the American Home, 1951–1961" includes nineteen photos, largely of individuals, but also of a female trio and two male quartets. These were the artists, composers, and arrangers who had made WORD what it had become in its first decade. Many of the artists were already hard at work when WORD came into being, certainly so by the time Kurt arrived. WORD recorded their songs and their singing as supplemental to those ministries, and foundational to WORD's work. Kurt's photo and name are included but are no more prominent than any of the others on this album cover. His presence was equal in proportion to The White Sisters trio, the Haven of Rest quartet, the Melody Four, pianist

Charles Magnuson, and arranger/conductor Dick Anthony. His light was no brighter or dimmer than soloists Frank Boggs, Bill Mann, Greg Loren, J. T. Adams, Claude Rhea, Bill Carle, Bill Pearce, Fague Springman, Joe Ann Shelton, or Ronnie Avalone, even though some of those names had approached the level of mentor for Kurt. What's more, Kurt's name and picture were the same size as Ralph Carmichael, who Kurt had admired for some time. Kurt's contribution to this album was a piano duet with Charles Magnuson, playing "Go Tell It On The Mountain."

That was the commemoration of the tenth anniversary of WORD. At only three years in, Kurt was still "new" to the company. It was a significant milestone for WORD, not for Kurt. What was its significance for Kurt? The company had a history that only barely included him. His contributions would lie ahead of him. The occasion called for pondering, even if for a passing moment: could he make a difference here?

But how could he be in doubt? Jarrell McCracken, president of WORD, had come to Chicago to seek out the young Kurt Kaiser, who already had a reputation as a great musician. Kurt had been discovered and hired. He was in an arena of heightened expectations. And as he had seen, and would continue to see, he was one of many. Remarkably talented people would come and go through WORD, many of whom would start their own recording companies or write or record with other companies. How would he fare as the continuous parade passed through WORD? Kurt had confidence, but he would have to call on more of it than in the past. The parade of future "loyal opposition competitors" passing through would include Fred Bock, Billy Ray Hearn, Buryl Red, Ken Medema, Mark Hayes, John Purifoy, Robert Sterling, and others. Each of these comings and goings was significant in its own way for Kurt. Staying was a renewed commitment each time a coworker came, learned, and left.

Kurt *became* WORD in the 1970s and 1980s. He had confidence in himself and in God's leadership. The "parade" was an opportunity to teach and bless. There was no crisis, no need for uncertainty. In 1974, WORD expressed their confidence in Kurt by building an office bungalow for him in his own backyard (literally). He paid half, and WORD paid half.

The twenty-fifth anniversary of WORD was something of a midpoint marker in Kurt's career with the company. In 1976, WORD Records produced the three-record LP collection *Word 1951–1976*. The set contains no commentary or attributions other than the statement "Twenty-five years on the growing edge of faith." The back liner simply lists the artists and song titles for each record. The name Kurt Kaiser and the title "Pass

It On" appear exactly in the center of the three lists, poetically in the middle of it all, record two, side two, cut one. It is a captivating arrangement and performance of the iconic song. Kurt, taking his own sage advice, plays "all the notes, but not too many notes" at the piano with light and delicate accompaniment from bass guitar, modest (almost embarrassed) bongo drum, and synthesizer strings. There is both meekness and majesty in the moment that is created, confidence and gratitude. Both icon and conscience are present, alive, and well at the halfway point. "Oh, How He Loves You and Me" (sung by Evie) and "Bring Back the Springtime" (sung by The Hawaiians) round out Kurt's recorded contributions to the twenty-fifth anniversary "Ebenezer" album. Kurt's work is duly represented, the "anniversary questions" separated and quieted.[20] His work appears prominently throughout a companion twenty-page, full-color promotional booklet titled "1976 A Record Year." Page five, the first of his appearances in the booklet, has large pictures of Kurt, Bev Shea, and Evie.

Kurt's backyard office bungalow in Waco, financed 50/50 by Kurt and WORD.

On page five, along with those pictures, George Beverly Shea's album *Angels Shall Keep Thee* is hailed as "the most unique album released in 1976." Kurt wrote the album's title song especially for Bev. It was Kurt's only song of the project. Kurt, of course, had signed Evie, a key move for the company. Her album *Evie: Gentle Moments*, introduced on page five with the bold-letter announcement, "Evie Has a New One," also includes only one Kaiser tune, "Pass It On." The symbolism of the page is nearly inescapable. On a single page, Kurt Kaiser, like WORD itself, reaches *back* to what Christian music evangelism had been (Shea), boasting Kurt's *newest* song, and reaches *forward* to what Christian music evangelism was becoming (Evie) with the mundane inclusion of one of Kurt's older songs. It was a dizzying pinnacle of time and trajectory for Kurt and for WORD. Kurt's picture and contributions were icons at WORD's silver anniversary. But, when a pinnacle is reached, when the peak is achieved, movement can only be in one direction, and standing still is not an option.

A modest yet full color brochure, "Picking Up the Pace," marked WORD's entry into its 30th year (1981). Black and white photos of the WORD staff are placed humbly among the pages that highlight, in color, WORD's "stable" of recording artists. At the bottom of the first page, three vice presidents are pictured: Carol Kilpatrick, VP for Production, Word, Inc.; Kurt Kaiser, VP for Music, Word Music Group; and Buddy Huey, VP for A&R, Word Record and Music Group (Kurt's original title and responsibility). Kurt's picture and influence have been reduced, but only slightly at this point.

The artists pictured in the thirtieth anniversary brochure include many of the best-known names in the late 1970s and early 1980s: Evie, The Bill Gaither Trio, The Imperials, The Mighty Clouds of Joy, Dion DiMucci, Amy Grant, Larry Norman, The Happy Goodmans, Shirley Caesar, Benny Hester, Chuck Girard, Leon Patillo, David Meece, Denny Corell, Bob and Pauline Wilson, Al Green, and The Rex Nelon Singers. Near the end of this list of artists, the written narrative states, "Adding their song-writing skill to their performing talents are artists like Michael and Stormie Omartian, David Meece, and Ken Medema." Additional black and white photos include those of Stan Moser, Senior Vice President, Word Records, and Chuck Fromm, President of Maranatha! Music.

Four other persons are listed on subsequent pages as vice presidents of varying facets of the company's operation, along with an assortment of directors. Kurt had friendships and warm working relationships with many of the directors, such as Piers Bateman, Dennis Hill, and Bruce Howe. The group of directors includes John Purifoy, Director of Music Publishing, Word Music Group. We single Purifoy out here because John, as an accomplished composer in his own right, would later start his own successful publishing company. By that time Kurt had become a mentor to John, a relationship that lasted throughout the remainder of Kurt's life.

A curious recording, released in 1985, is *A Musical Tribute to Kurt Kaiser*. Ten artists are featured, each singing a Kurt Kaiser song.[21] Who proposed this compilation of previous recordings six years before his dismissal, and why? We are left to wonder why a tribute was needed. Was it a pat on the back to bolster a fading star? Was someone trying to make a point or a case concerning Kurt's contributions to the company? We press on.

In 2011, WORD's sixtieth anniversary marked the fourth and final major opportunity for Kurt to consider his contributions to the company. Kurt had a storied career with the company. His impact on WORD, the Christian music recording industry, and Contemporary Christian Music itself was unquestioned. His contributions are brilliantly summarized in the early pages of the anniversary celebration's combination story/song book *WORD: The Story, the Songs*, authored by Deborah Evans Price. There Price connects Kurt's name with Tennessee Ernie Ford, George Beverly Shea, Ralph Carmichael, Ken Medema, Evie, The Mike Curb Congregation, Burl Ives, Anita Bryant, Wayne Newton, Carol Lawrence, Russ Taff, and others of similar renown.[22] But what of the Medallion Series, its artists, and the other classical work that Kurt had done?

It was a large poster, with art that matched the sixtieth anniversary commemorative book, that allowed the question to rise. Copies of the large, framed poster distributed across the WORD world featured the autographs of scores of artists, but not Kurt's, nor those of the classical artists. It featured scores of pictures of people on album covers, three that are the result of Kurt's work in A&R and producing, but not his name in autograph, nor his picture on an album.

True, Kurt may have been more administrator to WORD than artist, but he was an artist whose picture did appear on album covers across the years. The absence of his name and picture on the large sixtieth anniversary poster, combined with the absence of any of his classical work, somehow dimmed the presence of his name and picture in the sixty-year book. Did he care? Not even Pat knows the answer to that question.

It would be unfair conjecture to conclude that Kurt was intentionally snubbed. Now, well past the sixty-year commemoration, the name Kurt Kaiser remains an icon of the glory days of WORD. His contributions go without saying. But Kurt Kaiser was also the name of a human being. Don Cason, who rose from music editor to president of WORD during Kurt's time there, noted that "many of Kurt's era were not included on the poster." He stated conversationally, warmly, and authentically that "Kurt surely felt rejected, but he was a respected gentleman. After Kurt, no one was left who was both manager and top producer."[23]

Kurt had slowly moved to being an artist for WORD toward the end. Joni Eareckson Tada was the last of Kurt's enlisting and developing artists for WORD. Cason stated that respect, more than strategy, was the motivation for allowing Kurt to move from administrator to artist. Kurt had his own schedule (again, as he had at the very beginning). Kurt also went to the Estes Park, Colorado, showcase event as a Christian artist because he had moved to a freelance artist relationship with WORD. "It was a heart-warming time as he ended his time there with 'Oh, How He Loves You and Me.' The conferees loved him, the song, and the moment. He was seen as an elder statesman. He became an ambassador for WORD in the 1980s. Kurt was the last of a certain breed of persons at WORD."[24]

Kurt *separated* from WORD Music on December 17, 1991, after more than thirty years with the company. An icon was moved from display case to shelf, but the icon was not destroyed. The biblical scriptures 1 John 3:2 and 2 Corinthians 3:18 were especially meaningful for Kurt in that moment. Tom Stanton, a WORD executive from 1973 to 1995, summed up his thoughts about why Kurt separated from WORD: "Kurt was one of the old guys. Kurt's graciousness and contributions seemed to matter less and less."[25]

Can even the most respected elders lose a step or two from their earlier pace and grace? Yes, of course, and Kurt knew it. Reflecting on the changes that took place as new management replaced the original, Kurt said that at first things didn't change very much. "If something came in that I really liked, I'd play it for somebody in the music side of things, and say, 'Isn't this nice, it really turned out well,' you know, all this kind of stuff. And then they left here, and that was kind of a family here, but then they left here and became a corporation." That's when the company moved to the Dallas/Fort Worth metroplex. Again, in Kurt's words, "Coppell [actually Las Colinas], and then particularly now, in Nashville, they spend the money on an album, lots of money, and they throw it out there, and if it doesn't work, then well, that's the end of the artist. Well, my deal was totally different than that. Mine was ministry-driven . . . If this person had a good ministry with people, I would record them. It wasn't hinged to sales. But everything now is connected to sales."

When asked whether he thought that his mindset from when he first started with WORD would work in the present (2008), Kurt replied, "No, I don't think so." And then he made this candid and remarkably objective observation. "No, I don't think so . . . In other words, I wouldn't buy stock in a company where I was involved, because I'm not interested in selling. I was interested in . . . churches."[26]

Kurt's recognition of the dynamic tension between the concepts of a business doing ministry and a ministry doing business can be seen as the pronouncement of a bitter blessing on the company that left him behind. Kurt felt he could no longer stay with WORD Music and, at the same time, be a proper steward of his divine call. Also, he did not want to leave Waco. As difficult as the separation from WORD was, it was also simple.

TRANSITION SOUNDTRACK

Looking back, we detect an unintended soundtrack to Kurt's business and relationship struggles described above. Focused on Kurt Kaiser's time of having *become* WORD Music (mid 1980s), we can see the peak of his impact, and its mirrored upslope and downslope. The soundtrack can be seen/heard in the span of four CD recordings: (1) *In Heavenly Love Abiding*, Kurt Kaiser Music, © WORD, 1985; (2) *Kurt Kaiser: Psalms, Hymns, and Spiritual Songs*, The Sparrow Corporation, © 1993; (3) *The Lost Art of Listening*, Kurt Kaiser Music, 1995; and (4) *Hymns: Christopher Adkins, Cello, Stephen Nielson, Piano*, Kurt Kaiser Music, © 2006.

These recordings are high on the slopes, either side of a peak. The word "peak" is used to describe the 1993 recording above because it won Kurt the GMA's Dove Award for Best Instrumental Album of the Year in 1994. The story is "sounded" in copyrights across the arc of these four recording projects stretching from 1985 to 2006.

Kurt speaking upon receiving the Dove Award, 1994

Admittedly, this is a twenty-year span, and movement is difficult to detect over a long stretch of time while living it. But movement is more clearly seen by an observer who intends to be objective, many years later.

In the 1985 recording, *In Heavenly Love Abiding*, Kurt Kaiser Music was an established label whose logo is boldly present on the product. Yet WORD held the copyright. In effect, Kurt Kaiser Music was, for a season, a division of WORD. Allowing Kurt to establish his own recording entity while still an employee of WORD was a clear indicator that things were deteriorating in his relationship with the company. The recording features Anne Martindale Williams, cellist, and Stephen Nielson, pianist. It was one of the Medallion Series projects. In addition to being the producer of this recording, Kurt arranged all the hymn settings. There are several aspects of the product that speak to a transition freshly, but certainly, underway. The artists recorded here met Kurt's requirements for musical giftedness and excellence in the stewardship of that giftedness.

Anne Martindale Williams was the principal cellist of the Pittsburgh Symphony Orchestra. She was often a featured soloist in Pittsburgh, and in New York at Carnegie Hall and Avery Fisher Hall (renamed David Geffen Hall in 2015). She had collaborated with guest artists such as Yehudi Menuhin, Andre Previn, and others of similar renown in numerous chamber music performances. She also taught cello at Carnegie-Mellon University and gave solo and chamber music performances. She was a graduate of the Curtis Institute of Music. Her husband was the Director of Student Ministries at Beverly Heights United Presbyterian Church in Pittsburgh. She knew "church."

Stephen Nielson, a Steinway Artist whom Kurt deeply admired as a person and a performer, and upon whom he called for many recording projects, is a graduate of Indiana University. He is a distinguished concert artist, both as a soloist and in ensemble, having performed in the great music cities and centers around the world. He played for decades as a member of Nielson and Young Duo Pianists. He also teaches piano privately and in university settings across Texas and in Illinois.

Kurt said that *In Heavenly Love Abiding* was the only project of which he was a part in which he would not change one note. This is an astounding statement in that it suggests that even Kurt has written arrangements that he would, perhaps, change if given a chance. Kurt worked with a few violinists in whose musicianship he delighted. He worked with two or three cellists whose mastery of the instrument took him back to his high school orchestra dreams. But Stephen Nielson was the first and foremost, and perhaps the only, pianist to whom Kurt would turn if Kurt, himself, were not going to be the artist.[27] Stephen Nielson called Kurt a "true artisan, an artisan of the highest level who savored before serving. There will be none other like him."[28]

The second in our transitional soundtrack group of CDs is *Kurt Kaiser: Psalms, Hymns, and Spiritual Songs*, © 1993 by The Sparrow Corporation of Brentwood, Tennessee, a company founded and owned by Billy Ray Hearn. The recording won a Dove Award for Best Instrumental Album of the Year in 1994. There is no doubt that Kurt was worthy of a Dove Award. It can be debated, however, whether this recording was worthy of a Dove Award. It certainly isn't a bad recording. In fact, it's a good recording. But it is not Kurt's most notable solo piano recording.

Billy Ray had been an employee of WORD in years gone by and had worked closely with Kurt and Ralph Carmichael on the *Tell It Like It Is* project. Billy Ray's admiration for Kurt was always present but had deepened as the years went by. Kurt's release from WORD was still fresh, and the transition was not easy. Billy Ray knew that and was aware that Kurt still had some inertia built up for writing, performing, and producing. So, at Billy Ray's request, Kurt was the arranger, performer, and producer of this CD, with Billy Ray Hearn listed as Executive Producer. Billy Ray had immense influence in the Dove Award facet of the Gospel Music Association. It may well be that the GMA selection committee was influenced by Billy Ray to consider Kurt's album for recognition, perhaps even as a lifetime achievement recognition. We must also allow for the fact that the committee may have been sufficiently impressed with the recording on its own merit. But while we are considering possible answers for our question, "Why this album, at that time?" another option arises: gratitude. The album and the award, both very much within Hearn's sphere of influence, were a gesture from mentee to mentor, perhaps even a confession.

In February 2006, Billy Ray Hearn and his son, Bill, were selected to receive the National Academy of Recording Arts & Sciences Presidents Award of Merit. In an email to Kurt, dated January 26, 2006, Billy Ray reminisced and wrote:

Dear Kurt,

If you read the blog, you will see that Bill and I are being given the NARAS Presidents Award of Merit on Feb. 4th. In my little "Thanks" speech of 4 minutes I say that I want to thank several people who meant a lot to me and helped me in my early days. You are one of those and I always say so to everyone who will listen. As I get older, I realize how much you, Ralph and Jarrell opened the doors for me and forgave me, or at least were patient with my many mistakes. Looking back, I can see that all I really had going for me was enthusiasm, energy and passion. So, before it is too late, I want you to know how much I love you and Pat. You set the standard, musically and spiritually in those early days and faithfully stayed the course. You were a great mentor. Honestly, you should be the one getting this award.

Sincerely,
Billy Ray

Might we call Kurt's Dove Award the Icon & Conscience Award presented by Billy Ray Hearn on behalf of the whole of Contemporary Christian Music?

The Sparrow label is neither WORD nor Kurt Kaiser Music. It is, however, in the family, even as Billy Ray was in the family. This CD was an encouragement to Kurt that he was not suddenly relegated or confined to his own "vanity" recording label, but that he was still recognized and respected in the larger Christian recording world. By means of this recording, Billy Ray sent a message to Kurt and the industry: Kurt Kaiser did not need WORD to be Kurt Kaiser.

Third in the chain of transitional soundtrack CDs is *Kurt Kaiser: The Lost Art of Listening* (Kurt Kaiser Music, 1995). There is no mention of WORD in the copyright statement on the disc or the case. Yet every song carries the following inscription: "Written by [or Arranged by] Kurt Kaiser, Word Music (a div. of Word, Inc.)." There is one exception: "A Quiet Place," written by Ralph Carmichael, Communique Music. Transition is indeed messy. An August 1999 letter of clarification from WORD Entertainment in Nashville, Tennessee, to Kurt, explains that the 1995 agreement related to *The Lost Art* was to allow "you to manufacture and sell the product, not a transfer of ownership."

According to Robert Sterling, chosen by Kurt to be the producer of this album, someone realized that Kurt still "owed" WORD a recording, so this project was the solution to the situation. Sterling is an accomplished composer in his own right who worked for seventeen years as an "assigned writer" to WORD.

In this recording, Kurt is the artist, but all nature sings, joining him in something of a creation duet. Kurt's playing is seasoned by the occasional short insertion of a voice or additional instrument. In the case liner, Kurt wrote:

> For me, sound has its beginnings in silence. Music is an awakening from stillness . . . I decided to play fewer notes and so give more importance to those notes played. And what a pleasure it was to work with Rob Sterling. Together we'd build and change and form what has become *The Lost Art of Listening.*
>
> Kurt Kaiser

Kurt couldn't deny his part in contemporary music's rising tide, although he would downplay his impact. What he could do, and did in this recording, was stand as an icon and declare as a conscience that silence and discretion still matter and can be seen as creative and relevant.

The fourth of our four transitional soundtrack CDs is *Hymns: Christopher Adkins, Cello, Stephen Nielson, Piano,* © 2006, Kurt Kaiser Music. Kurt wrote the arrangements, and there is no mention of WORD. The product/company/identity transition is complete. Similar to the first of this soundtrack group, the arrangements are for piano and cello, Kurt's instruments of prayer and dreaming. The pianist is, again, the distinguished artist from Dallas, Texas, Stephen Nielson. The cellist on this recording is Christopher Adkins, principal cellist of the Dallas Symphony. Christopher Adkins received his musical training at the University of North Texas and at Yale University. During his tenure at Yale, Mr. Adkins held the position of principal cellist with the New Haven Symphony. In 1987, he returned to his native Dallas to occupy the chair once held by his former teacher, Lev Aronson.

The songs recorded on this CD are standard hymns, as the title suggests, except for two of Kurt's compositions, "In His Love and in His Pity," from the musical *Just for You* (WORD, 1979), and "Long Journey–for Chad," written in response to the death of his nephew.[29] "Long Journey" echoes the pathos of Handel's "Ombra mai fu" from the opera *Xerxes* and Elgar's "Nimrod" from the *Enigma Variations.* In this time of deep sorrow, Kurt, in spirit, "sat in"[30] with these classic composers. Adkins and Nielson performed the two Kaiser compositions at Kurt's memorial service.

A TALE OF TWO SECOND STANZAS

Kurt's two most iconic songs, "Oh, How He Loves You and Me" (1975), and "Pass It On" (1969), received unexpected attention in an unlikely place, their second stanzas. The second, and any additional stanzas of songs, live in the shadow of the first stanza. The status of second stanzas is akin to that of the second child in royal succession: important, even loved, but only faintly associated with the title. This is especially true in the case of popular songs and hymns. Kurt's work is no exception. The expectation level is lowered for the poetry and imagery of second stanzas, compared to what is expected of the opening lines. Forgiveness abounds for the relatively mundane craft of second stanzas if the first stanza is a memorable work of art.

"Oh, How He Loves You and Me": There is a law of physics that has its own mantra: "The universe abhors a vacuum." It seems this axiom includes the absence of a second stanza if a song is to be taken seriously by authorities such as hymnologists and copyright officers. Praise choruses were suspect in the early days of their being considered for inclusion in hymnals, being labeled "ditties" by hymnological purists. Evidently, the U.S. Copyright Office agreed with the hymn singers. When Kurt sought a copyright of his song, "Oh, How He Loves You and Me," he was informed that the lyrics of the piece (what was to become the first stanza) were too short to warrant a copyright. In order to get it copyrighted, he would have to lengthen the lyric. In church music terms, he had to write a second stanza. In fact, it was not simply about its length; the U.S. Copyright Office said that there was not enough original material in the first submission to warrant a copyright. Kurt quickly remedied the situation and returned the song to the D.C. office. It worked. He obtained a copyright. He would later say that the second stanza was not meant to be sung. Yet, in several subsequent recordings and in hymnals, the song appears with this stanza that "was not meant to be sung." Have we discovered here an inconsistency in Kurt? If so, we can forgive him. He was human. Perhaps we should be more generous and consider the possibility that this discrepancy is a simple strategic compromise.

Compromise is not a bad word, despite how it has come to be used in modern politics. The answer to the question of why declare the second stanza not to be sung, and then record it and publish it many times, is found in Evie's album *Evie Again* (1975). That album contains a cut that is Kurt's arrangement of "Jesus Loves Me," the children's hymn long in the public domain, combined with Kurt's "Oh, How He Loves You and Me," one stanza only. When Kurt wrote this arrangement, he did not have to worry about a copyright for "Jesus Loves Me." It was old enough to be comfortably in the public domain. But he didn't want to expose "Oh, How He Loves You and Me" to potential piracy should the song be covered by the copyright of the arrangement only. Kurt's song needed to be copyrighted as an entity unto itself, then, subsequently covered additionally by the copyright of this arrangement. Therefore he submitted "Oh, How He Loves You and Me" to the U.S. Copyright Office, to have that protection in place. He would write a second stanza for the copyright office, but he would not write a second stanza for the arrangement. He would stay loyal to the complete and right arrangement that he had heard in his head and written for Evie to sing; thus, his later statements that the second stanza was not meant to be sung. It was the truth. It wasn't meant to be sung. The arrangement has Evie repeat the (now) first stanza twice. That's what Kurt wanted. That's how he composed it. That's how it would be recorded. The second stanza was not meant to be sung on this album. The fact that the second stanza now appears in other settings and projects lies outside this hurried and pragmatic exchange between Kurt and the U.S. Copyright Office. The time pressure was related to the production and release schedules of the album *Evie Again*.

Even though the stanza was written for the U.S. Copyright Office and not for the Church, it stuck due to common expectation and usage. The people in the pews were well practiced at accepting second and third stanzas of lesser art, if they were attached to a strong first stanza with a first line that served, also, as the title of the song. The second stanza is awkward in its structure, but the congregational singers could handle it. "Jesus to Calvary DID go," while theologically and historically accurate, is not carefully wrought poetry. It served its immediate purpose and then slipped, somewhat unnoticed, into several hymnals and record albums. It is difficult to "undo" a less-than-stellar line in a lyric once the song informally, but with certainty, belongs to the people. The writer must, at that point, be thankful for the public's positive reaction, and determine to be a bit more careful next time.

"Oh, How He Loves You and Me" governmental bureaucracy calls "insufficient." God says, "inexhaustible," and Kurt knew it. The following newspaper excerpt provides evidence that the people who sing the songs are the final critics:

> In the first verse we sing about the ultimate sacrifice of our Lord: "He gave his life, what more could he give?" The second verse captures the fullness of that loving sacrifice: "Jesus to Calvary did go, His love for mankind to show. What He did there brought hope from despair. O how He loves me, O how He loves you. O how He loves you and me."
>
> From the Gospel of John, in 15:9, we read these words that Jesus spoke to his disciples: "As the Father loved me, I also have loved you, so abide in my love." It is glorious to know that Jesus loves me and loves you.[31]

In the case of *Pass It On*, the second stanza brings additional glory to its masterful title and first stanza. In the multimedia project *Windsongs*, published in 1989 by Tyndale House Publishers, distinguished calligraphy artist Timothy R. Botts was taken by Kurt's second stanza. In the *Windsongs* book, Botts wrote, "The second verse of 'Pass It On' by Kurt Kaiser presents one of the best metaphors for Christian conversion—the season of spring. The excitement of this new life I pass on to you."[32] One grimaces only slightly at the closing pun.

The *Windsongs* project includes "sixty calligraphic interpretations of hymns and spiritual songs with notes by the artist" in a "coffee table" sized book, and a VHS format *Windsongs* that included "meditative, instrumental arrangements of the world's best-loved hymns and spiritual songs. Featuring the calligraphy of Timothy R. Botts and musical arrangements by Kurt Kaiser." Commentary on the back of the VHS box includes this paragraph:

> *Windsongs* is a living psalter, enhanced by magnificent scenic footage of God's creation and the art of calligrapher Timothy Botts. The music of *Windsongs* has been arranged by award-winning musician Kurt Kaiser, who uses his special talent to emphasize the meaning and strength of the world's most inspiring and beautiful music.

Here the second stanza is discovered, uncovered, and mined, bringing to light its rich contribution to the hymn—yes, "hymn." The correct category of congregational song for "Oh, How He Loves You and Me" is "chorus," even with its two "stanzas." In that case, as we saw, the second stanza was forced, weakening the structure of the song. In "Pass It On," the second stanza supports and enhances the whole. Kurt knew the difference between "chorus" and "hymn." He respected both forms of communal singing and excelled in the writing, arranging, and performing of both genres. In "Oh, How He Loves You and Me," Kurt compromised with reality yet kept the original content, and intent, intact. In *Windsongs*, Kurt released "Pass It On" to the empowerment of other art forms. Both second stanzas present moments of decision concerning the protection of his art. In both cases he was a good and faithful steward of his God-given art, without worshiping it. Encasing in one instance, releasing in the other, both were offerings to God and God's mission through the Church. Was Kurt aware of all this, or was he just being pragmatic in both cases and forms? It doesn't matter. Either way, it all happened through his habitual discipleship and life-governing commitment. And it all happened through the second level of his work, below the headline. Shall we call that the deeper level, or the mundane level? It is at the level of work after the initial inspiration.

KURT KAISER MUSIC, INC.

Kurt Kaiser Music had an awkward beginning. It was not a stumbling procedural awkwardness; it was an uncomfortable relationship awkwardness. Friendship chafed against business. Respect chafed against prudence. As we have already seen, Kurt Kaiser Music, Inc. began while Kurt was still at WORD. On September 7, 1990, a little more than a year before Kurt's dismissal, WORD Music agreed to assign 50% of some of Kurt's music to his new label. As would be expected, WORD kept all rights to the most popular of Kurt's existing songs, dividing the income from his less popular songs. Kurt's creative work during the transition was eligible for the KKM label. This was a complex and delicate situation, awkward.

First and foremost, Kurt Kaiser Music was a holding company for copyrights transferred or newly registered. Secondarily, the new company was for Kurt a platform for recording the music that he wanted to record. His aim was not competition; it was, rather, freer expression in making the case that quality still existed and was valued. A third reason for the new company was, of course, to continue to create and produce, to stay in the conversation concerning the state of Christian music.

On May 1, 1991, KKM signed an agreement to provide music for Paul J. Meyer's *Success Motivation* videos. On May 26, 1994, Lewis M. Kirby, Chairman, Christian Music Publishers Association Membership Committee, informed Kurt that Kurt Kaiser Music had been elected to membership in the Church Music Publishers Association. These were affirmations that Kurt was still recognized as a significant contributor to the industry's mission.

In 2002, Kurt Kaiser Music released the CD *Dana Stephenson: In God's Time*. Kurt was still in his A&R mode when he signed Dana Stephenson, former Miss North Carolina, to make this recording. Kurt was the producer and arranger of all the selections except "The Lord's Prayer" (Malotte) and "Traveling Mercies" (Billy Crockett). In this project, Kurt Kaiser, the conscience of Contemporary Christian Music, was rather pointedly reminding its recording industry of their responsibility to keep music standards at a high level. In cut number 7, Kurt's medley arrangement of "I Love You Lord" and "As the Deer" elevate these praise chorus classics to the level of art song. In like manner on cut 9, Kurt's arrangement also lifts the esteemed hymn "Holy, Holy, Holy" to the level of art song. It is no accident that Kurt brings praise choruses and hymns together, in humility for both, as they approach the realm of art song. He did not ask praise choruses to bow before hymns, nor for hymns to acquiesce to praise choruses as the new standard. Rather, he reminds both of their obligation to give their very best as an offering, and does so by clothing them in art song raiment. Some will argue with this thinly veiled suggestion of style hierarchy. But it is authentic and consistent Kurt Kaiser. Subtle? Obscure? Annoying? Perhaps, but faithful to the conviction. The Christian music industry had to take notice and give consideration, whether or not they agreed. Dana Stephenson's performance throughout this CD is of the highest classical voice clarity and control. A subtle lesson had been taught by Kurt the teacher. Let those who have ears, hear.

Kurt Kaiser Music was beginning to stand alone when an additional new label opportunity presented itself. What would cause Kurt to start an additional label? What would this company accomplish that Kurt Kaiser Music wouldn't? The answer lies, in part, in the function of the two entities. While there was overlap, enough difference existed to place Kurt Kaiser Music and KNB music on similar but separate tracks. The overlap was recording.

KNB was the combined work of Kurt Kaiser (K) and (N) Brian Konzelman (B). Brian is Professor of Music Industry Careers at Waco's McLennan Community College (MCC). Kurt had known Brian's work as a performer, worship leader, composer, orchestrator, and sound engineer for a number of years. Brian had previous working relationships with WORD, Billy Ray Hearn's Sparrow Records, and Baylor University. Brian's "Back at the Ranch Studio" near Waco, and his "day job" at MCC combine to give him a unique sphere of influence in the recording industry. He and Kurt enjoyed mutual respect and admiration. They envisioned a place where their skill sets and experience could create a synergy, free from undue bottom-line pressures or obligations.

For awhile, Kurt employed one of Brian's students to transcribe his handwritten manuscripts. In a related effort, Brian gave Kurt some "Midi" (electronic keyboard transcribing) lessons in Kurt's backyard office. The enterprise was largely a labor of love. A couple of marketing ideas for their recordings didn't work out, but sales did happen, thanks to name inertia and genuine quality. In Konzelman's words, he and Kurt were "old musicians trying to be young businessmen."

An early KNB project from 1993 was *Seasonings: Spring*. The back liner states, "All performances by Kurt Kaiser and Brian Konzelman." The style of their music has the feel of improvisation, "easy listening," but not "Christian easy listening." The CD is an exercise in freed-from-productivity music, orchestrated for new electronic musical sounds. Kurt and Brian, congregational and stage church musicians, respectively, are on vacation here. "What-iffing" and "blue skying," as the expressions go. Kurt brought Bev Shea to Brian's studio, where Bev found the recording sessions to be enjoyable and of a more relaxed nature. The recordings are of well-known hymns and solos.[33]

Sitting in the dim light of an MCC recording studio, Brian shared, "I've never known anyone like Kurt. He stands taller in my esteem than nearly everyone I've ever met. I miss him." Then, after referring to Kurt as "extraordinary," and with tears in his eyes, Brian said, "I knew it while I was working with him. We communicated on a musical level—no words. He smiled and liked it: incredible affirmation."[34] Shared listening requires no verbal translation.

A person of soul and spirit similar to Kurt's is Billy Crockett. Creator and director of the Blue Rock Artist Ranch & Studio in Wimberley, Texas, Crockett was a longtime friend and collaborator of Kurt's. He is a songwriter and performer as well as a recording studio proprietor. He is perhaps best known in the Waco/Baylor world as the writer of the song "Traveling Mercies," also known by its lines "Take bread for the journey," and "Go in peace, live in grace."

In conversation with this author, Billy emphasized Kurt's engagement with listening as an art and Kurt's understanding of "listening" as a place of spiritual refuge. He spoke of Kurt's ability to stir conversations that created a community of listeners who shared his need for deep listening. To speak of "listening" here is not to speak of Kurt's perfect pitch or sense of blend and balance. It is to speak of listening to the hum of the Spirit in the music.

Billy refers to this level of listening as Kurt's "deep well." Such listening qualifies as a "thin place" between heaven and earth. Often these communities of listeners' conversations would happen in retreat settings such as Howard E. Butt Jr's Laity Lodge retreat center in that region of Texas known as the "Hill Country." Kurt was no stranger there.

Some would furtively call this relationship to listening mysticism. Here it is boldly identified as mysticism, understanding the Holy Spirit to be the agent, and Kurt to have valued it above perfect pitch.

3
ICON AND CONSCIENCE OF CONTEMPORARY CHRISTIAN MUSIC

> "CCM chose image and marketing over substance, eventually becoming a straitjacket that rewarded lowest-common-denominator thought and craft."
>
> Steve Taylor[1]

Many who knew and loved Kurt Kaiser and his music want to learn that he or his music started Contemporary Christian Music or Contemporary Worship. But the case simply cannot be made. Further, there was no way that Kurt Kaiser could condone or knowingly participate in the environment described in the Steve Taylor quote above. Kurt saw it coming. Kurt felt it coming. He heard it coming, and those who counted the transition as progress were forced, simply by his presence (no words needed) in the office, the conference room, and the recording studio, to consider what Kurt saw. They did not agree with Kurt. They could easily and respectfully attribute Kurt's opinion to that of an older man who was holding on to past convictions, and whose "celebrity" was waning even as CCM waxed ever brighter. But the new influencers and decision makers couldn't hush the silent commentary of Kurt's continuing commitment to high standards of musical excellence, congregational accessibility, biblical veracity, and established business guidelines. This dawning cast the shadows of evening for Kurt.

The 2017 book *Lovin' On Jesus: A Concise History of Contemporary Worship*, by Swee Hong Lim of Emmanuel College in Toronto, Canada, and Lester Ruth of Duke Divinity School, Durham, North Carolina,[2] two highly respected musicologists, makes no mention of Kurt Kaiser or his music. We must acknowledge this fact. There is, however, on p. 94 a quickly passing glance at Kurt in their book that could easily be overlooked: a reference to Campus Crusade for Christ's 1972 songbook, the title of which is *Pass It On*. Even then, Kurt's name is not mentioned. This reference appears as Lim and Ruth write of how few prayer songs were being published and sung in the early 1970s. If these two authors did not mention Kurt Kaiser in their study of contemporary worship,[3] what can we, here, make of Kurt's influence on that phenomenon? We begin by acknowledging that "influencing a movement" and "initiating a movement" are two important but significantly different roles. Rather than rush to Kurt's defense, which we need not do, we change the focus slightly.

As with other important moments and situations in the development of Christian music from the 1960s to the 1980s, Kurt may not always be front and center, but he is very often "in the picture." Even though his iconic name is absent, the title of his iconic song is voiced naturally in the study, the argument, the conversation that Lim and Ruth published. The mere title *Pass It On* suggests the nature of the content and intent of the entire Campus Crusade for Christ collection. Only an icon can represent so much in just a glance. In fact, that is the definition of an icon. Only the unofficial, but readily recognized, conscience of the movement could step back from the high accolades of having started contemporary worship, attributions that he knew to be well-intended but too hastily considered. Kurt Kaiser, icon in name and compositions, did not initiate contemporary Christian music or contemporary Christian worship. He knew it. He wasn't being self-effacing in his denials, he was being honest and authentic. He found solid simplicity in the truth.

He was co-writer of the musical *Tell It Like It Is*. He wrote the songs "Master Designer," "That's for Me," and "Pass It On," among other contributions to the musical. Later he wrote "Oh, How He Loves You and Me." These Kaiser songs are iconic, as are the name and face of Kurt Kaiser. His integrity in all facets of personal acclaim, biblical veracity of lyrics, excellence of music, and devotion to Church, though unintended and beyond his notice, served as the conscience of the movement that so many wanted to declare to be his invention. Kurt could not stop the deserved high praise related to *Tell It Like It Is*. Neither could he stop the overstated estimations of his singlehanded launching of the Contemporary Christian Music phenomenon. But he did know how to handle the cheers of the crowd. His father had taught him that lesson years before, on the way home from a large Youth for Christ rally in Chicago. The applause, the microphone, and the spotlight are focused on a gift from God. The audience may forget that; the performer must not. When one is called upon to bow, one must bow as a servant. The following is a sample of Kurt's ever-present, yet private, dilemma. It is the wording of a plaque.

CHRISTIAN ARTISTS

MUSIC ACHIEVEMENT AWARD

KURT KAISER

1984

For twenty-five years of outstanding achievement in the development

of contemporary Christian record production. And especially for his part in the musical

TELL IT LIKE IT IS that started

an era of church youth-music history that continues to affect the lives

of thousands of young musicians around the world.

KURT KAISER: Songwriter, Keyboard Artist & Originator of Chords & Progressions only he can play.

As we will see, Kurt was somewhat dismayed that "the Baptists" had started the youth musical movement with the publication of *Good News: A Christian Folk-Musical*, in 1967, by the Church Recreation Department of the Baptist Sunday School Board of the Southern Baptist Convention. He was convinced that "we could do better."

TELL IT LIKE IT IS

> "If the whole thing were Ralph, I think it would be, it might be, a bit superficial. If the whole thing were me, it wouldn't sell because it was too down, too serious . . . too churchlike."
> Kurt Kaiser[4]

All that has been written, or that ever will be written, concerning Kurt Kaiser exists under the pervasive presence of this one "folk musical about God." *Tell It Like It Is* stands watch over the pages of this book as well. Therefore, we stop here to acknowledge the banner that stretches from the first page to the last.

Kurt Kaiser, all else notwithstanding, is best known for this 133-page work, published in 1969 by Lexicon Music and distributed by Sacred Songs, a division of WORD Music. Better said, Kurt is best known for three titles: *Tell It Like It Is*, "Pass It On," and "Oh, How He Loves You and Me" (published after *Tell It Like It Is*).

The success of *Tell It Like It Is* resulted in an internal turning point at WORD. As sales of the musical soared, Jarrell McCracken revised Kurt's decade-long freedom to write for or publish with companies other than WORD. McCracken was becoming a more experienced businessman, and the gentlemen's agreement made when Kurt began at WORD had been of no consequence until now. Kurt understood. The conversation was between friends but left no doubt about WORD having "first refusal" rights to all that Kurt would write from that point forward. "Pass It On" did not, does not, belong to WORD since it is part of the musical. The new agreement was not the result of a mistake or misstep; it was the result of a mutual awakening. The restriction would stay in effect (now common industry-wide) until WORD allowed Kurt to establish Kurt Kaiser Music while still working for them, near the end of his time with WORD.

The musical, *Tell It Like It Is*, quickly became the glowing representation of its genre, even though it was not the genre's initiator. It can be argued that *Tell It Like It Is* was not the best of the Christian musicals, not even the best of Kurt's musicals. Even so, argue as one might, we must

Taping *Tell It Like It Is* at NBC studio in New York, 1969

stand atop "Mount *Tell It*" in order to look backward and forward across the full length and expanse of the history of youth musicals.

Kurt is often credited in casual conversation as *the* composer of this "youth musical." That attribution is only half right, but it is, indeed, half right.

Kurt Kaiser and Ralph Carmichael were co-composers of the musical that, by its daring and its immediate widespread acceptance, gave "permission" to composers of church music to freshen their work to the current cultural scene. Perhaps "challenged" composers of church music is the better way to express the awakening. The permission and challenge granted were encouragement that only a commercial (not denominational) publisher could give. Denominational publishers couldn't take the chance that a new genre with an "external to the Church" style might be misinterpreted as an encroachment by the culture. Some other entity, less beholden, would have to run that risk. Enter Lexicon Music, Inc., owned by a Pentecostal individual but not by a Pentecostal denomination. Lexicon teamed up with Sacred Songs/WORD, owned by a Southern Baptist individual, but not by the Southern Baptist Convention.

The nondenominational foray into the nascent folk experiment forced hesitant Baptists and others finally to release their singing teenagers from the choir loft, from robes and yellowed anthems. The new genre, taken to the "far reaches" that *Tell It Like It Is* dared to go, put both worship and outreach on notice: a fresh wind was blowing. Opponents were among the first to be awakened, suggesting that the new wind blowing was not necessarily the breath of God. A more thoughtful concern arose, as well, that enmeshed worship and evangelism/missions now had its own authenticating and energizing music. This concern of the 1970s, that evangelism would distract worship's focus on God, would come to be seen as an asset by the "Church Growth Movement" of the 1980s.

A revival was launched across the American religious landscape without tent, stadium, or evangelist. This revival stirred the Church, congregation by congregation, magnetically compelling teenagers to show up and sing. This phenomenon caused the Church's adults to be torn between being ever more alert to the outside world's influence and being thankful that their teenagers were finally engaged with the Church. Kurt was personally confronted by a mother caught up in this sudden dilemma. After an especially dynamic performance of *Tell It Like It Is*, she made her way to Kurt and demanded to know how Kurt was planning to keep her son in church, now that *Tell It Like It Is* had brought him into the church. It was a moment and a challenge that Kurt never forgot.

Good question: was the energy and draw of this new music sustainable? Could the music's "pied piper" effect lead the enthralled throughout their lives? Would this new music lead the young singers to find the timelessness, the eternal time*li*ness, of the gospel? Did *Tell It Like It Is* light the fuse that would explode into adult contemporary worship? Kurt consistently insisted "no." He was convinced that this new music did not have that capacity or staying power to carry worship on its back.

Southern Baptist congregations had experienced a preludial shock just two years earlier when the Church Recreation Department of their Baptist Sunday School Board in Nashville, Tennessee published the musical *Good News: A Christian Folk-Musical* (Broadman Press, 1967). The Sunday School Board's Church Music Department had been on guard ever since, set to protect music, and therefore worship, from the cultural revolution taking place in all other aspects of society. But *Good News* was in the style of folk music, as advertised: guitars, yes; "mod" (modern) dress for the youth choir instead of robes, yes. These changes to sanctuary decorum were disconcerting but not yet alarming, except, perhaps, for drums. The music of *Good News* was still within sight and reach of the hymnal and the anthem.

Even so, the slippery slope seemed to be just a step away. The Church Music Department of the Baptist Sunday School Board, guarding high musical standards, heard *Good News* and said "no," but ultimately they had no choice. Administrators higher up the "Board" structure, above the former ministers of music in the organization, decided that the Church Music Department did not have to publish *Good News*. However, they were directed to give music editorial guidance to the Church Recreation Department, which *would* publish it. The Church Music editor assigned to the cross-departmental project was Elwyn Raymer. He complied but kept his name from appearing anywhere on the printed score of *Good News*.

Kurt Kaiser, with the same musical standards as the Sunday School Board's Church Music Department (he referred to the staff of the Church Music Department as "The Baptists"), heard *Good News* and had a different reaction. He immediately saw that something better could be done. Standing at the same liminal point of response to pioneering work, two publishing entities with like mind, heart, talent, and ultimate goal, operated in environments of differing realities.

Kurt, we might say, was denominational (Southern Baptist) on Sundays and Wednesday nights (traditional prayer meeting and adult choir rehearsal schedule), but was commercial (WORD, Inc.) during the work hours and days of the week. In contrast, the musicians of the Baptist Sunday School Board were denominational during the work hours and days of the week, and nondenominational on Sundays and Wednesday nights, using the music of many publishers in their congregations. Kurt lived, worked, and worshiped across that entire weekly spectrum, becoming an icon of that period's dynamic tension. He was in a unique position to influence the thinking of both "sides." His discernment was the result of applied Christian conscience. This fluid juxtaposition of brothers and sisters in Christ, who admired each other's gifts and who were genuine friends, was a dance of sorts; a dance between business and ministry, between creativity and tradition, between risk and caution, between cultural art and liturgical function. How very much alike, how very different: a ministry doing business and a business doing ministry.

Good News was one matter, *Tell It Like It Is* was quite another, even though both claimed to be folk music. For Southern Baptists, folk music, actual "folk" music similar to that of the Appalachian and Blue Ridge mountains, had a recognizable regional flavor about it, despite political and cultural tags that were being applied to the genre "folk" by popular music groups such as "Peter, Paul, and Mary." The composers and promoters of *Tell It Like It Is* could not hide (nor did they try) its Broadway musical style. Broadway was show business, New York show business, and the "taint" stuck, no matter the Texas and California home bases of the musical's composers and companies, and no matter Kurt Kaiser's Southern Baptist credentials proffered by Seventh & James Baptist Church membership and Baylor University involvement.

What was Kurt thinking when, unimpressed by the respected fellow Baptist composer Bob Oldenburg's[5] *Good News: A Christian Folk-Musical*, he suggested, "We can do better"? Did "we" refer to Southern Baptist musicians who might be similarly embarrassed or unduly enamored? He was by all appearances a Southern Baptist church musician. Or did he mean Ralph Carmichael and himself writing for commercial companies instead of a denomination? It can easily and safely be assumed that Kurt's use of the word "we" was a combination of both possibilities, both identities.

Geoffrey Beaumont's *20th Century Folk Mass*, published in the U.K. in 1956, didn't cause Kurt to act (or react), even though he was surely aware of the composition and recording. John-Michael Tebelak and Stephen Schwartz's *Godspell*, and Tim Rice and Andrew Lloyd Webber's *Jesus Christ Superstar* would not appear until 1971. Those works could not have spurred Kurt's 1967 resolve to "write something [better] for the kids." The 1960s spirit of "antiestablishment" affected all areas of Western society and culture, including the Church, as evidenced by Vatican II decrees concerning music and cultural relevance. The Protestant Church could not look the other way while Catholics became more up to date than they in global outreach and evangelism. Neither could the Protestant Church in all its subsets deny the possibility that the Holy Spirit was calling Christianity, through the Catholic Church, to new expressions of the Old Story. There seemed to be a spiritual awakening stirring amid all the cultural protest, upheaval, and discontent. For the Church, this impatient "new wine" called for innovative "new wineskins": "something for the kids."

For Kurt there were two specific frustrations to be addressed: (1) the Southern Baptists' 1967 folk musical, for all its distinction from the sound and decorum of traditional church music, was still too much of an old wineskin, and (2) the Southern Baptists had made the first move, rather than WORD.

Bob Oldenburg did not and does not need defending for composing a groundbreaking work that was, by its very place and time, subject to criticism and improvement. Rather, he is to be commended for forcing open the front door of the Church and for prompting new work by Christian composers whose creativity needed to be loosed. Bob Oldenburg's work inspired Kurt Kaiser to shift into a new gear of bold writing in ways that other composers had not.

Kurt heard the call, saw the vision, and interpreted it in bigger and brighter expression. In the end, Christian writers in both denominational and commercial publishing houses would do better. The biblical verse Romans 8:28 comes to mind: "And we know that God causes all things to work together for good to those who are called according to His purpose" (NASB), admittedly remembered and included out of context.

Baptist musicologist and Baylor School of Music retiree Dr. David Music had this to say about *Good News*:

> Popular music often has a relatively short shelf life, and *Good News* was no exception. Its idiom quickly began to seem dated, and its meteoric rise to popularity was followed by a decline that was almost as rapid. Indeed, the whole genre of the youth musical lasted in popularity for only about twenty years.
>
> *Good News* and other works of its type, however, opened the door for two other kinds of popular music that had a larger impact on Baptist

church music: the scripture or praise chorus and contemporary Christian music (CCM).⁶

Kurt agreed wholeheartedly with the general appraisal and conclusion of David Music's analysis. Kurt frequently stated that he did not start the Contemporary Christian Music genre, nor its accompanying contemporary worship movement. His insistence was not one of humility, but of fact that could clearly and easily be documented. He was present at the beginning of CCM and its worship, but he did not create it.

Be that as it may, by any analysis, *Tell It Like It Is* was profoundly impactful. Kurt could not deny that. Who first thought to write this musical? Three characters appear in the scene of this musical's birthing: Ralph Carmichael, Billy Ray Hearn, and Kurt Kaiser. It is not at all surprising that the origin of the idea was remembered in differing ways. Ralph wrote this in his book *He's Everything to Me*:

> One evening Kurt Kaiser, Director of Music at WORD, and a fine composer and pianist, was having dinner with Mar [Ralph's wife] and me at our house in Woodland Hills [California]. The phone rang, and I excused myself to answer it. The spirited voice on the other end belonged to Billy Ray Hearn, who at the time was with WORD Records.
> Billy Ray said, "Hey, I've got a great idea."
> I said, "What's that?"
> He said, "You and Kurt should write a kids' musical."
> I said, "Well, Kurt just happens to be here. Let me get him on the extension." When Kurt got on the other phone, the three of us spent the next half-hour brainstorming the possibilities of what promised to be a most exciting project. That was the night *Tell It Like It Is* was born.⁷

In his copy of Ralph's book, Kurt wrote, "Kris—This is <u>not</u> how I remember 'Tell It . . .' getting started . . . But, oh well!" As it turns out, that's not exactly how Ralph always remembered the moment, either. On the back liner of the *Tell It Like It Is* record jacket (1969), Ralph wrote, "Kurt Kaiser . . . he started this whole thing. 'Let's say something to kids,' he said. And so we started to work . . . for almost a year."

In those same back liner paragraphs, Carmichael wrote, "I feel very fortunate (and I know Kurt feels the same) to have had Billy Ray Hearn's counsel and guidance throughout this project. With his background and experience in this field, he has made a valuable contribution. I'll say one thing . . . Mr. Hearn is not a 'yes' man. By the time he got through throwing out songs, making us rewrite lyrics, and change melodies, I felt like I had written two folk musicals." Why would Billy Ray Hearn be given such editorial authority? Here are some of the answers: Billy Ray was an erstwhile minister of music. He had participated in the development of the musical *Good News*. He knew congregational music ministry from a Southern Baptist viewpoint. He knew his way around a recording studio. He had music industry savvy.

Kurt remembered the birthing of the idea this way:

> Kris: Whose idea was it? [referring to *Tell It Like It Is*]
> Kurt: I'm sure there are at least three different ideas as to how it started. Ralph probably has an idea, Billy I know has an idea, and I have an idea.
> Kris: Well, I want to hear yours.
> Kurt: Yeah, I have it right, I mean, you know. So, I remember very, very well calling Ralph. I really admired him. I thought he was really something special, and I called him on the phone and said, "Ralph, let's make some, let's write something that makes it with the kids." I remember that very distinctly. And I said, "So how do we get started on this?" He said, "Well, why don't you write in Waco and I'll write here on the west coast and just keep writing and then when you come out here, we'll see what we've got." And I said, I remember this, too. I said, "Well, what about continuity between it?" And he said, "Nah, don't worry about that, but just keep putting parts together, we can always write the continuity." And so that's how that started.[8]

Acknowledging that the title should, in proper English, be "Tell It *AS* It Is," Kurt credits "Tell It *Like* It Is" to a member of *The Addicts*, nine former drug addicts who were now "clean" and had formed a gospel singing group. He had recorded them and recalled that "one of the guys came up with a phrase, or used a phrase, 'tell it like it is.' I may even have asked him what we should call it. He said, 'Well,' he was the one who told me, 'Tell it like it is.' That's a phrase the kids use, you know. And so that's, I thought, that's perfect; what we were doing."[9]

Kurt felt the musical had an important, but limited, place and purpose. He did not want *Tell It Like It Is* to be performed in the sanctuary of Seventh & James Baptist Church, even though Kurt and his family were members there. That is a fascinating statement for one of the co-composers of a hit Christian youth musical to make. There were a number of Baylor University faculty in the Seventh & James congregation, and Kurt did not want them to think that he was only capable of composing in that style, or that it was his preferred style. Neither did he want anyone to think that *Tell It Like It Is* represented what he thought worship music should be.

The success and widespread acceptance of *Tell It Like It Is* was causing the work to become Kurt's identity: "Kurt Kaiser, the man who wrote

Tell It Like It Is." The musical was a significant achievement, but Kurt did not want it to be his defining achievement. He wanted to keep his identity and future options more balanced in the eyes of colleagues, friends, and the Christian music industry at large. From the moment of this musical's success through the rest of his professional and personal life, Kurt would be in a struggle to demonstrate that he was more than a composer of Christian pop music for kids. He wanted the Baylor faculty and the wider classical music world to know that he was a "legitimate," classically trained, classically oriented, and knowledgeable musician. Furthermore, he wanted church musicians to know that he was a trustworthy traditionalist as well as an innovator.

Balance was all that he could ever achieve. For no matter the renown of the classical artists with whom he associated, recorded, or for whom he composed and arranged, he was always and ever also the composer of *Tell It Like It Is*, "Pass It On," and "Oh, How He Loves You and Me." Even though "Pass It On" and "Oh, How He Loves You and Me" became a unified phrase, "Oh, How He Loves You and Me" was not a part of *Tell It Like It Is*, but "Pass It On" certainly was.

Kurt and Ralph felt the need for a song that, in Kurt's words, would "button it up," that would function much like Fanny Crosby's "Just as I Am" did in the Billy Graham Crusades. It was determined that Kurt would write the song. On a cold Sunday evening Kurt was building a fire in the fireplace, stoking it and thinking, "It only takes a spark to get a fire going, and soon all those around can warm up in its glowing." Kurt and Pat decided to take a walk around the neighborhood. While on the walk, Kurt kept saying, "You know, Mommy,[10] that's really going to work." Returning to the house, Kurt again stoked the fire in the den fireplace. "It only takes a spark to get a fire going" was emerging and strengthening. As Kurt worked with the fire, Pat called from another room, "You know, you should say something about shouting it from mountains."[11] And he did. At the "pinnacle" of the hymn, the third line of the last stanza, "I'll shout it from the mountain top," has become the place for singers to add their unwritten, but heartfelt shout, "Praise God," in the two-beat rhythm of the half-note, and the following quarter rest. Praise God, yes, but also thank Pat.

Kurt wrote the song and shared it with Ralph, who immediately recognized the song as something special. It became the musical's "Just as I Am" and rivaled the old gospel song for "invitation" song of choice for specific age groups for many years. When, in her interview, Kris asked her father,

"So the feedback you got when *Tell It Like It Is* released was booming sales, what else?" Kurt quickly replied:

> Kids finding Christ, which was really, really nice. 'Cuz there was a kind of, there was a kind of apathy in the church, I think, and this helped revive all of that stuff, you know. And the "Pass It On" was the perfect vehicle to sort of draw in the net at the end of a performance. And one of the things I learned way back when, was every song needs to do something. Needs to go somewhere. And the "Pass It On" did that. It had this, there's nothing new about it, but it just said it in a different way with some rhythm. And it wasn't too obnoxious for people because the lines were easily sung. And it did what we wanted, tied it all together, you know.[12]

One needs only to listen to some of Kurt's own arrangements of "Pass It On" to hear the dynamic tension between popular and classical being played out in the space of three stanzas. His arrangement of "Pass It On" in the CD *Emmanuel*,[13] which features violinist Michael Davis, then concertmaster of the Louisville Orchestra, is full of the passion of reaching a younger generation with music from within the Church and, at the same time, salutes the supreme art of classical music as a gift from the Giver of All Good Gifts. The violin pleads, dances, dreams, and explores all that the simplicity of "Pass It On" can reveal in this collection of hymns and sacred songs. The musicianship of Kurt and Michael Davis moves from high confidence to introspective vulnerability before the Creator of Music. Here, Kurt's arrangement of "Pass It On" confesses a holy agreement between a humble response to a call and an extravagant stretch of genius. Indeed, the two ventures complement each other in one expression.

Kurt was not ashamed of his popular youth music. How could he be ashamed of what God had done through him? In fact, there were numerous moments of righteous pride that accompanied the widespread usage of his creative work. He certainly didn't stop writing in support of the Church's desire to be relevant in its outreach and worship. He simply wanted to keep a balanced reputation in place so that he could function with equal acceptance and influence in the traditional and classical worlds of the Church as well.

Tell It Like It Is changed the world in which Kurt lived and worked, as well as the world in which he worshiped. In good ways and in new frustrations, *Tell It Like It Is* became for Kurt a constant companion, an ironic source of both pride and humility, hesitancy and hope.

As has been established, the enthusiasm and genius that Kurt poured into *Tell It Like It Is* and similar works was motivated by a desire to connect young people to the gospel. He had no desire to update or bring any sort of showmanship to Christian worship. One hears at this point Kurt's father's admonition concerning accepting applause. Why, then, would Kurt seek the uncomfortable moment? To bring the musical into the sanctuary would be to invite applause into the sanctuary. It was difficult enough to accept and process applause in the concert hall. Neither was keeping *Tell It Like It Is* out of the sanctuary a conflict with his standard of connecting all new music to the church. Kurt was convinced that *Tell It Like It Is* could, and should, enhance the Church's outreach and cultural connection on various stage venues. *Tell It Like It Is* should send the Church out into the world rather than enticing the world into the sanctuary, the Church's foremost place of gathering for continuing transformation through the humble worship that takes place there. His drawing a line at the sanctuary's front door, dividing performance from worship, can also be seen in the premiere of his 1984 musical *The Pursuit of Excellence: The Way Out of Mediocrity*.[14] The performance took place at the national convention of the Christian Booksellers Association, meeting in Anaheim, California. Knowing this association included some very conservative groups, for whom dance was seen as something quite worldly and set apart from singing solos, Kurt was hesitant to include dance choreography. Yet he wanted to do so, felt led by the Spirit to do so. After praying with the dance troupe before the performance, he gave heartfelt approval for them to perform, even though he had not seen what they were going to do. Before the performance, Kurt read Psalm 150 on stage. The musical and the dance were well received. The performance was at a convention, not in a sanctuary on Sunday morning.[15] Kurt, fully given to conservative tradition in worship, was also fully capable of "living the questions" when the Spirit's urging challenged long-held answers. Seventh & James Baptist Church had taught him that.

Two insightful interviews conducted by Indiana University master's degree student Bruce Horner, one interview in July 1968, the other in July 1969, took place at the conference center in Winona Lake, Indiana, during international Youth for Christ assemblies. The dates of the interviews straddle the birth of *Tell It Like It Is* and reveal that Kurt was living the questions related to a culturally relevant philosophy of church music.

Kurt spoke bluntly, honestly, and with authenticity in his responses. His thinking aloud enunciated a conscience for others to consider, and not within YFC alone. The significance of his comments encompassed all the Church's music ministry. The fact that these interviews took place at a venue that had been so important to Kurt's spiritual development and musical opportunities adds to the weight of his reflection. When asked in the 1968 [before *Tell It Like It Is*] interview if he believed that Youth for Christ music affects what young people believe, Kurt replied:

> I think that in the emotion of the moment the music has a great part to play, but I think in the overall life span of a young person or even their young adult life the music probably has very little to do from a theological, philosophy point of view. I simply do not think the music has that much to say. Basically, it's pretty much "surfacy" kind of music. There aren't any great theological concepts given out in the music that's used primarily. Once in a while a nugget will come in, that even I can enjoy and appreciate, but as I think back in my own life, I can't remember anything of any Youth for Christ rally that had a profound, lasting effect on me. Oh, I enjoyed it at the moment, but beyond that I don't think so. I think it has to do with your home upbringing.

Later, Horner asked, "Is there something that you might like to add that would be pertinent as the people in Youth for Christ consider their music program and consider making changes?" Kurt replied:

> Well, this year I've only been around here for a few hours, but I've been pretty excited by the idea that they are trying to do a better-quality music. I directed the program for a couple of years and I tried, every now and then, to stick in something that had a little more body to it . . . But that's what I would do. I would try to, with all of the flash and the frill and the frosting, say something that had a little more body to it . . . something that really has some musical value inherent in it. That's what I would do, but I don't know if that's right.

A year later (1969), same venue, same interviewer, Kurt was asked similar questions. The first one was, "What do you think music should accomplish in the Youth for Christ program?"

> Kurt: Well, I think that the music (not the text) has to communicate in the language that the teenagers understand at the moment, and that is current in their listening and hearing habits. Now I think the message, the lyric, has to be such that it also is current. What I and other of my contemporaries

have tried to do is say things in the terminology that is understood and appreciated by the kids these days.

Horner then asks: "At the present time, Kurt, what kinds of music do you feel come closest to the purpose of communicating?"

Kurt: I think the "folk-country-rock" idea is about right for the YFC crowd. Some of the real message music that we hear these days makes it with kids. I think that the music which communicates best is that which has a melody line which is easily singable and which has a lyric that they can readily understand or even has some deep philosophical meaning and forces the kids to think. I've found that this kind of music they'll go for even if they don't understand it the first time around. Maybe in the third or fourth hearing they'll understand what's really being said and that's a kind of music that I think communicates.

Kurt is then asked what happened in the past year to make his answer to this question [above] different from that of one year ago.

Kurt: The primary difference is a folk musical that a real genius friend of mine, Ralph Carmichael, and I wrote titled *Tell It Like It Is*. *Tell It Like It Is* is a folk musical about God and that's exactly the way we stated it. We're saying things in it that couldn't have been said a few years ago but which need to be said in 1969. I've changed a lot of my thinking, I guess, because of the fact that even though the message of Christ is the same, the method must change to be contemporary. We've done some unbelievable rhythmics that kids can do. They may not be able to read them off the page, but once they hear them they'll know them because it's the kind of thing they hear all the time on the radio. I just think that we can say things now—regular message music that is religious, but not so religious that it turns off kids outside of the church. I know that *Tell It* works because I've just finished touring it for ten days with my group down at Baylor University . . . it was unbelievable the response that we got just because we were fresh in our ideas . . . Musically, it was new—it was right. Idiomatically, everything was correct—and kids just go for this.

Then Bruce Horner's last question from the interview of a year ago was asked in this interview: "If there are things not mentioned concerning music and reaching young people with it, would you add them at this time?" Kurt's answer laid bare the responsibilities that accompany upholding musical standards while desiring to speak to the kids of the current culture:

> I have a very great fear that people will get the feeling that this is the only kind of music that there is for kids and that, of course, is very, very wrong. I must say that *Tell It Like It Is* is not great music, for example. The folk music that these kids are singing is not great music. Most of it is often trite and it is often poorly conceived. I would like to see us be able to span the whole range of music because there is some marvelous sacred classical literature that could be very relevant, very meaningful, and really enriching in the lives of these kids.[16]

Forty-three years later, reflecting on the relationship of *Tell It Like It Is* to the music of its day, Kurt said:

> Well, it was late sixties, so I think there was a feeling in the country of promiscuity of every kind. And I think that was when Woodstock [August 15–18, 1969] took place. I think there's a lot of rebellion in our country about that time. And the churches were so happy, and here we come with this music, which is like the stuff you hear at Woodstock, or heard at Woodstock, but the churches are happy because we are providing them a vehicle that's not totally unlike what they would hear at Woodstock, and that doesn't defame principles or doctrines that are important to the church, and every pastor was really thrilled that we were doing that kind of stuff . . .
>
> . . . in the back of my mind I'm thinking to myself, Ralph [Carmichael] does his kind of music. I don't want to do Ralph's kind of music; I can't. I'll always remember when I heard what he did to start *Tell It Like It Is*, I thought, that is so good![17] And I was right. Kids could jump on that like crazy, what a great lead-in. Well, it was sort of incumbent upon me to write my kind of stuff, which had a little bit more substance to it, let's say. . . . both ways [music and text]. Ralph was very hip to what was going on, all around him, I thought. And I remember on *Natural High*[18] there's a tune called "Outasite." Well, he just said, "Kids say 'man that is out of sight." And I said to myself, see, I would never have thought anything like that. That's what he knew. He knew that kind of stuff. Maybe in collaboration with other people that always happens . . . but it was really wonderful for me to work with a guy up from the West Coast . . . Ralph was where it was happening, and that's what I thought was great.[19]

Kurt was not imagining, nor was he inventing, the weight on his shoulders as one of the key contributors to the Church's new culturally aware music. Neither was the weight lessened by the passing of four decades. Kurt's personal struggles with balance between entertainment and worship, between traditional and contemporary, reflect a conversation and conflict that has been common throughout the Church, Protestant and Catholic, for centuries. In Kurt's generation, in all aspects of worship and witness, the concern and conversation were reinvigorated by Vatican II (Rome 1962–1965). To embrace the culture with respect, freshness, and welcome, while at the same time embodying the Church's long-tested faith, doctrine, and theology, was to live the questions "How much?" "In what ways?" "According to whose guidelines?"

Many individuals, congregations, and denominations simply decided to stay traditional or to jump to contemporary, even though neither category was clearly defined. Others tried "blended" middle-of-the-road mixtures of traditional and contemporary components and sensibilities. Kurt was relevant across the spectrum. His personal espousing of worship that was true to the highest standards of music, congregational integrity, and biblical veracity seemed a noble attempt to bless the blended approach to community. But it was not that. It was more than that. It rose above the three categories of traditional, contemporary, or blended, or of classical, popular, or eclectic. His way rose above any three-item menu of cultural positioning. But rising above the obvious options was not always welcomed, for it seemed to reject the productivity of the energy to be found in any one of the three. In terms of sales and "branding," of church growth, stylistic devotion and development, rising above and across the three-option mindset was seen as idealistic or naive. Kurt was naive by virtue of deep commitments. That "naivete" became the conscience of his industry as it encountered and embraced the contemporary Christian music movement.

Warranted or not, the weight of icon and conscience of this new reality in church music was taking up residence within Kurt. Just one item of evidence, out of many that could be cited, surfaced in a conversation between this writer and the pastor, playwright, poet, and lyricist Ragan Courtney. As reported earlier, when asked if he had ever worked with Kurt, Ragan responded that he had not, but that he had always wanted to. Ragan further stated that in all of his own work he would think: at some point, Kurt Kaiser might see this. I wonder what he will think of it.

Kurt could not discard his standards, even if they were starting to isolate him from both "high church" and "low church." He could deny this role of champion of high standards, but the crown sat all the surer on his head each time he did so. His honesty ("I didn't start it") only convinced admirers that he was deserving of the accolade. At one level, Kurt is saying, "I didn't start it." At another level, he was forced to consider the possibility that "*we* may have started it."

Kurt was not simply an unofficial moderator and mediator in the competitions between adherents of traditional and contemporary; he lived the question. The struggle was internal for him, a dynamic tension within that motivated him and shaped his musical decisions in the studio and the sanctuary.

KURT KAISER MUSICALS (1969-1979)

The success of *Tell It Like It Is* (1969) rang the bells of evangelism, business, and the church growth movement. Motivations to write more musicals were varied, mixed, and mingled. The churches wanted more. WORD and Lexicon gave them many more, along with a number of additional publishing companies.

In 1970, again with Ralph's Lexicon Music, and again distributed by WORD, Ralph and Kurt published *Natural High: A Folk Musical about God's Son*. It was recorded by an auditioned group of Baylor University students recruited to become "The Kurt Kaiser Singers." This group included Tina English, who became a popular Christian music composer. The "world premiere" soon followed at Baylor's Waco Hall with Kaiser, Carmichael, and Jarrell McCracken in attendance. Another early performance of *Natural High* took place on October 24, 1970, sung by the Oklahoma Youth Celebration Choir, but Kurt couldn't attend because of heart difficulties. Yet another performance took place on December 12, 1970, in the Dade County (Florida) Auditorium, with the sixty-voice youth choir "The Minority" from First Baptist Church, West Palm Beach, Florida as the performing choir. This was the promotional pattern set by *Tell It Like It Is*. *Natural High* produced strong and impressive performance numbers, but fewer than *Tell It Like It Is*. Ralph and Kurt had set the bar, then in this second instance, fallen a bit short of it. *Natural High* was solid in its own right; however, the expectations and momentum of *Tell It Like It Is* could not be matched. There were no "takeaway" songs. "The Moment of Truth" (1970) did not match "Pass It On" (1969).

The slight downward trend sloped a bit more with the youth musical *I'm Here, God's Here, Now We Can Start* (1973), again composed by Kurt Kaiser and Ralph Carmichael, again published by Lexicon, again distributed by WORD.[20] Three titles may have given this musical something of a limping start. *I'm Here* would have been an intriguing title for young people searching for their identity. *God's Here* might have been a title to awaken young people to anticipate divine inspiration and guidance in life. *Now We Can Start* might have given permission to young people to venture forth on life's path. But, combined, the "three" had a difficult time functioning as "-in-one." The *I'm Here, God's Here, Now We Can Start* title

Kurt conducting the recording of *I'm Here, God's Here, Now We Can Start*, 1973

may well have cast some doubt on the strength of the work as a whole, predisposing ministers of music to see the three sections of the musical as more separate than was intended, indecision instead of confidence. Trust, so firmly established with the "cool" title of 1969's *Tell It Like It Is* thinned a bit. Yet we must admit that the three titles move more closely toward one, and clarity, in Ralph's lyric in the fourth song, "Now We Can Start to Hear Music." But it seems to be too little, too late. Perhaps that title should have been "the" title.

Does this chapter's three-title commentary sound a bit harsh? Have we, here, dented two haloes? No. Our observations are neither harsh, nor snide. The less-than-complimentary comments serve to balance and underscore authenticity in all that is written in these pages. If it were our purpose to prove Kurt Kaiser a saint above fallibility, we would have declared these triplets to be, in fact and intent, icons of the trinity. But canonization is not our goal. Unnecessary, effusive, inauthentic; these words would apply to any sort of blindness or tunnel vision that we might have chosen as a loving lens. These titles speak of a human phenomenon, inconsistency, not omnipotence. There is a difference between genius and omniscience.

The musical *I'm Here, God's Here, Now We Can Start* gave us lyrics that would make a compelling Bible study focused on the parables. But on the heels of *Tell It Like It Is*, followed by *Natural High*, ministers of music wanted to see an upswing, back to the heights of *Tell It Like It Is*. The later work, *I'm Here, God's Here, Now We Can Start* did not deliver that remembered, deeply gratifying experience. Were *Natural High* and *I'm Here, God's Here, Now We Can Start* lesser attempts on the part of Ralph and Kurt? Had this team of writers lost their creative touch or their ability to "read the market"? No. Their experience was a high-profile example of "the next one must be bigger and better" success trap. Human experience exposes the futility of the concept that bigger and better, more exciting, is somehow the trajectory of any and all ministries. They said "yes" to ideas and opportunities as Christ-followers should. But it must be remembered that Lexicon and WORD were businesses, companies that had to make a profit to stay at the task. The Church's businesses are in competition with the Church's call to find its fulfillment in obedience, not success. Church music, in this dance with its daughter, Contemporary Christian Music, presented the drama of the dilemma in a well-lighted arena. The final song of *I'm Here, God's Here, Now We Can Start*, "He'll Go with You" (1973), did not match "Pass It On" (1969).

In 1974, Kurt, along with his friend, coworker, and fellow church member Charles F. Brown, composed the young adult musical *God's People*, published by WORD.[21] Kurt and Charlie Brown brought the focus fully, and with freshness, back to the local church, one of Kurt's foundational pillars. He reached all the way back to his boyhood family walks to church on Sundays with the song, "Sunday Mornin'." Kurt brings the singers and listeners to the awe of the Sunday morning sanctuary with his song "His Will Our Own," and its telling phrase, "A holy hush comes over us and we behold in awe." This was the proper attitude, physical and spiritual, for worship in Kurt's mind and experience. Let us remember that Kurt did not want *Tell It Like It Is* to be performed in the sanctuary at Seventh & James. Further, the song underscores what Kurt considered worship's proper end result, "He makes His will our own," a weekly recentering of priorities brought about by worship focused on God and nothing, no one, else. The choral benediction of *God's People* is beautiful, reverent, and memorable. It would become a familiar benediction at Waco's DaySpring Baptist Church in years to come. The little chorus is full of peace and hope, but "The Lord Whom We Love" (1974) did not match the widespread acceptance or impact of "Pass It On" (1969).

In 1979, Kurt composed for WORD the musical *Just for You: A Loving Adventure with God . . . A Joyful Occasion with One Another*.[22] There was no other company involved. There was no co-author. This was his, and his best. It did not set any sales records, but it held high the banner of his foundational principles of excellence in music, biblical veracity, and connection to the Church. If we wanted to, we could give this multigenerational musical a similar evaluation to that of *I'm Here, God's Here, Now We Can Start*. That musical had three titles. *Just for You*, it could be said, has an ending section that includes five songs. But the culminating songs, one after the other, are more like encores of the Spirit, rather than the earlier three-titles' functional crafting.

The wonderful five-song ending section of *Just for You* might have included an admonition to ministers of music to "choose one." But that task was impossible for Kurt, and it would be impossible for the choir director. There is the Ken Medema solo, "Be Joyful," the children's choir anthem, "Commit Thy Way," and the adult choir anthem, "The Final Victory." Those songs are numbers one, two, and five of the concluding sequence. Number three is Amy Grant's solo "Precious," and number four is the adult choir anthem, "He Careth for You," in which the audience/congregation is invited to sing along.

Kurt, like all believers, understood that the sometimes-biting concept of "ending" is tamed by the promise of beginnings. Every ending is a beginning. Every ending sprouts new, green-edged thoughts of next and more. Members of the listening congregation, as well as members of the performing choir, might be experiencing a variety of "endings" within their ranks. Did Kurt simply not work hard enough to create the one proper ending for this musical, or did he at some depth sense that each ending had its potential place in a musical titled *Just for You*? *Just for You* had to have a last page, but the musical refuses to quit without this artful protest to the concept of an end to what God has started, and equal protest of the thought that everyone faces the same closures within life at the same time and in the same way.

In *Just for You*, Kurt gave us the magnificent middle section songs "Sing O Heavens," "Forgiven," "It Is Finished," and "In His Love and in His Pity." This was the height of Kurt Kaiser's combined work as a choral composer, record producer, and church musician. In the recording, Kurt enlisted one of the finest local church choirs of the time, the First Baptist Church Choir of Richardson, Texas, under the direction of Bill Green. Kurt enlisted soloists Barry McGuire, Dave Boyer, Robert Hale, Ken Medema, and Amy Grant, each a recording artist of the first order. The narrator of the commentary woven within the choral pieces was the renowned pastor and preacher Dr. Jack Flanders of First Baptist Church, Waco. The orchestrator was none other than monumental composer and arranger Bill Pursell. And, again, Kurt called upon his friend Bruce Swedien, this time to be the "mixdown engineer." At every point, Kurt recruited the best.

Yet another Kurt Kaiser accomplishment here is the joining together of apparent opposites: artist and amateur, the joining of skilled and unskilled singers, of children, youth, and adults. This is a picture of the Church, its song, its reach both outward and inward. Kurt Kaiser stood in the midst of all of it, with giftedness and confidence on display, to bring the entire project and all that it represented into harmonious union.

If monumental change is going to be successful, it will have icons that communicate in memorable representation the heart of a people and of a movement; where it has been, where it is going, and sufficient assurance that the transition is good and possible. The closing takeaway song "He Careth for You" (1979) was memorable but did not match "Pass It On" (1969). What shall we say of no endings, however beautiful and memorable, ever matching "Pass It On?" We would do well to revisit the wedding at Cana (John 2) where Jesus performed his first miracle. We revisit the scene as servants, Kurt with us. We carry water, as instructed by the Lord, sometimes just a cupful, sometimes a pitcher full, ending after ending. He turns the water into wine ("Pass It On") according to his time and purpose.

One musical remains to be considered, but outside of the five above. It is the senior adult musical *You Are Special*, published in 1989 by "Genevox Music Group," a new division of the Southern Baptists' publishing business/ministry. The musical score was in large print, and the recording was available in cassette tape only. Lyricist Bob Woolley was the Director of the Church Music Department of the Missouri Baptist Convention. He was known for his sense of humor, which comes through in his light-hearted lyrics. Kurt's music (composition and piano accompanying) matches the moods of the lyrics, from "fun" to "thoughtful." One wonders why Kurt would be a part of this project, except that it might represent a capstone (a musical for senior adults) to the process that began with "doing something for the kids" two decades earlier. Senior adult ministry is a legitimate facet of the life of the Church, often more sophisticated than this musical. Did Kurt do this musical out of friendship, out of Southern Baptist loyalty, as a later-ministry blessing? The "conscience of the Contemporary Christian Music movement" may well have felt obligated to walk the entire distance of the Christian musical journey. He was at the beginning. He would see the journey through.

THE TERM "CONTEMPORARY CHRISTIAN MUSIC"

This bold and daring new sound in the music of the Church, according to WORD Music executive Stan Moser, didn't have a suitable genre identification until, in a 1975 marketing meeting, he suggested that "what we have here is Contemporary Christian Music."[23] Moser played a role in creating the atmosphere of WORD Music around the time of Kurt's stepping away. Yet in his book *We Will Stand*, Moser acknowledges the early and sustained shaping and strengthening of the company that came about because of Kurt Kaiser's work. It is not uncommon that one who stands between two differing worldviews, extending a hand to each side, is seen as indecisive. But at the peak of Kurt's creative output, he was admired by both sides (traditional and contemporary) as a man of courage, willing to risk musical derision for the cause of unity with integrity. Later in his book, Moser wrote concerning a difficulty that has encompassed all of Contemporary Christian Music since its inception and before its naming:

> [Cutting edge releases] were often in conflict with established church leadership. The backlash from church leaders was strong and relentless. I didn't blame them. Sometimes it was difficult for me to accept radical rock music as a viable tool for communicating the gospel. But it was. (145)

Kurt had the musical talent, even genius, to analyze the music theory of Contemporary Christian Music's most intricate rhythms and harmonies. CCM's electronic keyboards could never surpass Kurt's piano skills. But his soul could not and would not climb over or circumvent standards that were increasingly seen as barriers to the industry. His presence was an iconic reminder and persistent conscience of a bygone era of artistic and ecclesial decorum. Both parties breathed easier when the man and the company parted ways. But the larger movement, Contemporary Christian Music, could not dismiss its icons. Kurt's name and songs grew dusty perhaps, but they were and are still in place and speaking.

In his 1999 book *At the Crossroads*, award-winning recording artist, producer, and songwriter Charlie Peacock had this to say:

> It is biblical and essential to communicate the gospel. In this, Billy Ray Hearn, Ralph Carmichael, Kurt Kaiser, Elwyn Raymer, and the Southern Baptist leadership were indeed faithful. All Christians, even the nastiest

critics of CCM, must acknowledge that God has used these enthusiastic and imperfect men to add to his kingdom. This is reason to give God praise and honor and glory. And, it is reason to honor these men and their contributions to the church and to contemporary Christian music.[24]

It is naive to think that a company will not change over time. It is equally naive to think that definitions of foundational words will not change over time. We need only to look at the definition of "hymn." It has changed from "strophic poetic text to or about a god or hero" to "a congregational song of prayer, praise or testimony." "Pass It On" and "Oh, How He Loves You and Me" are now considered hymns by virtue of being included in hymnals. So too does the definition of "Contemporary Christian Music" change via expansion over time as styles that are "not traditional" follow each other in a never-ending sequential parade of rejection, innovation, and acceptance.

No one should ever question or be surprised at Kurt's ability to move from one genre of music to another, to move from knowing conversation with an artist of one style to informed conversation with an artist of another style. Kurt could move in and out of what might appear to be opposing styles of music because his focus was on the essence, the art, the authenticity. Every genre of music has at its core an honesty of expression. That's where and how any type of music gets its start and its momentum. Kurt's concern and currency was not with the novelty of emerging music, but rather with its human heartbeat and foundational principles.

From chant to electronic, Kurt knew that creative people served the common human desire to explore and know and create. He connected with that impulse. It made his communication current and much of his music timeless. The soul that made humans human, the creativity that was born of the Creator's image shaped in flesh, the kernel at the core of the creative spirit is of God. Kurt knew that and respected it. Sometimes worshipers exhibit an exclusionary musical zeal that God will not own.[25] With his eyes on the gifting God, and his ears attuned to creation itself, Kurt did not allow lesser concerns to deter or distract him from embracing the divine essence in the music of others. Like new islands rising up from within the sea in praise and testimony of the Creator, so too new music can rise up from within the Church in praise and testimony of the Creator.

Kurt knew that one of the distractions or concerns that bothered traditional congregations was a perceived "air" or attitude in those who were the "celebrities" and proponents of Contemporary Christian Music. (Of course, traditional musicians were just as susceptible to this tendency.) Kurt had absolutely no tolerance for self-imagined importance and said so in no uncertain terms. Rather, a countenance that Kurt did see and understand, in much of early CCM, was enlivened synergy of creativity and opportunity, enthusiasm concerning new possibilities for the Church's music. This state of anticipation and motivation is sometimes observed with a measure of disdain by those who do not possess it, but it is recognized and embraced with a sense of knowing by those who do possess it.

Even Kurt was rightly criticized for being aloof or arrogant on rare occasions as this new music met growing acceptance. But his life made up for this occasional misstep.

The acknowledging of one artistic spirit by another is not the insider greeting of a clique. Musicians in general, as with any guild, have a language and vocabulary that they, alone, understand. Yet, the church music guild's unity was strained, if not outright divided, by the rapid emergence and popularity of Contemporary Christian Music and its seemingly unquestioned access to both stage and dais. Kurt sensed the potential destructiveness of the unrest and sought to put it to rest by personifying balance and openness.

What the faithful feared would be lost in CCM was not properly balanced with what could be gained by the emergence of fresh Christian expression. Those were two different conversations, being held in emerging and diverging camps. Kurt found himself playing the role of the playground daredevil who stands on the fulcrum of the teeter-totter as both sides go up and down. Giving equal weight and attention to both "traditional" and "contemporary," he tried to infuse evidence of quality and mutual respect for, and into, each side. All facets of composition and performance were to Kurt components of prayer, a part of the obedience that the co-creating composer owed to the Creator of All Things.

For Kurt, style and genre were opportunity-specific manifestations of a shared call and commitment to the highest offering one could present to God. Sometimes pastor, sometimes prophet, Kurt was, unknowingly, received as both with authenticity and integrity within the movement and the industry. He did not even entertain the thought that he might be seen as responsible in any way or degree for bringing about the change from traditional to contemporary in church music. In fact, he did not see CCM as change or exchange but rather as an expansion of the Church's song. A lowering of standards would certainly be a reason for concern, but new music that exhibited those standards was something he welcomed. He participated with dedication, innovation, and excellence in the CCM movement in its early days, but in his eyes that was quite different than launching the movement. Stewardship of his giftedness and the exercise of creativity were acts of love and worship. His decision to "write something for the kids" (*Tell It Like It Is*) was about outreach to a restless and troubled generation. His intention was to be a channel for the Spirit's fresh breeze, already, and equally, present and available in the Church's traditional song and worship.

Indeed, for many of those who were influential in the shaping of the emerging genre of Contemporary Christian Music, their peer Kurt Kaiser was the movement's conscience in matters of musical integrity, biblical veracity, congregational commitment, and personal walk with God. But this was not an assumed role. Nor was it a position or station formally assigned by Kurt's peers. It was an observed presence. He was this "person among people" because of his walk with his Lord. He could not hide it. He could not fake it. While, as stated earlier, his demeanor was on the rare occasion interpreted as arrogance, it was far more often and rightly seen as the peace and assurance of a disciple. Kurt's ability to politely deflect the effusive compliment was well rehearsed.

Kurt had high expectations for professional musicians. Music was their gift, their call, their profession, their advertised primary mode of expression. He expected the same of himself. But his lofty and continuous goal for the professional musician was matched by his concern for the accessibility and the enriching musical experience of the amateur musician. Even so, on occasion he would slip into studio mode while rehearsing a volunteer church choir. Students in transition from amateur to professional were susceptible to first experiencing professional expectations from Kurt the conductor of the Baylor Religious Hour choir, and Kurt the classroom guest speaker. In like manner, Kurt expected professional church musicians and Christian recording personnel, those who were ushering the Church into a new era, to take their call and responsibility seriously. His expectations showed respect for the persons involved, and for their call to the sacred task at hand.

His own skills and standards of high-level musicianship gained Kurt entrée into the unofficial but widely recognized role of musical coach. His dedication to the highest levels of morality, devotion to marriage and family, and Christian discipleship gave him similar credibility and presence as spiritual coach for those with whom he worked. His work as a record producer, and his ability to spot and call forth young talent with exceptional potential, ushered him into the position of example and coach for many in similar positions throughout the CCM world.

4
ADOPTED SON OF WACO AND BAYLOR UNIVERSITY

THE CITY OF WACO

As was mentioned in the introduction of this book, the headline of the Tuesday, November 13, 2018, *Waco Tribune-Herald* newspaper announced, "KURT KAISER: 1934–2018: Composer's Work Helped Shape Worship Music." Reporter Carl Hoover and the editors knew that no citizen of Waco would question this being the lead article. A favorite son had died, a beloved adopted son had died. The first line of the article identified Kurt Kaiser as "Waco composer and pianist." His transplanted roots were acknowledged in the fourth paragraph:

> The Chicago-born musician moved to Waco in 1959 with his wife Pat and family and lived here, becoming deeply involved with Baylor University, which their four children attended. He was also involved in the Waco Symphony Orchestra and in Seventh & James Baptist Church before helping to start DaySpring Baptist Church, where he and his wife Pat are members.

The January 2000 issue of *Waco Today* included the article "Letter from Sweden," written by Kay Olson, wife of then U.S. Ambassador to Sweden, Lyndon Olson. Lyndon is the brother of Charlie Olson, Kris Kaiser Olson's husband. Describing a busy holiday season, Kay wrote:

> For Lyndon and me, the holiday season started in early December with the annual Nobel ceremonies in Stockholm. As is often the case, Americans were among the Nobel laureates, and—as is the custom—we hosted them and their families at a luncheon at our residence . . . Three days later, Pat and Kurt Kaiser arrived. Kurt needs no introduction, but I must say, if Waco were to catalogue all its treasures—from the Brazos River to those of the human kind—Kurt definitely would be among them. Pianist, composer, conductor, arranger, and more—Kurt's light has been brightening Central Texas and all of Christendom for decades . . . That light shone brightly again the evening of December 13 [1999], a major holiday in Sweden. It's the day of St. Lucia. (p. 84)

Kurt conducted, from the piano, a holiday concert with a chamber orchestra at the Museum of History in Stockholm. He was a part of the American ambience provided by the embassy. That night he was Waco's ambassador.

Kurt entertaining at the U.S. Ambassador's Christmas Program in Sweden, 1999

The July 2008 issue of the *WACOAN: Waco's City Magazine*, featured an article by Baylor professor Robert Darden that declared Kurt to be "Waco's most beloved musician." The article, "Tell It Like It Is: An Afternoon with Waco's Most Beloved Musician," featured a large picture of Kurt at the piano in his home. The article is a short interview that covers Kurt's life in a nutshell, and Kurt's love for Waco shines forth when he calls Waco a "perfect place to raise kids" (pp. 79, 88–90).

These articles are sufficient evidence that Kurt was adopted as a son by the city of Waco, and that he and Pat had adopted Waco in return. But they are bolstered by, of all things, authorized graffiti, sophisticated French graffiti, not unlike the work of England's "Banksy."

On November 22, 2018, Creative Waco, under Executive Director Fiona Bond, posted on its blog that the week prior Xavier Prou, the world-renowned street artist from Paris better known as "Blek le Rat," used as his canvas six walls in the downtown cultural district of Waco. The artwork was layered stencil spray paint. Blek was in town at the invitation of art collector Brian Greif and others. Photos of the artist at work appeared alongside the *Waco Tribune-Herald*'s front page article, "Art of the Rat."[1]

One of the six works, the one at 324 South 6th Street, is titled *In Honor of Kurt Kaiser*. The other five are *Violinist, Selfie-Rat, Young Chopin, Young Picasso,* and *Victor Hugo*. This artist from Paris confirmed in paint that Kurt Kaiser was one of Waco's beloved sons. The image is of an angel (made obvious by the wings) wearing tennis shoes and holding a conductor's baton. The tennis shoes are a rather poetic link to Kurt's love of Baylor basketball.

Mural by Parisian artist "Blek le Rat" dedicated to the memory of Kurt Kaiser. Located at 324 S. 6th St., Waco, Texas.

In a March 5, 2019, email response to Kurt and Pat's son Craig, the artist wrote:

> To answer to [sic] your question, you know sometimes in life we feel the need to do something that we don't know the reason why. In last September when I was working on the project to paint Nashville and Waco, I had the feeling to work on an image of an orchestra conductor. I can't tell you the reason why. Then I ask to my son Alex to pose for an image this is the reason why the character wear tennis shoes. As I was painting in the character in Waco someone told me about the history of your father, I thought the coincidence was really amazing. During the conversation with the person I said I think it's probably a tribute to Mister Kaiser that I wanted to make. Since then I have read the history of your father on internet. He was a great man! Kind regards, Xavier.

Kurt died on Monday, November 12, 2018. The Waco newspaper reported Kurt's death on Tuesday, November 13, and then reported on "Blek le Rat's" work in the Thursday, November 15, edition. Kurt's memorial service was on Friday, November 16. For many in Waco, the coincidence of the painting was a poetic and timely way of mourning and commemorating the passing of a son.

Kurt and Pat were consistent supporters of the Waco Symphony Orchestra in both attendance and donations. They held season tickets for years, and during the 1986–1987 season, Kurt served the Waco Symphony Association as Vice President for Planning. During the 1999–2000 season he served as the Association's President. The October 12, 1999 concert opened with Kurt's "Millennium Fanfare I," composed for the occasion, and the March 29, 2008 concert closed with Kurt's setting of the Mary Landon Darden lyric "Coming Home," again, composed for the occasion. The program notes for the 2008 concert proudly proclaim Kurt to be "our own."

Kurt needed music as art. His functional vocational and worship music needed art's refinement and freedom. His soul needed art's inspiration. His gift needed the master composers' humbling. He inhaled and exhaled that quality of life that can only be breathed in a musical community.

Baylor professor Maestro Stephen Heyde, conductor of the Waco Symphony for thirty-five years, enjoyed with Kurt a friendship of mutual respect and admiration. He considered Kurt one of the best musicians he had ever known and said that Kurt had "ultimate ears—more than perfect pitch. It is the ability to know what harmony might be more effective." But within and beyond music, Heyde felt that Waco was fortunate to have Kurt, who had "moved into a role that is very becoming to him—being a community leader."[2]

To be a leader in the Waco community is to know and nurture its important components. McLennan Community College is one of those components. Excerpts from a 2020 letter take us into the Kaiser home and the depths of their Waco citizenship:

> Your warm acceptance and sunny dispositions not only made our jobs easier but also made them most enjoyable. Your home is absolutely beautiful, warm and inviting. But your willingness not only to host our special event but also provide the entertainment sealed the success of the entire evening! I wish I had a more complete mastery of the English language so that I could enhance the "thank you" that comes so sincerely with this

note. But I hope you know just how much we truly appreciate all that you did for McLennan Community College and our students in hosting this once-in-a-lifetime celebratory affair for our All-Steinway initiative.

Warm regards and many thanks,
Harry I. Harelik, MPA, CPA, CFRE
Executive Director
The McLennan Community College Foundation[3]

BAYLOR UNIVERSITY

Baylor's "adoption" of Kurt as a son was duly documented and certified. On May 13, 1995, Baylor University bestowed upon Kurt Kaiser the honorary degree Doctor of Humane Letters. The prelude to this recognition was Kurt's receiving Baylor's 1993 W. R. White Award for Meritorious Service. The underscoring of it all was in 2017 when Baylor University bestowed upon Kurt the "Pro Ecclesia Medal of Service." Baylor gave Kurt one each of everything it had to give to a nongraduate. Kurt's engagement with the life of Baylor spanned decades and disciplines. He moved comfortably in and out of Baylor's life and work, formal and informal, in the spotlight and behind the scenes.

Kurt receiving the honorary degree Doctor of Humane Letters (LLD) from Baylor University President Dr. Herb Reynolds, 1995

During the second half of the culturally turbulent decade of the 1960s, Kurt conducted the Baylor Religious Hour Choir, learning, as well as shepherding, the college students' new-music impulses. BRH was not and is not a part of Baylor's renowned School of Music. Rather, it started in 1948 as a facet of the weekly revivalistic, student-oriented Baylor Religious Hour gathering at First Baptist Church, Waco. That gathering is no longer in existence. However, the choir continues as a source of tradition, ministry, and public relations, exhibiting across the years a once/always esprit de corps.

Those who have sung in the BRH Choir wear the experience as a badge of honor. The names of those who have conducted the BRH Choir comprise an elite list in the history of the university. Kurt's conducting of the BRH Choir is additional evidence that he was an adopted, even favored, son of the school. The fact that he was the first conductor never to have been a Baylor student underscores the intertwined creative family relationship between three separate Waco establishments: Baylor University, Seventh & James Baptist Church, and WORD. He personified the connections. Kurt conducted the choir and was a high-profile member of the church and a dedicated employee of the company. Kurt's 1995 honorary doctorate citation includes this sentence: "From 1965 through 1970, Kaiser served as director of the Baylor Religious Hour Choir."[4] It was a big deal.

In June 1966, Kurt took the BRH Choir on a tour of Mexico, holding concerts in the cities of Monterrey, Saltillo, Mexico City, Guadalajara, León, and Torreón. Kurt's extensive international travel experience equipped him for confident leadership of university students experiencing a journey into a new culture. The in-country coordinator of the tour was Baptist missionary J. T. Owens, a professor at the Mexican Baptist Theological Seminary in Torreón. The BRH students recognized that this tour, and the choir's spring break trips, were major commitments on Kurt's part, investments in their lives.

When in 1967 WORD Records recorded *Cliff Barrows and the Gang: Along the Trail*, the "Gang" was the BRH Choir. The students were impressed that Kurt knew the Billy Graham Crusade's Cliff Barrows. Thanks to Kurt, they now knew him, too.

In November 1969, the BRH Choir videotaped Kurt and Ralph Carmichael's musical *Tell It Like It Is* in NBC's Brooklyn Color Studio in New York. The ticket into the studio read "'Tell It Like It Is,' Presented by The Southern Baptist Convention." The information packet for the event declared on its front cover, "Produced by the National Broadcasting Company and

Southern Baptists' Radio-Television Commission, . . . Paul M. Stevens, Executive Director." The production aired on NBC-TV across the nation on February 1, 1970, at 3:30 p.m. CST. One can only imagine what the Church Music Department of the Baptist Sunday School Board must have thought about that. A mild "explosion" must have rocked 127 Ninth Ave North, Nashville, TN 37234. The SBC's Radio and Television Commission gave valuable national exposure to the product of a competitor of the Baptist Sunday School Board's Church Music Department. In the Southern Baptist Convention structure, the Commission and the Department were separately purposed and separate operational entities, but the letters "SBC" connected them. Paul Stevens probably gave little thought and lost no sleep over any music industry misstep the telecast may have caused. The NBC opportunity seems to have been initiated by a family connection: a sister in the local Waco NBC television affiliate, and her brother in the New York company office. Kurt Kaiser stood as an unassailable conscience in the middle, braiding competitive commerce, choir, and convention into something for the kids, for the sake of spreading the gospel.

Kurt's first heart surgery marked the end of his tenure as director of BRH, but not of his ministry to those who had sung during his tenure, and to their families, even in times of deepest sorrow. In 1980, Kurt played for the funeral of one of his former BRH members who died by suicide. Kurt's presence and his piano touched the family's hearts.

Lines of separation often blurred between the BRH Choir, the Seventh & James Baptist Church college choir, and temporary demonstration recording choirs needed by WORD. Students moved in and out of the choirs and back and forth across James Avenue as need and opportunity arose. Kurt was at home in any of the Baylor, WORD, and Seventh & James Baptist Church situations or combinations. His presence was an affirmation that the choir and the project were current and worthwhile. One such needs-based singing group was the "Sing 'n' Celebrate Chorus of Baylor University," directed by Kurt. In 1972, Kurt directed this occasioned choir in recording *Sing 'n' Celebrate: A Double Album Singalong*, containing "Forty-four selected songs from the Songbook SING 'N' CELEBRATE, published by WORD Music."[5] The recording was produced by Billy Ray Hearn, the "third party" in the *Tell It Like It Is* concept and project.

In 1973, Kurt directed this choir in recording *Sing 'n' Celebrate: Volume 2: A Double Album Singalong*, which was "Fifty selected songs from the Songbook SING 'N' CELEBRATE!" This project, which completed the recording of the entire *Sing 'n' Celebrate Songbook* series, was produced by Charles F. Brown, who was as involved in Baylor University, WORD Music, and Seventh & James Baptist Church as Kurt. The double album format was designed to allow the listener to hear the instrumentalists and recorded singers, or to hear only the background instrumental track. The local church and its choir directors were always in Kurt's heart and mind. These recordings and the collections they accompanied would be profitable for the company. Kurt knew that. He also knew they would enhance music ministry.

On the dates of February 2, 4, 5, and 6, 1982, Baylor University and the Baylor University Alumni Association presented Orlin Corey's play "The Towers of the Brazos." The play, performed at Baylor's Waco Hall, had musical accompaniment and depicted the history of the university. The music was composed by Kurt, Bill Pursell, and Ted Nichols. Kurt was also the conductor. They had no illusions that the play would become a hit. Yet great talent was assembled and focused on this limited time and place project. It was good for Baylor and its students. Kurt's involvement afforded additional gravitas and validation. The story continues.

On the evening of October 29, 1988, Community Hospice of Waco presented the show "An Evening in Concert with Kurt Kaiser and Baylor ShowTime!" in the Waco Hippodrome. The twelve-member song and dance troupe ShowTime! was organized in 1980 as a public relations ensemble. Dr. Leta Horan, a member of Baylor's piano faculty, became the ensemble's director in 1983. The printed program for the evening was general in nature, listing only the following pieces: "Broadway Rhythm," Baylor ShowTime!; "Reminiscences of New England 1988," Kurt Kaiser; Intermission; "Gospel Music," Kurt Kaiser; and Finale, "Sound of Music Medley," Kurt Kaiser and Baylor ShowTime!

Kurt Kaiser and ShowTime! were highlighted in Community Hospice's special event to garner support from Waco citizens. Two major sponsors, and the number of advertisers in the evening's booklet, suggest that the effort was a huge success.

August 27, 1994, was a big day at Baylor. The Ferrell Center was the venue for a sesquicentennial celebration gala. Baylor enlisted Kurt to arrange several elements: first, the opening sequence of "God Bless America," "My Country 'Tis of Thee," and "All Creatures of Our God and King"; second, the *Pro Texana* patriotic medley of "God of Our Fathers," "Eternal Father Strong to Save," "Stars and Stripes Forever," and "Baylor Blessing"; third, the *Pro Ecclesia* hymn medley of "Amazing Grace," "How Firm a Foundation," and "How Great Thou Art"; and fourth, the postlude. Lydia Bratcher played the organ and Kurt played the piano in the "Stars and Stripes Forever" arrangement. Katy Stokes wrote the words for "Baylor Blessing," and Kurt wrote the music; the song was performed by a "Select Student Choir." The Baylor University motto, *Pro Ecclesia, Pro Texana*, and now *Pro Mundo*, appears on the university's official seal. Whether for Texas, for the Church, for Baylor, or for the world, Kurt qualified on all counts.

Things That Endure: Kurt Kaiser & George Stokes, a CD produced by Kurt Kaiser Music in 2001, is the result of creative work done by three friends connected to both Baylor University and DaySpring Baptist Church. The recording brings pause to all that speeds through the mind, through the filling of days with business. Burt Burleson, pastor of DaySpring Baptist Church at the time of the recording and, later, Baylor University Chaplain, had a good idea. It was to record two of his senior adult church members in a mosaic of spoken words and carefully crafted music. They were to contemplate "things that endure" audibly, in mild and gentle tones. Burt imagined the triad of (1) the Texas drawl and deep measured voice of George Stokes, (2) the thoughtful "not too many notes" of Kurt Kaiser at the piano, and (3) the sound of wisdom. The energy was that of shared reverence for Church, friendship, and Baylor.

George was known as "The Voice of Baylor" because he announced Baylor's football and basketball games for twenty-six of his thirty-one years at the university. He earned a master's degree in speech from Baylor, and a doctorate from Northwestern University, Kurt's alma mater. During his Baylor career George served as director of broadcasting, director of the Baylor Alumni Association, and head of the department of communication studies. Kurt described George as his closest friend, no small accolade. On the back liner of the CD case, Kurt described a somber and profoundly timely series of events:

> On June 18, 2001, following a routine medical checkup, George was told that he had a form of cancer of the blood. After receiving two blood transfusions, he seemed to have renewed energy, so, on July 1, we went into the studio and recorded these excellent readings. He died on the 14th of July. The "Voice of Baylor University" was stilled. I have completed this project in honor of our friendship and so that the entire Baylor family can experience what is very special to me.[6]

The disc label promises "A Moving Collection of Poetry and Scripture Read by George Stokes. Piano Underscoring by Kurt Kaiser." The CD also includes readings from essays that were neither scripture nor poetry. In Burt

Burleson's estimation, George had "saved" Kurt after his dismissal from WORD. Like a big brother, George had also kept Kurt's feet on the ground during times of great success and recognition. On one occasion, George suggested to Kurt that the composer of "Oh, How He Loves You and Me" should not disparage the simplistic and repetitive lyrics of praise choruses.

By now we recognize the name Billy Ray Hearn, Kurt's friend and Baylor alum. Billy Ray financed two conferences at Baylor University, both titled the "Hearn Symposium." These conferences brought together key leaders in CCM and "traditional" protestant worship music. The dates were October 7–9, 2002, and October 4–6, 2004. Some thirty years into the "worship wars" these important formal conversations were conceived and presented under the leadership of Dr. Randall Bradley of Baylor's School of Music. Baylor University seemed a uniquely appropriate venue given its history of academic and practical connections to both traditional and contemporary musical energies. In the first conference, even though the focus was on current leaders, Kurt Kaiser's presence in the history of the subject, in the town of Waco, and on the Baylor campus seasoned the environment.

The 2002 conference broke the ice that had kept CCM and traditional music influencers largely talking *about* each other instead of *with* each other. Their willingness to share and listen was impressive and strangely heartwarming. Even so, a criticism of the first conference, voiced by veteran Minister of Music Merril Smoak, of the Trinity Baptist Church of Livermore, California, was that actual ministers of music were basically confined to the audience. That was a fair criticism, even though the conference was conceived as a service to, and a gift of respite for, ministers of music who had to struggle with the contemporary/traditional question each week. Representatives of academia, the current CCM publishing and recording industry, and the Hymn Society of the United States[7] stood before the ministers of music who had gathered to share their views and motivations concerning Church, worship, trends, culture, purpose, and the spiritual formation of the Church. The perspective and focus were largely protestant.

Two years later, in the second conference, Ralph Carmichael and Kurt Kaiser joined Billy Ray (the "let's do something for the kids" trio) as "eyewitnesses" in a Q&A titled "Cutting Edge in the 1970s: A CCM Retrospective." Just an hour earlier the three had joined current leaders in CCM to form a panel whose conversation was given the title and subject "It Only Takes a Spark: Why Then/What Now?"

The second Hearn Symposium was meant to continue the conversation begun two years earlier, a passing of the baton of sorts. This second generation of leaders in places of influence met with the "legends" of the earlier generation on Baylor's stage. But the energy level of the first gathering was absent in the second. The wound had been healed in the family reunion atmosphere of the 2002 "Music and the Church: Relevance in a Changing Culture" symposium. There was energy and emotion in that somewhat anxious reuniting. Curiously, the 2004 Hearn Symposium, "Music and Worship in an Emerging Culture," did not generate the same soul-deep intensity.

In 2004, the right people were in the right place. The right questions were asked and the right issues were addressed, but the healing did not need to be repeated. The separate trajectories had been somewhat reconciled and blessed. The questions addressed in 2002 and 2004 were similar, but a significant difference was that the "worship war" veterans of 2002, who had been asked to look backward, were asked in 2004 to do the more difficult work of explorers, looking forward. The "cleared air" of what had been was replaced by the fog surrounding what would be. Kaiser, Carmichael, and Hearn faithfully shared their wisdom and blessing. They were revered and heard. But the conferees seemed to lack the personal confidence and the corporate cohesiveness needed to accept and steward well that blessing.

A single question hovered over both conferences: "What now?" But in the 2004 gathering, the question was explicitly addressed in the session mentioned above, "It Only Takes a Spark: Why Then/What Now?" Kurt's song was in the title; he was on the panel. He was icon and conscience in face, name, wisdom, and song: present. The new guard knew that the old guard could not march with them. There was a bright spot, though. There was hope. The three legends embodied the truth that God works through the Church, through persons willing to listen and then to act boldly in new ways on what they have heard. That lesson alone, passed from one generation to the next, was worth the effort of gathering and the risk in dispersing.

Kurt's friend and fellow church member Robert Kruschwitz was the Director of Baylor's Center for Christian Ethics (later, Senior Scholar of the Institute for Faith and Learning), and Professor of Philosophy. His responsibilities included editing the Center's quarterly journal, *Christian Reflection: A Series in Faith and Ethics*. Beginning in 2009, Kurt contributed to three issues of the journal. Even though it was, for him, a relatively small and "off stage" vehicle, Kurt considered the work of the Center to be worthwhile. One of the 2009 issues focused on prayer and included two hymns, "When Gathered Saints in Common Praise" (words by Burt L. Burleson, to the tune "Gathered Saints" by Kurt Kaiser) and "Waiting Here, In Silence" (words by Terry W. York to the tune "Waiting Here" by Kurt Kaiser). The 2015 issue focused on generosity included the hymn "All Who Thirst" (words by Anthony Carl, to the tune "All Who Thirst" by Anthony Carl and Kurt Kaiser). Then, in 2016, an issue focused on chastity included the hymn "Intense the Love God Molded" (words by Terry W. York, to the tune "Anniversary" by Kurt Kaiser). Kurt's music planted seeds that would bloom into bouquets, as well as seeds that would bake into bread. Both were acts of obedience. Both provided nourishment. Both were from God's bounty.

A three-day conference for senior adults, held at Baylor University on October 18–20, 2012, "Oasis: A Gathering of Well-Seasoned Souls" was one of the more public moments in the fading of Kurt's stage appearances and performances. Its final session was "Ken Medema in Concert: Special Guest Appearance by Kurt Kaiser." It is fitting that the conference took place in Waco, Texas, specifically at Baylor University, and in the company of senior adults. There could not have been a more comfortable environment for Kurt once again to shine as a bright, if now somewhat dimmer, light. More than that, it was fitting that Kurt was invited onto the stage, and then off the stage, by Ken Medema, one of the most enduring of Kurt's recording artist successes.

Ken had been asked to provide the music, both entertainment and worship, for the event. One of the first things he did in this capacity was to invite Kurt to make an appearance as an accompanist, and as a performer in his own right. Ken knew that Kurt was by then receiving fewer and fewer invitations to speak and perform. He knew that Kurt was receiving rejection notices from publishing companies as he submitted new compositions and arrangements. Ken was delighted to have this opportunity to bring Kurt to the stage, but not out of pity. He invited Kurt because of who Kurt was and who he had always been. He invited Kurt because he knew the conferees held him in highest regard. Kurt's appearance was a rite of remembrance, a blessing of excellence, and a bestowing of Christian grace.

It was a poignant moment, indeed, when in the final session Kurt came on stage, before an audience warmed by several of Ken's song-stories. Hearts were full. Then came Ken's uplifting introduction of Kurt. The audience certainly knew who Kurt was, even as they knew who Ken was.

But they didn't know the breadth and depth of Kurt's role as Ken Medema's mentor, coach, teacher, friend, and encourager. Neither did they know that Kurt was responsible for Ken's first recording contract and his first opportunity to sing at a Billy Graham crusade, along with other early and foundational moments in Ken's career.[8]

With Kurt on stage, Ken shared that often when he and Kurt were together, including on occasion in the recording studio, they would talk to each other with exaggerated German accents, given their shared German lineage. Reminding each other of the rules of a musical game they had played in several concert settings, they sat on two side-by-side piano benches facing the same keyboard. Ken informed the audience that the two of them would play four-hand, on the "fly," arrangements of songs that came to mind as they played. The main stipulation was that one would play from middle C down, and the other would play from middle C up on the keyboard. To begin, Ken was on the lower half, Kurt on the higher half. Ken got things started with the lively march "Stars and Stripes Forever." From there they moved through "Leaning on the Everlasting Arms," "Austrian Hymn," "Joyful, Joyful We Adore Thee," "Pass It On," and "Make Me a Blessing." Abrupt key changes came as challenges, back and forth, with not one note or rhythm missed. In the midst of the continuing music and strained German accents, they swapped positions at the keyboard. Ken scooted to his right and Kurt got up and moved around to the left, again, no notes or rhythms missed. The mutual love and respect were deep, authentic, all-encompassing, and obvious. The audience was captivated.

The novel challenge ended, and Ken stood to sing his beloved song, "Come, Let Us Reason Together." Kurt accompanied him in a smooth jazz style that turned the performance into a duet of combined worship. When the solo ended, Kurt spoke his praise and admiration for Ken.

Then, just before Kurt left the stage, the two Christian music giants, now of equal recognition and stature, recounted the story of Ken's audition for a recording contract in Kurt's office many years before. They told the story of Ken's audition selections becoming part of his first album. They also told the story of Kurt crying at the depth and beauty of what he heard in the audition. But they didn't tell the audience exactly what phrase Kurt had used in that contested moment of response years earlier. Kurt left the stage to rousing applause and a heavy reminder that things change. In years past, the concert would have ended with *Kurt's* exit. But this time Ken stayed on stage to end the concert. His ending included his masterpiece, "Moses."

In the Christmas season of 2015, Kurt and his daughter Kris broadcast and taped an interview on Baylor University's public radio station KWBU. Their discussion was woven around carols recorded on the 2015 Kurt Kaiser Music CD *Olde Carols Ever New*,[9] but the program cannot in any way be construed as a promotional piece. The flutist, Helen Ann Shanley, and the clarinetist, Richard Shanley, were retired members of the Baylor Music faculty. Kurt at the piano completed the musical texture of the trio and the program, "Sharing Traditions and Carols of Christmas."

The hour-long conversation is warm, casual, and relaxed and settles deep into what's best about Christmas. Kurt reminisces about the Christmas of his childhood, citing aromas of the seasonal treats and dishes that his mother prepared. The city of Waco fell in love with every aspect of this interview. First aired in 2015, it has been aired each Christmas season since. A blend of Waco, Baylor, and family, the father/daughter interview has become one of Waco's Christmas traditions.

Kurt's insider comments about how songs were selected and arranged include unadorned practical considerations across the full spectrum of Christmas. Waco loves the authenticity. The interview and the music are revisited each year like heirloom Christmas ornaments and recipes. The program is a reminder of important things. Kurt Kaiser Music was created to accommodate such recordings, gifts free of commercial concerns.

Kurt's friendship with Baylor faculty members was an integral part of his support network. Dr. Donald Bailey was the Director of Choral Activities at Baylor from 1993 to 2008. When he started at Baylor, he was a bit skeptical of the musical relationship Kurt had established with the university and its music faculty. But Donald and Kurt would become close friends, caring for each other during times of health issues and connecting in deep discussions of music and theology. They developed an authentic respect, even admiration, for each other's musicianship. When Donald injured his shoulder to the point that he could no longer conduct, Kurt became his only personal contact. During the last few months of Kurt's life, Donald was one of Kurt's only contacts, moving the nature and venue of their lunch meetings to "take out" brought to the Kaiser house.

Lunch had become for them a significant, if not sacred, time of communion. Donald, Robert Young, and Harry Elzinga, all three Baylor music professors, along with chemistry professor David Young, and Kurt, constituted a daily "lunch bunch" for a number of years. The lunch group even spanned employed and retired status. Over lunch they talked about music, performances, and composers, with Kurt recalling, "we lie a lot, you know . . . it's just a lot of fun . . . we've been eating at El Charro's every day for years."¹⁰

When Robert Young died, the remaining four met less often, but Kurt and Donald continued the daily lunch routine. It was over lunch that Kurt first learned of Donald's early health concerns, and over time the two moved from hesitancy to vulnerability. Trust deepened as Donald learned that Kurt had never intended for his musicals to be used in worship, rather to draw kids in. He was impressed with Kurt's almost singular ability to be in the forefront of music's trend toward the contemporary, while at the same time holding to the highest standards of musical quality. This set Kurt apart. But "unique" can be a synonym for "alone," like a chess master seeking an opponent.

Donald considered Kurt to be a lonely person. "We were both lonely. Kurt had lots of friends, but not many musician friends on his level. Kurt brought something to Baylor that has faded away. The seminary helped a bit to bring it back. Baylor is a unique school."¹¹

Donald did only two recording projects with Kurt. Both were of hymns for Baylor's Chamber Singers ensemble to use in nursing home singalongs.¹² The academic and the record producer led each other to hymnody.

Kurt connected with the heart of Baylor, not its fringes, and nothing and no one was closer to the heart of Baylor than Dr. Joyce Jones, professor of organ at Baylor for forty-three years, beginning in 1969. She first met Kurt in 1970 when she was working on a recording with her Baylor colleagues pianist Roger L. Keyes and cellist Lev Aronson.¹³ The organ portions of the album were recorded at Southwestern Baptist Theological Seminary in Fort Worth, Texas. Kurt had recovered just enough from recent heart surgery to be up and around, but he could not yet drive. So Joyce drove Kurt and herself to the recording session some ninety miles away. He was the producer of the recording. Her children were most impressed that she had spent the day with the composer of *Tell It Like It Is* and recent director of the Baylor Religious Hour Choir.

Joyce Jones, a world-renowned recitalist, was on the unofficial organist-as-needed list for Kurt and WORD. She played, for instance, on the 1974 recording of *God's People*, the adult choir musical by Kurt and Charlie Brown. In the summer of 1995, Kurt and Joyce were scheduled to do a combined Summer Sounds Concert at Indian Springs Park in Waco, but plans changed due to rain. On the day of the concert, it was moved indoors to Baylor's Jones Hall. In this "backup" venue, the program would now be played on a pipe organ and a Steinway piano, upgrades from the park venue instruments. Joyce was aware of only one person who was unhappy about the change of venue—a man with his dogs.

Waco loved both performers and anticipated something akin to "Flight of the Bumblebee" played on the pedals versus "Oh, How He Loves You and Me" played as a fugue. That would have been enough, but the concert turned out to be much more. Mutual respect, and admiration for each other and for the music itself, shaped a program that ranged from classical to hymns, to Broadway show tunes, to Handel's Hallelujah chorus, to patriotic song. Jones Hall was packed, so they did two more summer concerts over the next few years. Their concerts were "fun and funny," to the delight of their audiences.

On June 1, 2009, Kurt and Joyce did another joint concert, again in Jones Hall, their fourth. It was the opening concert for Baylor's *Pipe Organ Encounter Plus*, sponsored by the Waco chapter of the American Guild of Organists. Again, their concert was relaxed, full of excellent music, warmth, and charm.

"We were never *great* friends [voice inflection suggesting "close friends"], but Kurt would come over to my house to rehearse."[14] (Joyce had a pipe organ in her house.) Her statement leaves something of an empty spot in the hearts of those who loved and respected both heroes. While we might have wished for "we were dear friends," she and Kurt were not members of the same congregation and both had extensive travel schedules. Her statement does highlight one of their similarities: musical genius, stellar performances, sense of humor, authenticity, and . . . simple, foundational, honesty. While Joyce and Kurt were "never *great* friends," she was disappointed that she was not asked to be the organist at Kurt's memorial service.

5
A CHURCH MUSICIAN

I was serving as minister of music at First Baptist Church, Temple [Texas], in January, 2010, when the sanctuary and most of the buildings were destroyed by fire. We lost everything, all music, all equipment, all instruments, everything. In those early weeks we were scrambling to have the resources to hold a meaningful worship service.

In late February, I was working from my home office and my cell phone rang. I picked it up and answered it as I always did, "Hello, this is Gary." On the other end was a deep voice that began with, "You don't know who I am, but my name is Kurt Kaiser. Is this Gary Anthony from First Baptist Church, Temple?" I choked back my surprise and answered, "Hello, I certainly do know who you are!"

After a moment of silence, Kurt continued. "I heard about the fire and I'm so very sorry for your loss. I'm a music director of a small church in Waco and I often write some music for my little choir. I would certainly like to share some of that music with you, if you think you could use it. I will be glad to send it to you and you can make as many copies as you need." After telling him I would be honored to receive it, he asked for my address, gave me a word of encouragement, and we hung up.

In just a few days I received a packet of music from him, all handwritten and copied on manuscript paper, with a very kind note. He assured me that he would be praying for us and that he was hopeful some of the music might be helpful and encouraging to us as a choir.

I still have the note and the music; it's in my files for safekeeping. I was touched by his generosity and support during those days.

Gary Anthony
Worship & Care Pastor
First Temple[1]

Kurt was a minister of music at heart, a minister of music on special assignment. Success and fame in the recording industry present temptations to turn away from or lose sight of Christian music's home base, the Church and its local congregations. But the distractions didn't turn Kurt Kaiser's focus. His successes were nestled in the mission and message of the Church. The congregation was not his launching pad to be left behind and below. Rather, it was his shelter, the pathway of his journey, his earthly base and community. For Kurt, if the Christian music industry should cut its ties with local congregations, it would have lost its way.

CHURCH OF THE AIR, BILLINGS, MONTANA

As a high school student, Kurt's congregational responsibilities as pianist for The Church of the Air in Billings were part of a package that also included radio broadcasts and evangelistic meetings. He did not experience the weight of what became the full congregational responsibilities of a "traditional" minister of music. What he did experience was an expanded understanding of how music could function and of what congregations were capable of doing and being in the name of ministry outreach. He learned that however alike they may be, congregations are unique in opportunities and inherent giftedness. Yet, in all of the diversity that he saw and imagined, his understanding of music in the context of worship stayed simple (not simplistic), focused, and set apart from the experimentation and novelty allowed in the Church's outreach to surrounding cultures. At age sixteen, these concepts and possibilities were being observed, gathered, and considered. He did not yet have the experience, nor did he have the time and resources, to test them. But his own core understanding of church was solidified, and his creativity was sensitized toward possibilities that were God's.

BETHEL COMMUNITY CHURCH, CHICAGO, ILLINOIS

Kurt served Bethel Community (Evangelical Free) Church in Chicago for five years while a student at Northwestern University. He started as the pianist. As he advanced in school, finishing his bachelor's and master's degrees in music in 1958 and 1959, he also evolved from pianist to organist to Minister of Music at Bethel. His responsibilities eventually included writing for and conducting the congregation's band on Sunday nights. Being newlyweds, the church salary was a welcome supplement to Pat's income as a nurse. The congregation took Kurt and Pat under their wings, throwing a baby shower for Pat in anticipation of Kris' birth and allowing Kurt to take a summer international ministry tour with Bob Pierce for additional experience and income.

Writing from Langoon in "dark, heathen" Burma on August 13, 1958, Kurt composed a letter addressed to the "Dear ones at Bethel." He painted for them a picture of the awakening in their young minister of music's worldview. Thanks in part to their investment of time and money, Kurt was seeing Christianity in a culture that made no pretense of being Christian. He was in awe of pastors who had traveled from three to seventeen days by foot, train, and boat to attend the Pastors' Conference for which he was providing music. His Western eyes saw "filth," while his Christian eyes saw a humbling "zeal for the things of the Lord." His naivete cracked and fell away under the pressure of Christian commitment viewed starkly against a Buddhist background. "We have found that denominations mean very little when the joy of winning the lost is the primary objective."

As he traveled, he searched and mingled the vocabularies and concerns of music, politics, economy, and spirituality, attempting to reconcile his simple theology and missiology with a complex environment. Touring evangelists, career missionaries, Burmese Christians—a unified community of Christ-followers? Hear the struggle in Kurt's one-sentence penultimate paragraph: "Again, may I ask prayers on our behalf." For Kurt the word "our" was expanding. No culture could claim to own God, or even to possess the best understanding of God. Questions outpaced and outnumbered answers.

The typed letter, in Kurt's possession until his death, was *from* him, not *to* him. It is properly folded, but there is no envelope. It contains eight penciled-in typographical corrections. Did he send the congregation a corrected copy? Did he decide not to send the letter after all? The question remains unanswered, but at one level, the answer doesn't matter. What does matter is that Kurt wrote the letter in the context of congregational responsibility and identity. He needed to capture, and perhaps share, his deep ponderings. He held the thoughts communally, congregationally, globally, whether or not he actually sent the letter. Bethel Community Church facilitated a local/global capstone for Kurt's education.

SEVENTH & JAMES BAPTIST CHURCH, WACO, TEXAS

It was at Seventh & James that Kurt was ordained a deacon on November 3, 1965. In Baptist life, being ordained a deacon requires no specific theological or ecclesial training, nor is it clerical in nature. Rather, deacon ordination is a solemn ceremony in which the candidate's ongoing volunteer service to and within a congregation is acknowledged as servant ministry. A similar position in other settings is "elder." Though candidates are certified by local congregations, the recognition is honored by Baptist congregations everywhere.

Kurt and Pat joined the Seventh & James Baptist Church when they moved to Waco, because Kurt "liked the music there." He recalled, "As you know, I was raised Plymouth Brethren in Chicago, and I really wanted to get away from that, and coming to Texas gave us a brand-new kind of life."[2] Another influence was the fact that Jarrell McCracken, Kurt's boss, was an active member at "Seventh." Many of the congregation's ministries and activities were new to Kurt and Pat, including the style of worship. But the newness was in keeping with the freshness of the new town, region, and opportunities that they found so invigorating.

Under the watchful eye of Dr. Euell Porter, Kurt, along with WORD colleagues Charlie Brown and John Purifoy, started a college choir as one of the ministries of the church. Dr. Porter, beloved head of choral music at Baylor, was the part-time Minister of Music at Seventh & James. Forming the choir was a natural and obvious course of action given the scores of Baylor University students who would formally join the congregation when school came back into session. In addition to their college Sunday School classes and fellowship (socializing) activities, the college choir generated a great deal of energy that arced like a rainbow connecting the buildings of Baylor and the buildings of "Seventh." The college choir would frequently serve as something of a test group, a laboratory or demonstration group, for the music that its directors were writing, publishing, recording, and distributing as employees of WORD. The church's college choir had a university twin, the Baylor Religious Hour Choir. Twin choirs of differing origin, but similar purpose and readiness, "stood guard" against musical stodginess on both sides of the street.

For Kurt, Seventh & James "opened our minds a great deal to what Christianity is; as opposed to being captured, this was open, everything was open-air, blue-sky. And that was . . . new. And I loved that, I thought it was just great. And so it did, it opened up our thinking—Mommy [Pat] and my thinking—about what the Christian life is, and what the Bible is, you know."[3]

In selecting Seventh & James Baptist Church as their new "home" church, Kurt and Pat became Southern Baptists. "Southern Baptist" had long since ceased being a geographic designation. Rather, it was an identity found in missionary efforts and a curious sense of ecclesial completeness within the denominational world that the title creates. Southern Baptists are not a cult, but they are proud and sure. Kurt and Pat co-taught a college Sunday School class at Seventh, though Pat did most of the teaching with Kurt providing support and music. On Sundays and on Wednesday nights (prayer meeting and choir rehearsal) Kurt would join his boss Jarrell McCracken as a Southern Baptist. However, during the work week at WORD, Kurt joined Jarrell and others in being "not Southern

Baptist" but, rather, friendly competitors and rivals of the Southern Baptist Convention's music "business," the Church Music Department of the Baptist Sunday School Board in Nashville, Tennessee.

The Baptist Sunday School Board was a company and a complex so large that it generated enough incoming and outgoing mail to be given its own zip code (37234). This weekly back and forth, them and us, existence for the Southern Baptist church members who worked for WORD was heightened in its ironic complexity by Seventh & James Baptist Church's and WORD's relationship with Baylor University. At the time, Baylor University was an entity of the Baptist General Convention of Texas, an autonomous affiliate of the Southern Baptist Convention. Many Baylor University faculty and students walked back and forth across James Avenue literally and figuratively, as if the church and the school were parts of a shared whole. Baylor students who were members of Baptist churches "back home" flocked to Seventh & James Baptist Church to perform the ritual of joining a local congregation of "like faith and witness," by "moving their letter" (official congregational membership) to this university-savvy congregation.

If Baylor University, WORD, and Seventh & James Baptist Church were somewhat braided in purpose, commitment, and engagement, WORD Music and Southern Baptist music interests were similarly entwined in the eyes of Baptist congregations across the nation. The major difference between WORD's work and that of the official Southern Baptist music entity was that Southern Baptists were focused primarily, if not solely, on the music ministries of Southern Baptist congregations. The major "leak" from Nashville out into other denominations was the outstanding children's choir curriculum produced by Southern Baptists. WORD had no such obligation or affiliation.

Yet, the Waco Trilogy (WORD, Baylor University, and Seventh & James Baptist Church[4]) reflected the structure and offerings of the larger, national Southern Baptist Convention. Aware of each other, and watching each other in a furtive sort of way, Waco's WORD Music and Nashville's Church Music Department (CMD) existed informally as brothers (the appropriate metaphor for the time) in the same family.

The Nashville "brother" was an authorized representative of the family. The Waco "brother," with the same blood in most of his veins, was unauthorized but loved, and exercised a greater freedom to experiment and explore. They knew each other well, respected each other, and, two days a week (Wednesday and Sunday), worshiped together. Church musicians of denominations outside the Southern Baptist world neither knew nor cared about this Waco/Nashville relationship. They knew, and felt their own kinship with, WORD.

Kurt was a "Waco Trilogy" Baptist, a brother who was deeply respected by the Nashville brothers. The Secretary (Director) of Nashville's Church Music Department during the years of its youth musical competition with WORD was Dr. William J. Reynolds. During those years, Kurt, the Southern Baptist who worked for WORD, and "Bill" Reynolds, the Southern Baptist who worked for the Southern Baptists, were captains of competitive (if not opposing) teams in the same "game." They oversaw the provision of music that would supply the church music ministries of the more than 30,000 Southern Baptist congregations throughout the United States. As has been established, both entities sold their products beyond Southern Baptist congregations, but the SBC congregational market was large and boastfully autonomous. Southern Baptist church musicians could buy their music, even hymnals, from whomever they wanted.

Both Kaiser and Reynolds, however, would leave, under less than happy circumstances (Reynolds in 1980, Kaiser in 1991), the enterprises they had led so brilliantly.[5] In late December of 1979, it was internally announced that Bill Reynolds would retire effective April 30, 1980. It was not announced externally, but Kurt heard the news. On February 2, 1980, Kurt received this handwritten note from Bill:

Dear Kurt,

Bless you for your thoughtfulness. I appreciate very much your interest in my creative writing—

I am trying to put the pieces together for the future and it looks fantastic—God is great and his mercy endures and endures and endures—I know and I know you know!

Cordially,
Bill

Obviously, Kurt had reached out to Bill concerning the future of Bill's work as a composer. They were now brothers with no competition between them. The unique feature of Bill's note was this: after his signature, Bill drew a three-measure music staff with the melodic notation of the first line of "Oh, How He Loves You and Me." The opening line of the song was an icon that even a former competitor recognized, symbolizing a message that both men needed.

These two retired giants stayed in touch, though infrequently, across the years. In 1990 Reynolds sent Kurt an autographed copy of his new book, *Songs of Glory*,[6] with the inscription, "To Kurt Kaiser in gratitude for his gifts, his spirit, and his friendship." Reynolds, also in his own handwriting, directed Kurt to pages 143 and 199 in his book. There, Reynolds had written about "Pass It On" and "Oh, How He Loves You and Me" (first stanza only). Another warm contact from Bill Reynolds is his September 5, 2001 letter to Kurt:

Dear Kurt:

CONGRATULATIONS!

I just read in today's [Fort Worth] *Star Telegram* [newspaper] that you have been elected to the Gospel Music Association's Hall of Fame. That's wonderful! For at least twenty-five years I have been an elector of the Hall of Fame for the GMA. Several weeks ago, I received a list of names of those nominated for the 2001 Hall of Fame. I marked your name and several others. (I didn't vote for ELVIS!).[7]

I am very proud of you for this recognition, and it is well deserved. Give my regards to Pat.

Cordially,
Bill

DAYSPRING BAPTIST CHURCH, WACO, TEXAS

There came a time when Kurt and Pat grew dissatisfied with changes that had come about at Seventh & James Baptist Church. It wasn't what it used to be. Similarly, Kurt and Pat had grown in their understanding of what Church could and should be. For them, Seventh & James had lost its desire for freshness.

When Kurt, Pat, and six other families (twenty-three people in total) broke away from Seventh and started DaySpring Baptist Church in October of 1993, they had a significant opportunity and responsibility to make a statement about worship. When all around them new congregations were forming with the idea that contemporary worship would build large churches in a short time, this breakaway group founded a new congregation on the concept of "unplugged," contemplative worship with a considered slow liturgical pace, including scheduled moments of silence. Attracting large numbers of attendees was not in the calculus.

With the same heart and mind that had Kurt help start a church not based on contemporary music or structure, he was also respectfully careful concerning contemporary church music in the recording projects that he did for WORD. He balanced projects between classical music and contemporary, between celebrities, veterans, and newcomers. Kurt's musical, biblical, ecclesial, and ethical standards remained intact and influential at work and worship. While some of the new-sound songs he wrote and recorded found their way into worship, he never launched them thinking that they would strip the sanctuaries of "traditional" worship.

In this way Kurt remained an ever-present conscience, keeping his head when it came to evaluating new music, new worship, or a new congregation as fresh, fad, or trend. His consistency proved that new music could be adopted with discretion; it didn't have to take over. He proved that church planting could have more than one musical/liturgical soundtrack. He proved that college students were not monoliths, responding to only one Sunday morning sound. Kurt's consistency and confidently pressing ahead served as a model for many who sought balance. Those same attributes, however, were considered by some advocates of the church growth movement to be old-fashioned, stubborn, even anti-evangelistic.

Kurt, calling forth the silence that marked the pace of worship during his childhood in the Plymouth Brethren Church, described the DaySpring approach as follows: "A lot of silence. That's what I incorporated into our worship at DaySpring, I think. And I like that silence."[8] A man remembered for his music offered silence to the thoughtfully crafted worship of this new congregation. Beautiful music ushers and shapes meaningful silence, and then is born of that silence. While the congregation was hearing Kurt's music, he was sensing the silence that enveloped it. There was no rush after anthem, hymn, or offertory. "A holy hush comes over us, and we behold in awe."[9]

The following paragraph appears on the case liner of the CD *Kurt Kaiser: Oh, How He Loves You and Me* (Kurt Kaiser Music, 2005):

> Like many of you, Kurt's music was a part of my pilgrimage for a long time. I grew up singing his songs and have so many memories, mountain top experiences, where Kurt was present long before I met him. However, for the past ten years, it's been my privilege to work side by side with him as we plan and lead worship for our church where our motto is "sacred and simple." Our worship is a time for renewal and healing. Kurt's talent and intuition are, in large measure, responsible for this contemplative spirit. He knows! He just knows at some deep, gifted level, how to play in such a way that the soul gets soothed. People settle down spiritually when Kurt leads worship. They take a deep breath and remember what matters most. They

hear things. Preaching after Kurt plays . . . it's often unnecessary, icing on the cake at best.

—Burt Burleson, Pastor, *DaySpring Baptist Church*

Kurt began what continues as a meaningful close to DaySpring's Easter services. To end the service, the congregation gathers around the piano to sing Malotte's setting of "The Lord's Prayer."[10] When this practice first began, it was quite easy for the entire church family to fit around the piano. Now, the much larger congregation moves forward toward the piano, engulfing it, with most of the people only symbolically nearer. The arrangement is played, the congregation sings the Easter celebration to its completion, the ritual enriches all hearts, and the older eyes shed tears. They remember that Kurt conducted the choir, accompanied the congregation, played for weddings and funerals, and, with a chainsaw as his "second instrument," cleared brush on church property. He did all of this as a church member, not a celebrity.

There is much to learn by observing Kurt's life through the lens of those who lived in congregational proximity to him. One of those living lenses is Kathy Gladen Johnson. Kathy was a choir member and frequent substitute for Kurt at the piano, and she is an excellent composer and arranger in her own right. She was the obvious "next-in-line" at DaySpring's piano when Kurt's health demanded that he "retire from the bench." By means of the 2017 two-piano CD, *Come Away: Offertories by Kurt Kaiser & Kathy Johnson*,[11] Kurt blessed and enshrined the transfer. The recording also capped the influence of his congregational music soul on her soul, a process, as we shall see, that began in Mexico decades earlier.

Kurt's influence did not create Kathy Gladen Johnson's musicianship. Hers, like his, was a well-stewarded gift from God. Kathy's own giftedness resonated with the essence of Kurt's holy jazz, chordal soul, and considered keyboard touch. Mentoring Kathy, Kurt left what he could of his music ministry in a place of safekeeping. One must listen with a sophisticated and experienced ear to the last cut of the *Come Away* CD to discern which two hands are Kurt's and which two hands are Kathy's. It is not that Kathy was finally playing *like* Kurt, it was that she was confidently playing piano *with* Kurt. This is mutual achievement: mentor and mentee.

There was a profound mentor/mentee moment for Kathy in the *Come Away* project, recorded at Billy Crockett's Blue Rock Studio in Wimberley, Texas. During the recording of one of her solo pieces she played a "superfluous grace note or two" that she knew Kurt would question. Even so, she played on, completing her arrangement. When she finished, Kurt called her into the production booth and asked for the engineer to go to an exact spot in what had just been recorded. It was as Kathy anticipated. Kurt had, of course, heard it. Now he was about to question it. How painful would the reprimand be? She was an adult, and she had played her arrangement. But he was Kurt Kaiser, after all, and they were in a recording session. She steeled herself for the sting. Kurt said, "Listen to this. Do you really want to hear that six months from now?" He sent her back to the piano to record the song without the grace notes. He told her she could decide which recording to keep. She chose the second recording.

The question respected the quality of her musicianship while pointing out a flaw. It was the question of a teacher, a mentor. It was a question for the conscience. It was the question of an artist who assumed that Kathy's mastery would continue into the future. Kurt felt that artists should try to distill their music to the purest sound possible. The standards of past and future were brought into the present, summoned by a simple question. Kathy recorded the song again, loving it then and six months later. Even now, years later, she listens for the moment and hears more than music in the chord.

Kathy first met Kurt when she was an MK (missionary kid) in Mexico where Kurt had taken the BRH Choir in 1966. Later, in 1972 as a Baylor University student, she would see Kurt in action as a composer who was held in high esteem at both Baylor and Seventh & James Baptist Church. Kurt wore a mantle of esteem afforded him in the doubly rarified atmosphere of academia and music recording. Somehow, for Kathy, the glow of fame didn't match the aura of humility that seemed to surround him in the Mexico mission field. She processed the difference as arrogance on Kurt's part. He was conductor, guest teacher, composer, performer, producer, and publisher who, she would discover, wasn't even required to write in legible words or notes on the musical score. Lesser musicians would just have to figure it out.

Yet, she, a student, was offered and accepted work as a copier of Kurt's handwritten manuscripts, translating them into words and notes that others could read, play, and record. Doing so, she learned more about orchestration and music theory than she ever did in formal classroom settings. She also learned more about Kurt, the person.

Later, while serving as Administrative Assistant to the Dean of Baylor's School of Music, and as Kurt's substitute and successor as pianist at DaySpring, she learned that Kurt wasn't arrogant. He was often visiting the future while those around him were only in the present moment. His "arrogance" was an energy that called for musicians to experience the "more" that was in them. He was praying at the piano and calling others to prayer, a posture easily misunderstood when first encountered. But it wasn't arrogance. It was being a step, or a sound, or a season, ahead of the current pace. It was a summoning to follow Kurt while he could still lead. He knew it wouldn't be forever. It was mentor calling forth effort worthy of a true musician's offering to God. His "arrogance" was the beginning of a deep compliment. It was Kurt, in the present, not saying "lean on me" but rather "lean into your future," into the full stewardship of your talent: respected musician to respected musician.

As Kurt neared death, and DaySpring Baptist Church held its breath, Kurt called his daughter Kris and his mentee Kathy to his hospital bed. This was before his final days in hospice at home. In his hospital room, Kurt, Kris, and Kathy discussed the details of his impending memorial service. He knew the songs that he wanted to be played and sung, and he assigned the keys in which they should be performed. Arrogance? No, a gift to those who would attend: final blessing of the minister, final lesson of the teacher, final project of the producer, final example by the mentor.

Carlos Colón, born in Chalchuapa, El Salvador, was another of Kurt's church-related mentees. He and Kurt first met in August 1990 when Carlos was a student at Baylor and a choir member at Seventh & James. After graduation from Baylor with a master's degree in music, Carlos moved to Florida, where he served several churches. He moved back to Waco in 2002 to become Assistant Director of Worship and Chapel at Baylor University, and Resident Scholar at Baylor's Institute for the Studies of Religion. He also joined Kurt and Pat in the life and worship of DaySpring Baptist Church.

In 2003 Carlos also began working for Kurt, transcribing his musical scores. His proficiency with Finale, a software program used for musical notation, got him the job. He found Kurt's instrumental work to be "amazing" and was happy to count Kurt as a mentor in instrumental music.

The transcription process was that Kurt would give Carlos a handwritten score for Carlos to read as Kurt played it on the piano. Kurt would then ask Carlos if the score conveyed what Kurt had just played. The process led to some changes, with one or both of them hearing mistakes. Carlos worked like this with Kurt for about seven years, observing that "to watch him make music is like watching a child at play."[12]

The work became private lessons for him. But Kurt was aware of Carlos' efforts as a composer, and as a mentor he encouraged Carlos to work at finding his own voice as a composer. Even though it was gradual, there was a mutually agreed upon parting of the ways so that Carlos would have more time to devote to his own compositions. Carlos began amassing an impressive list of publications, largely Latino choral music, from hymn arrangements to a requiem about which Kurt said, "You will be remembered for this."

Most notably, Carlos Colón was commissioned to compose two works for the canonization of St. Oscar Romero: one by the Archbishop of El Salvador and one by the Vatican. When asked if Kurt was present at the canonization ceremony, Carlos replied, "No, but his shadow was, through one who found his voice under Kurt's tutelage."[13]

Some lessons were more difficult than others. Once, at an international conference held at Baylor, Carlos used a Kurt Kaiser arrangement without Kurt's knowledge. Kurt had given Carlos permission to use his music in the routine work of Baylor activities but felt that this conference was above and beyond routine. Kurt thought that Carlos should have notified him about the extraordinary event. Kurt sent Carlos a handwritten confrontation regarding the incident. Carlos replied with a handwritten apology; two notes between friends. Their friendship continued without either of them ever speaking of the incident. This was another formational moment for Carlos Colón at Kurt's hand.

Kurt's wisdom drew pastors to him, as well.

DaySpring Baptist Church was without a pastor for the first year of their existence. The delay was intentional so that they might establish an identity before inviting a pastor to join them. The year also served as a time of grieving and processing for those who had left Seventh & James Baptist Church.

Pat was in charge of enlisting preachers for each Sunday of that year. When the congregation finally did look for a pastor, they found Burt Burleson, one of their first-year supply preachers. He started on February 3, 1995. His youth and poetic bent reflected the freshness that the small congregation had established and was determined to maintain.

Burt was very much aware, and somewhat in awe, of who Kurt Kaiser was. A couple of years into his pastorate, Burt began to write poetically crafted readings and litanies that he thought their worship needed. Kurt soon realized that Burt's gift had the potential also to produce organic music for the young congregation and its small choir. Burt was nervous at first, wondering if the renowned musician would think his lyrics were worth setting. Indeed, Kurt did not like everything that Burt wrote. In similar fashion, Burt, on rare occasions, would tweak the theology in some of Kurt's lyrics. And once Burt respectfully reprimanded Kurt after he had become frustrated with the choir in a *Messiah* rehearsal.

But Burt realized that Kurt was in the clearly present "DaySpring groove, its DNA," so they planned worship together in the early days. This led them to write DaySpring music (some twenty hymns, anthems, choruses, and service pieces) for DaySpring's people. In Burt's words, "The community of faith called it out of us."[14]

These "Kurt and Burt" songs were not all that the young congregation sang, but their frequent presence as an enhancement to worship was an affirmation that the Holy Spirit was at work in the new church enterprise. Three service pieces, "Take Up Your Cross," "Show Me Your Ways," and "Draw Me," were especially meaningful to the DaySpring congregation. Kurt continued as church pianist, choir director, and musical collaborator with Burt, even when he had ceased helping to plan worship. "The Lord Whom We Love," one of Kurt's songs from the musical *God's People*,[15] remains in DaySpring's frequently sung benediction repertory.

When Burt Burleson resigned from the DaySpring pastorate to become University Chaplain at Baylor in October 2007, the second search for a pastor began. The church knew not to look for another Burt, but they did want another refreshing and creative "fit." They were looking for someone who would understand the church's vision statement—"sacred, simple"— without need of explanation. They found the quiet, comfortable, and confident fit in Eric Howell. He began as pastor in 2008.

When Eric came to DaySpring Baptist Church, Kurt was still directing the choir and playing the piano. But, as his health continued to decline, DaySpring member and retired high school choral director Susan Thrift became the choir director. As a segue into the early days of a new pastor, Kurt planned worship with Eric. But they did not write together as much as Kurt and Burt Burleson had. Kurt was interested in helping Eric with the "flow" of worship that DaySpring had come to expect. Eric listened to the suggestions and to Kurt's orienting stories, earning Kurt's deep respect and the respect of the congregation.

Kurt was a regular attendee at Eric's Friday morning lectionary breakfasts, even though he was there for the fellowship more than in-depth theological discussion. The same was true of the Men's Bible Study that Eric began in 2014. Kurt attended, liked it when Eric would say, "I don't know. What do you think?" again enjoying the fellowship more than the Bible study.

Eric wasn't aware of Kurt's fame when he first became his pastor. He was educated along those lines when a writer from a national pastoral leadership periodical interviewed him about DaySpring's contemplative Baptist worship. When the interviewer asked, "What's the name of your pianist again?" his response to Eric's answer was, "THE Kurt Kaiser?" Eric continued to lead the congregation and plan their worship through a careful theological lens, while Kurt continued to plan according to intuition: "This feels right" or "This feels lumpy." By then Kurt's theology, settled deep within, nestled near his intuition.

In his remarks at Kurt's memorial service, Eric shared this precious moment:

> On the day before he passed, when he was barely conscious and unable to speak most of the time, he lay still, his whole body, but one finger. Moving, conducting music only he could hear. Someone roused him, "Dad, what are you doing? What do you have going on there?" He said, with eyes still closed, "Ja. I've got something. I think it's going to work up there." If you're anything like me, you can't wait to hear it. Alleluia. Amen.[16]

HYMNALS FOR CONGREGATIONAL USE

"For congregational use" may seem obvious when one speaks of hymnals. But congregational accessibility in content, song structure, key signature, vocal range and tessitura, and rhythm cannot be assumed. Kurt certainly did not make such assumptions. Some new hymnals are designed to lead a denomination, or the Church in general, to new musical and/or textual expressions that uncomfortably stretch congregational levels of music and doctrine. Often the theologians and musicians who are on committees tasked with the development of new hymnals lose sight of their pastoral role in the excitement of a once-in-a-lifetime opportunity. This temptation never overtook Kurt. He knew music, he knew the human voice, and he knew congregational capacities. Kurt knew the difference between soloists in the studio and church members in the sanctuary. He knew that songs made popular by commercial recordings had to be carefully ushered into corporate singing, lest they inadvertently discourage congregational participation. He knew the difference between a congregation and an audience, writing memorable Christian music for both entities.

Kurt served on the executive committee for the development of *The Hymnal for Worship & Celebration* (WORD Music, 1986), a book that contains seventeen entries attributed to him. Sometimes an executive committee exists primarily for the purpose of lending their names to the prestige of the new book, and they are traditionally not as involved as are other committees in the nuts and bolts work of compiling a hymnal. But Kurt's name brought more than celebrity for promotional purposes. His name also brought assurance of a trusted governing presence, a reliable conscience as well as an acknowledged icon, to the hymnal production process.

WORD's *Hymnal for Worship & Celebration* (1986) moved unchallenged into Southern Baptist churches whose most recent denominational hymnal at the time was the *Baptist Hymnal* (1975). The force of denominational "brand loyalty" sales had dwindled to a trickle. Then came the unveiling of the Southern Baptists' new book *The Baptist Hymnal* (1991), at the Opry House in Nashville, Tennessee, on March 14, 1991. A dwindling brand loyalty would enjoy its final surge with the 1991 book. It might also be said that the quality of the 1991 *Baptist Hymnal* was the final point of unified pride for Southern Baptists. The immediate acceptance of that edition tipped the hymnal-in-the-pew rack "teeter-totter" back in favor of "the Baptists" in Southern Baptist congregations, and away from WORD's 1986 book. Wesley L. Forbis, who followed William J. Reynolds as head of the Southern Baptist's Church Music Department, was the editor of the new Baptist hymnal. Forbis, while earning his master's degree at Baylor University years earlier, had been an early director of the BRH Choir. The strangely close community and competitive interaction between Baylor University, the Southern Baptist Church Music Department, and WORD appears again, here in the slow pendulum swing of hymnal publication.

The 1986 WORD hymnal was not Kurt's first encounter with the birthing of a new hymnal for congregational use. His father had, in both direct and indirect measures, prepared him for the task. Ever since the applause episode at the Youth for Christ rally in Chicago, Kurt knew that his father remained mindful of Kurt's response to fame. In addition, the biblical veracity and theological moorings of Kurt's published lyrics were of equal importance to Otto. Even though the applause question had been settled, there was a continuing theological conversation between Kurt and his father concerning Kurt's lyrics. From time to time, the father would question, or the son would consult; they took turns restarting the conversation. It was respectful and good-natured, but either way, the father was instructing the son. There came a time when the weight and tenor of the conversation would find a new balance.

Otto Kaiser chaired the hymnal committee that produced *Hymns Selected and Revised in 1928, Tunes Added in 1970*, published by Believers Bookshelf of Sunbury, Pennsylvania. In actual practice, Kurt served as the music editor for this hymnal. In his words, Kurt "put music to the text, . . . and decided finally upon the music for which text . . . so it was a little bit more orderly . . . mostly like the harmonies, fixed the harmonies. And fixed how it looks, how the thing appears." When asked if he had written any of the hymn tunes, Kurt replied quickly and decisively, "Oh no, never. I just took, . . . I wasn't worthy of that."[17]

The names of the committee members are not included in this hymnal. To list names would have been to invoke the spotlight of vanity, especially because the chair of the committee and the music editor were a father and son team. Even so, there is precious recognition of Kurt in his personal name-embossed copy of the hymnal. This handwritten inscription from Kurt's father appears on the blank inside cover page:

"Sing unto the Lord. Sing
unto the Lord a new song,
and His praise in the
congregation of the saints."
(Ps. 149:1)

This advanced copy is
dedicated to you

Mr. Kurt Kaiser

for your labor of love to edit
the harmonies for the tunes used
in this hymnbook with which
you are familiar since your
childhood.

For the Hymnbook committee,
Otto Kaiser

Chicago, Ill.
May 23, 1970[18]

To have received this gift from his father must have been for Kurt a blessing of the first order and of significant depth. The embossed hymnal was a gift. But Otto's handwritten inscription was the real gift. Hear the respect and humility in "dedicated to you Mr. Kurt Kaiser." Hear the affirmation of Kurt's musical skill, commitment, and perspective in "for your labor of love." Hear the father's humility in the reference "since your childhood." Might that harkening back actually establish a new relationship . . . adult to adult? We will not put words into Otto's mouth. But we will read his words through what we have come to know of Kurt's eyes and heart. His father's signature is simply "Otto Kaiser," not "Mr. Otto Kaiser." Surely Kurt must have read the inscription as blessing, admiration as well as love, gratitude and wings.

Otto Kaiser had asked for Kurt's help in a monumental task. That help was acknowledged in humility, respect, and ink. It was a moment that echoed throughout the rest of Kurt's life. Kurt was symbolically invited to "sit with the men," something that didn't happen for him back in the Chicago Plymouth Brethren Church. It was a moment cradled in a hymnal. Otto's watchful eye over his son's theology morphed into discussions between peers. The icon and conscience of Contemporary Christian Music had received his earthly father's blessing.

There was a second hymnal project in which Kurt and his father would collaborate, editing the music and, in this case, obtaining and acknowledging copyrights. In October of 1973, Otto was one of some eighty men who met in Toronto to prepare for an expected reunion of two estranged groups of Plymouth Brethren. In St. Louis, Missouri, in February of 1974, the "Booth" brethren and the "Kelly-Continental" brethren were united in one company again. Otto recalled,

> Since we were now one company, the desire was for one hymnbook. At a brother's conference in Kenosha, I was charged to form a committee to work with the one in the United Kingdom. The task before us was much more difficult than choosing tunes, as in the former work. Editing the text of the 500 hymns chosen was a formidable undertaking. It took a great deal of correspondence with the English-speaking brethren worldwide, to have them have a part in making this new hymnbook acceptable. The Lord gave great grace and a text edition was printed in 1978.
>
> The task of choosing tunes was still before me. I asked four brothers to help me. Kurt edited the music and helped with the copyrights, etc. I enjoyed this work much, and the Lord was guiding step by step. We all use this new hymnbook, "Spiritual Songs," since 1981.[19]

While Otto's scrutiny of Kurt's work had grown into conversation between equals, Otto was still Kurt's father, free to initiate theological debate between them. Kurt's song "Bring Back the Springtime" had grown in popularity from the time it was copyrighted in 1970. It had been recorded by such notables as Anita Bryant, Wayne Newton, Ray Price, George Beverly Shea, The Hawaiians, and Tennessee Ernie Ford. Kurt also recorded "Bring Back the Springtime" twice on instrumental-only albums.[20] But when "Bring Back the Springtime" appeared in *The Hymnal for Worship & Celebration* (WORD, 1986), with the lyrics now promoted to the status of hymn text, Otto spoke up. In his copy of the commemorative edition of the new hymnal, Kurt's father wrote suggested word changes to the second stanza and the refrain, in his hand, in ink. This copy remains in Kurt's library.[21]

Even though mutual theological respect had been established, and the hymnal had been published, Kurt tried to implement his father's suggested revisions: (1) in stanza two, change "Of the streams that flowed from Calvary" to "Of the precious stream filled with your love," and (2) in the chorus, change "O return to me sweet Holy Spirit" to "O refill me now, sweet Holy Spirit." Let the reader study the nuances. Kurt was told that the corrections would appear in subsequent printings, but that never happened.

Kurt was, no doubt, pleased to have this song included in the hymnal. Yet the joy was tempered. "Bring Back the Springtime" and its "flaws" now "belonged" to the congregations. The tempering tension between joy and chagrin was keeping celebrity in check. In 2004, via Kurt Kaiser Music, Kurt "published" the corrected text of "Bring Back the Springtime" in an anthem arrangement written for the DaySpring Baptist Church choir. The suggested corrections also appear in *The New Church Hymnal*, Lexicon Music, 1976, a company owned by Ralph Carmichael.

CONCLUSION

At one of the junctures where WORD Records sensed the need to move on toward what it *might become*, Kurt Kaiser had become an icon of what WORD Records *had been*. His own success had frozen him in time, no matter his continuing talent and vision. The icon that was Kurt could not be stretched into a future where enacted principles would become even more elastic than the flexibility that he had helped bring about. Kurt Kaiser, icon and conscience of a specific and dynamic moment in the history of sacred music in America, gave everything to that time and ministry; everything, including his last ounce of influence. He gave everything to the Source of his giftedness and the Scope of his vision. His influence flourished in a particular time, and it belongs to that time, yet it shines from then to now. Forward movement may diminish the champions of its past, but it also proceeds in the glow of their contributions.

In the course of his 2008 interview with his daughter, Kris, Kurt said, "The God I know is a God of relationships and of love and fresh air." Kurt believed that breathing God's fresh air could overcome fraying in human relationships and love. Kurt breathed that air, exhaling for us God-fresh songs to sing.

Breathing God's fresh air ensures spiritual consistency, even in the midst of culturally aware creativity. For all of his giftedness and creativity, consistency was Kurt Kaiser's brilliance among us. His consistency is why we sensed that we should write of Kurt's presence among us and absence from us. Consistency at times looks like stubbornness, at times like compromise, at times like leadership. Consistency is not the death of creativity; it is the measure of one's conscience. If compromise means working in a way that complements and encourages the good work of those around you, Kurt compromised. If compromise means contributing effort toward the common good, Kurt compromised. But when compromise is dimmed to its lesser definitions—abandoning one's core values, or simply putting those values at risk—Kurt did not compromise. Whether facing the hazards of success or failure, celebrity or obscurity, influence or marginalization, Kurt pressed on. He was consistent in his convictions and commitments. His colleagues were often convicted through his moral consistency.

Kurt was consistent in the authenticity of his humanity as well. He had little patience for sloppy musicianship by professional musicians, yet admiration for the honest striving of the committed amateur. He had no patience for the arrogant. Kurt inherited but overcame prejudice against Catholics, evidenced in part by his several recordings of the Daughters of St. Paul. His bent toward allowing physical attractiveness (or lack of it) to color his first impressions of potential artists or performers—reinforced somewhat by entertainment culture—persisted but lessened over the years. Kurt Kaiser was human.

Pat was always a bit nervous about what Kurt would say when he stood before a group of people. Kurt possessed a bluntness born of an entrenched, somewhat naive, honesty. For Kurt, who heard the color of keys and chords, his artistic refinement was in singularity with his occasional social coarseness. Bad music was bad. Good music was good. Notes were sharp, flat, or in tune. Where is the offense in that? Where is the prejudice? Where is the slight? Pitch was his only perfection.

We often speak too soon and too lightly of eras at the birth or death of persons. We do so out of either admiration or disdain. Was the death of Kurt Kaiser the mourned end of an era? What of his departure from WORD? Was his pioneering work the beginning of an era? We cannot make such claims, for he was not alone at important musical times and places. But he was present, inescapably present. Kurt's presence and consistent influence mattered to those around him and with him at significant beginnings and endings. But at any time, and in any group, he was an icon of the best motivations and principles.

If Kurt's death was not the end of an era, how then shall church musicians of all skills and stations speak of the significance of his parting from us? His death was felt, reported, and noticed so far beyond his immediate family that it surely must have been an event of unusual magnitude. A life lived as committed as humanly possible to high standards in multiple, overlapping, and enriching arenas of nobility may or may not constitute an era. We may exaggerate what we see in someone like Kurt Kaiser. We may underestimate. But we cannot look away. Kurt's life compels us to know it, to learn from it, to hope that we might in some measure emulate it. We are forced to admit, again, that a life of integrity and consistency has unusual gravitas in any and every human era.

Change in church music is inevitable and constant, but it need not be a degrading of what is left behind. Kurt Kaiser was dedicated to change that flowed without ebbing, a timeless tide of quality, heritage, and biblical veracity.

It may well be that the best way to approach, embrace, and recount the life story of Kurt Kaiser would have been to do so by way of a symphony, *The Kurt Kaiser Symphony*, for first and foremost, he was a performer and composer. Perhaps that recounting will come someday. It may be that an epic poem would have been a better approach, words that do not attempt to capture and catalogue as we have done here, but, rather, to simply and profoundly point to a life that existed beyond words. Should this writer live long enough to become an actual poet, perhaps he might honor Kurt with *The Kurt Kaiser Saga*. But within these pages, a mere rhymer presents his prose in a faithful attempt to provide a prologue for future and greater scholars in their deeper telling of Kurt's life. Kurt's was a life of accessible poetry and musical improvisation that maintained the integrity of the melody. He did not attempt, in his own strength, to convince us of anything. The standards did the convincing, established the boundaries. The high standards encouraged the amateur, the skilled, and the gifted toward the full measure of their capacity.

Giving himself to these foundational standards, not as their guardian but as their prophet, gleaned for Kurt significant, unsought recognitions: National Evangelical Film Foundation Instrumental Album of the Year Award (1963); honorary Doctor of Sacred Music from Trinity College, Deerfield, Illinois (1973); Christian Artists Music Achievement Award (1984); American Society of Composers, Authors, and Publishers Lifetime Achievement Award (1992); Baylor University's W. R. White Award for Meritorious Service (1993); Gospel Music Association's Dove Award (1994); honorary Doctor of Humane Letters (LLD) from Baylor University (1995); Christian Booksellers Association Hall of Honor Award (1999); Gospel Music Association Hall of Fame (2001, along with Elvis Presley and a few others); Texas Gospel Music Hall of Fame (2007); Southern Baptist Church Music Conference Hines Sims Award (2011); Baylor University's Pro Ecclesia Medal of Service (2017). In light of such an impressive list, we might well say that Kurt Kaiser taught us how to respond to the applause at the end of our "fifteen minutes of fame."

Kurt left us with something that we feel we should explore, not because of celebrity or recognition, but because of a pulsating essence that we instinctively know is important. We leave this brief look at Kurt's life with a confession borrowed from 1 Kings 10:7, "The half has not been told."

APPENDIX

Kurt Kaiser Memorial Service
November 16, 2018
First Baptist Church, Waco, Texas

The Worship of God

In Celebration of the Life of Kurt Frederic Kaiser

    Gathering Music
        Kathy Johnson, piano
        Eugene Lavery, organ

    Seating of the Family

    A Musical Offering
        Kathy Johnson

    Call to Worship and Invocation
        (from Psalm 46)
        Eric Howell

    Hymn 345
        When Morning Gilds the Skies

    The Ministry of Silence
        (from Psalm 150)

    Reflections from the Family
        Kent Kaiser, Craig Kaiser

    Witness of Faith
        In His Love and in His Pity
        Christopher Adkins, cello
        Stephen Nielson, piano

    In Remembrance
        Terry York

    Instrumental Meditation
        Long Journey
        Christopher Adkins, Stephen Nielson

In Remembrance
    Burt Burleson

Scripture Reading
    Psalm 95:1–7
    Romans 8:31–39
        Brett Kaiser, Anne Olson

Pastoral Meditation
    Eric Howell

Congregational Response, 309
    When in Our Music God Is Glorified

A Musical Benediction
    Ken Medema

Blessing
    Eric Howell

Recessional
    There's a Sweet, Sweet Spirit in This Place
    Kathy Johnson

AFTERWORD

We are a composite of all we hear and experience. There are so many echoes in my lifetime of relationships with people and music. I find myself listening to other pianists, especially jazz pianists, who have something to say. Reflecting on imperfections in his recordings, the great Keith Jarrett said recently, "What matters is the spirit kept." I like that notion. I learn from listening and try to communicate more than just the notes. Music is born out of silence. The space before and around each note is what gives it meaning. So, I take my time and say all I need to say, with as much simplicity as I can find. Famed recording engineer Bruce Swedien once said to me, "It's not corny to begin and end in the same key."

Here are many of my favorite hymns, played with fewer notes, and dissonances that don't always resolve. You will have to resolve them yourself. These are not played as a performance, but as a reflection. Happy Listening!

Kurt Kaiser
CD Case Liner
Legacy
© 2013 Kurt Kaiser Music, Inc.
Waco, Texas

NOTES

INTRODUCTION

1. Pat remembers that when they were driving to Waco she had "two babies, and two dresses to my name." She also remembered that it took fourteen quarts of oil to get "the old Pontiac" from Chicago to Waco.
2. "Bucky" is Andrew Lance "Andy" Anderson, Pat's brother. From an interview with this writer: Kurt and Andy became good friends as well as brothers-in-law. Andy and his wife Mariejanne watched Kurt record Ernie Ford, Wayne Newton, and Burl Ives in Chicago recording sessions. Kurt would sometimes stay with the Andersons when working in Chicago.
3. Though Kurt's education is woven into the narrative of his younger years, we pause here to summarize: McPherson Grammar School, Chicago, Illinois, was just a fifteen-minute walk from his house. Lane Tech High School, Chicago, Illinois, was a large, all boys school where Kurt played cello, was a member of the Student Council, and was on the skating team. American Conservatory of Music, Hammond, Indiana, is where Kurt first studied after deciding to pursue higher education, but after two years he realized that the school's focus did not align with what he understood to be the best use of his musical talent. He transferred to Northwestern University, Evanston, Illinois. Northwestern University is where Kurt earned the bachelor's and master's degrees in music, tutored the basketball team, and conducted the men's chorus.
4. Kris Kaiser Olson interview, 2008–2009.

1 OWNING THE GIFT

1. Otto Kaiser, *Otto Kaiser: His Story*, family compiled and printed memoir (Chicago, Ill., July 2001), 61. This book, coupled with the Kris Kaiser Olson interviews, was exceedingly helpful in recounting the early Kaiser/Chicago story.
2. O. Kaiser, *Otto Kaiser: His Story*, 75.
3. It is interesting to note here that from the late 1980s through the early 1990s, Kurt produced at least six recording projects with the Daughters of St. Paul in Boston. Most of the songs were from within the Roman Catholic tradition. See the Recordings by Title section of the bibliography.
4. Martin Kaiser remembrances shared, in writing, with the author.
5. Martin Kaiser remembrances shared, in writing, with the author.
6. Walter Gast remembrances shared, in writing, with the author.
7. Walter Gast remembrances shared, in writing, with the author.

8 "Sunday Mornin'" by Kurt Kaiser, in *God's People* by Kurt Kaiser and Charles F. Brown, WORD, 1974.
9 Kris Kaiser Olson interview, 2008–2009.
10 Kris Kaiser Olson interview, 2008–2009.
11 Kris Kaiser Olson interview, 2008–2009.
12 Handwritten letter to Kurt dated September 20, 1980.
13 Phone interview with this author.
14 Kurt would later, as a college student, help edit the Christmas cantata *The First Christmas*, compiled and edited by James W. Brewer, choral arrangements by Kurt Kaiser (Billings, Mont.: Accent Music Publisher, 1955). That same year, two recordings would feature Brewer as the organist and Kurt as the pianist: Bill Carle, *Bill Carle's Favorite Gospel Songs*, and idem, *Songs from the Redemption Story* (Carletone, Bill Carle Sacred Music Foundation, Hollywood).
15 The studio was Sumet-Bernet Sound Studios, then located on Twin Hills Avenue in Dallas, Texas.
16 An interesting artifact from this Youth for Christ convention is the LP *Youth for Christ International Official Album*, choir, brass band, and musicians directed by Paul Mickelson; Kurt Kaiser, organ; Donna Maines, piano, WORD Records, 1958, recorded in the Billy Sunday Tabernacle at Winona Lake, Indiana, during the Youth for Christ International Convention, June 29–July 13, 1958.
17 Tim Kaiser phone interview with this author, February 18, 2022.
18 This event is recorded on *Preludes to Faith: Kurt Kaiser, Pianist, with the Tokyo Symphony Orchestra*, conducted by Ralph Carmichael, Sword Records, Waco, Tex., c. 1961.
19 Ralph Carmichael and Kurt Kaiser, *Tell It Like It Is: A Folk Musical for Choir and Solos*, Lexicon Music, Waco, Tex., 1969.
20 Ralph Carmichael and Kurt Kaiser, *Natural High: A Folk Musical about God's Son*, Light Records, Lexicon Music, 1970.
21 Kris Kaiser Olson interview with this author.
22 Kris Kaiser Olson interview with this author. Kent added that this gesture was something that the "now Rev. Donald Hooks and the other black teammates remember to this day."
23 *Praise the Lord: 500 Mennonite Men*, WORD Records, 1973.
24 Letter from Kurt to Kent Kaiser, July 31, 2007.
25 Craig Kaiser interview with this author.
26 O. Kaiser, *Otto Kaiser: His Story*, 33–34.
27 We step away from the pain and creativity conversation for a moment to think about this composer with perfect pitch talking about how sound *tastes*. This was not an uncommon metaphor for Kurt. In his commentary on the jacket of the album *Evie* (1974), Kurt wrote, "The tasty arrangements are by a young Swedish arranger whose name is Lennart Sjoholm. It's exciting for me to meet new Christian artists—Evie and Lennart are two for whom I predict great things." Whatever the artist's mode, when the gift is called upon to perform, it rallies all of the artist's senses, even taste, demanding that each contribute to the essential expression.
28 *Kurt Kaiser Piano: A Part of Me*, WORD Records, 1981.
29 June 8, 2021, email to the author.

30 Kurt's personal manuscript for that event.
31 Kris Kaiser Olson interview, 2008–2009.
32 Kris Kaiser Olson interview, 2008–2009.
33 *Hymns: Anita Kerr, Kurt Kaiser*, WORD Records, 1977.
34 *Keyboard Legends: Masterful Arrangements Performed by Four Renowned Pianists*, Fred Bock, Kurt Kaiser, Max Lyall, and Don Wyrtzen, WORD Music, 1996.
35 This is an echo of the line "When I rise to worlds unknown," from the third stanza of the Augustus M. Toplady hymn "Rock of Ages." In the hymn the reference is to heaven, not to the lower worlds of recording and academia.
36 By his own count, Kurt recorded sixteen solo albums at the piano (not all with WORD).
37 *Kurt Kaiser, Piano*, WORD Records, 1960.
38 Tom Bledsoe phone interview with this author, August 3, 2021. Tom's wife, Teresa, had been in the Baylor Religious Hour Choir at Baylor University and had babysat the Kaiser children.
39 *Limited Edition, The Crusade of a Lifetime: A Musical Tribute to Billy Graham*, Brentwood Music, 1996.
40 *The Addicts Sing: Nine Former Addicts*, WORD Records, no date. See below for more information about this group.
41 Kris Kaiser Olson interview, 2008–2009.
42 *Kurt Kaiser Piano: A Part of Me*, WORD Records, 1981; and *Kurt Kaiser: Oh, How He Loves You and Me*, Kurt Kaiser Music, 2005.
43 This account is based on the article "What Really Happened at Explo '72," in CRU online magazine, October 15, 2015.
44 "Improvisation on a Groove," Kurt Kaiser, unpublished cassette tape, March 21, 1997.
45 For an account of Swedien's wide reach in the highest echelons of American popular music (although Kurt is not mentioned therein), see Bruce Swedien, *Make Mine Music* (New York: Hal Leonard Books, 2009). Swedien worked with artists such as Quincy Jones, Michael Jackson, Paul McCartney, and many more.
46 *Strength for Today, Bright Hope for Tomorrow: Bill O'Brien with Kurt Kaiser at the Piano*, Kurt Kaiser Music, 1999.
47 *Just for You: A Loving Adventure with God . . . A Joyful Occasion with One Another*, by Kurt Kaiser, orchestrated by Bill Pursell, WORD Records, 1979. This recording features Dave Boyer, Amy Grant, Robert Hale, Barry McGuire, and Ken Medema as soloists. The choir is The First Baptist Church Choir, Richardson, Texas, Bill Green, Director. (This title should not be confused with the earlier album *Just for You: Song Stylings by Dick Baker*, produced by Kurt Kaiser, WORD Records, no date.)
48 Jeff McGarvin phone interview with the author, May 26, 2022.

2 WORD MUSIC AND KURT KAISER MUSIC

1 Letter, dated August 27, 1957, from Jarrell F. McCracken to Kurt Kaiser, 5811 W. Henderson St., Chicago, Illinois. The letter mentions McCracken's pleasure at meeting Kurt and Pat and says, "I am looking forward with great anticipation to working with you on many recordings in the future." A photocopy of

a letter dated September 14, 1957, from Jarrell F. McCracken to Bill Mann at First Methodist Church of Houston, Texas, references Kurt's work as choral and instrumental arranger, and producer for a recording session in Chicago on "September 23 or 24."

2 Robert Frost, "The Road Not Taken."
3 Kris Kaiser Olson interview, 2008–2009.
4 Aaron E. Sanchez, Bob Dylan's Overlooked Christian Music, *Sojourners*, September 3, 2019, https://sojo.net/articles/bob-dylans-overlooked-christian-music. Sanchez does not mention Kurt's encounter.
5 One of these concerts was recorded as *Bill Mann & Kurt Kaiser: On a Sunday Evening*, WORD Records, no date.
6 *Moments for Meditation with Bill Mann, Lyric Tenor*, WORD Records, no date, back liner notes.
7 *Bill Mann*, WORD Records, back liner, no date.
8 Not to be confused with the recording of the 1979 Kurt Kaiser musical with the same title.
9 Scallon, Rosemary, with Lucy Elphinstone, *Dana: An Autobiography* (London: Hodder and Stoughton, 1985), 142.
10 Barry Liesch. *People in the Presence of God: Models and Directions for Worship* (Grand Rapids: Zondervan, 1988), 219.
11 Kris Kaiser Olson interview, 2008–2009. Billy Crockett did make three recordings for WORD on their "Dayspring" label. Kurt was involved only as upper management at the time
12 *Ken Medema: Fork in the Road*, WORD Records, 1972.
13 Phone interview with this author, July 16, 2021.
14 "Spirit Wings," words and music by Claire Cloninger and Michael Foster, from the album *Joni Eareckson: Spirit Wings*, WORD, 1982.
15 Savage Club, Berkeley Square, London, http://www.savageclub.com.
16 Savage Club Rules as revised 8th May, 1973, "Object."
17 For a short but insightful interview with Kurt concerning this dilemma, see Carol R. Thiessen, "Kurt Kaiser Reaches for the Higher Notes," in the May 21, 1982 issue of *Christianity Today*.
18 Kris Kaiser Olson interview, 2008–2009.
19 *Celebrate Life*, youth/young adult musical, music by Buryl Red, book and lyrics by Ragan Courtney, Broadman Press, 1972.
20 The complete list of performers in this twenty-fifth anniversary collection is as follows, in order: Frank Boggs, Bill Pearce & Dick Anthony, Anita Bryant, Ralph Carmichael, The White Sisters, Ohman Brothers, Melody Four Quartet, J. T. Adams, Paul Mickelson, Lew Charles, Dale Evans & Roy Rogers, Cliff Barrows and the Gang, Alan McGill, Jack Holcomb, Burl Ives & The Korean Children's Choir, Bill Mann, Les Barnett, Old Fashioned Revival Hour Quartet, Ethel Waters, Don Hustad, Jerome Hines, Kurt Kaiser, Gloria Roe, Norma Zimmer & Jim Roberts, Bud Tutmarc, Mary Jane & Gene Gaither, Rudy Atwood, George Beverly Shea, Evie, Tom Netherton, The Hawaiians, Carol Lawrence, Larnelle Harris, The Anita Kerr Singers, Dave Boyer, Ken Medema, Honeytree, The 2nd Chapter of Acts, The Happy Goodmans, The Inspirations, The Florida Boys, and Reverend Cleavant Derricks and Family.

21 The artists, in order of appearance: Dana, Joni Eareckson Tada, Frank Boggs, Anita Kerr Singers, Robert Hale, Larnelle Harris, Anita Bryant, Dave Boyer, Bud Tutmarc, Evie.
22 Deborah Evans Price, "History of Word Entertainment," in *WORD: The Story, the Songs: Celebrating Six Decades of Hits*, WORD Music, 2011, 7–9.
23 Phone interview of Don Cason by the author, July 7, 2021.
24 Phone interview of Don Cason by the author, July 7, 2021.
25 Interview with this author, June 8, 2021.
26 This entire conversation is from the Kris Kaiser Olson interview, 2008–2009.
27 A year later, in 1986, Kurt would produce the recording *Stephen Nielson: Music of the Masters* on his Kurt Kaiser Music label.
28 Interview with this writer, September 9, 2021.
29 Son of Kurt's sister Sigrid Kaiser Schultz.
30 To "sit in" describes an outsider being invited to join a jazz artist or ensemble in the performance of a song or a session of songs.
31 Lucy Adams, "Oh How He Loves You and Me," *The Enterprise Mountaineer* (Waynesville, N.C.), March 17, 2004.
32 Timothy R. Botts, *Windsongs* (Wheaton, Ill.: Tyndale House, 1989). Pages unnumbered.
33 Titles are included in the Recordings section in the back of the book.
34 Brian Konzelman interview with this author, October 31, 2022.

3 ICON AND CONSCIENCE OF CONTEMPORARY CHRISTIAN MUSIC

1 Quoted in Mike Cosper, "Defiant Joy: Shaped by Grief, Buoyed by Faith: Bono Discusses Four Decades of Art and Activism," *Christianity Today*, December 2022, p. 37. In this article, musician Steve Taylor is described by Cosper as "an outsider's insider in CCM through the 1980s and 1990s, skirting the edges of acceptability with satirical and edgy post-punk and alternative music."
2 Swee Hong Lim and Lester Ruth, *Lovin' On Jesus: A Concise History of Contemporary Worship* (Nashville: Abingdon, 2017).
3 It is this author's opinion that Kurt would completely agree with this silent affirmation of what he professed at every opportunity, namely, that he did not start the Contemporary Christian Music genre, neither by design nor by coincidence.
4 Kris Kaiser Olson interview, 2008–2009; Kurt is speaking of *Tell It Like It Is*.
5 Composer Bob Oldenburg was the compiler and arranger of *Good News: A Christian Folk-Musical*. Other contributors included Bill Cates, Frank Hart Smith, Johnny Fullerton, Cecil McGee, and, interestingly, Billy Ray Hearn.
6 David W. Music, "Turning Points in Baptist Church Music," *Baptist History & Heritage*, vol. 52, number 3, fall 2017, pp. 65–77.
7 Ralph Carmichael, *He's Everything to Me* (Waco, Tex.: WORD Books, 1986), 145.
8 Kris Kaiser Olson interview, 2008–2009.
9 Kris Kaiser Olson interview, 2008–2009.
10 Though this conversation took place in private, those who knew them well know that Kurt had no qualms about calling Pat "Mommy" or "Baby" in any public gathering.
11 Kris Kaiser Olson interview, 2008–2009.
12 Kris Kaiser Olson interview, 2008–2009.

13   *Emmanuel: Fantasia for Violin and Orchestra*, Michael W. Davis, violin; Kurt Kaiser, composer/conductor, City of Prague Philharmonic Orchestra, Kurt Kaiser Music, 2005.
14   Kurt Kaiser and Bryan Jeffery Leech, Chancel Music (a division of WORD).
15   For a fuller account of this event see: Barry Liesch, *People in the Presence of God: Models and Directions for Worship* (Grand Rapids: Zondervan, 1988), 217–19.
16   R. Bruce Horner, "The Function of Music in the Youth for Christ Program," unpublished Master of Music Education thesis, School of Music, Indiana University, 1970, pp. 169–73.
17   Kurt is referring here to the opening, title song "Tell It Like It Is," in which he has the choir speak in rhythm for two and a half pages before they sing.
18   *Natural High: A Folk Musical about God's Son*, composed and conducted by Ralph Carmichael and Kurt Kaiser, Light Records, Lexicon Music, 1970.
19   Kris Kaiser Olson interview, 2008–2009.
20   Ralph Carmichael and Kurt Kaiser, *I'm Here, God's Here, Now We Can Start*, Lexicon Music, distributed by WORD, 1973.
21   Kurt Kaiser and Charles F. Brown, *God's People*, WORD, 1974.
22   Kurt Kaiser, *Just for You: A Loving Adventure with God . . . A Joyful Occasion with One Another*, WORD, 1979. This musical's book and recording are not to be confused with the album *Just for You: Song Stylings by Dick Baker*, produced by Kurt Kaiser at WORD nearly two decades earlier.
23   Stan Moser, *We Will Stand: The Real Story behind the Songs, Artists and Executives that Built the Contemporary Christian Music Industry* (Brentwood, Tenn.: Christian Music United, 2015), 39.
24   Charlie Peacock, *At the Crossroads: An Insider's Look at the Past, Present, and Future of Contemporary Christian Music* (Nashville: Broadman & Holman, 1999), 6.
25   With apologies for this strained reference to Frederick W. Faber's great line, ". . . we magnify His strictness with a zeal He will not own" from his hymn "There's a Wideness in God's Mercy" (1854).

4   ADOPTED SON OF WACO AND BAYLOR UNIVERSITY

1   Carl Hoover, "Art of the Rat," *Waco Tribune-Herald*, November 15, 2018, with photos by Rod Aydelotte. Photos of the artist at work were also posted on Creative Waco's blog for November 22, 2018, "Thanksgiving, a Rat, and a Waco Treasure Hunt."
2   2020 interview with Nan Rentz.
3   Letter dated October 18, 2010, addressed to Mr. and Mrs. Kurt Kaiser.
4   "The Baylor University Honorary Doctor of Humane Letters" section of *The Sesquicentennial Commencement, May Thirteenth, Nineteen Hundred and Ninety-Five*, printed program, p. 11.
5   *Sing 'n' Celebrate!* compiled by Kurt Kaiser, Sonny Salsbury, and Billy Ray Hearn, WORD, 1971. The success of this collection led to the publication of two additional collections in a series: (1) *Sing 'n' Celebrate! Volume 2*, compiled and edited by Kurt Kaiser, Sonny Salsbury, Billy Ray Hearn, Charles F. Brown, and Robert C. Black, WORD, 1975, and (2) *Everybody Sing 'n' Celebrate!* compiled by Cliff Barrows, Bruce Howe, Kurt Kaiser, and John Purifoy, Rodeheaver

Company, Sole Selling Agent: WORD, 1979. The collections in this series comprise a repository of the popular Christian songs and choruses spawned by youth musicals and related publications.

6   *Things That Endure: Kurt Kaiser & George Stokes*, Baylor Alumni Association, 2001.
7   Currently The Hymn Society of the United States and Canada.
8   It could not have been known at the time, of course, but Ken's introduction of Kurt was a harbinger of "A Song for Kurt," that he would write, record, and sing in person for Kurt at his home in Waco some six years later as Kurt neared death. The song includes the line, "I sought to be like you." Kurt again cried upon hearing a Medema song.
9   *Olde Carols Ever New*, Helen Ann Shanley, flute; Richard Shanley, clarinet; Kurt Kaiser, piano, Kurt Kaiser Music, 2015.
10 Kris Kaiser Olson interview, 2008–2009.
11 Phone interview with this author, September 8, 2021. The seminary to which Donald Bailey refers is Baylor's George W. Truett Theological Seminary, established in 1993.
12 One of those singalong recordings is *Songs of Faith for Singing and for Listening*, WoodSong, 2000. It is an excellent example of the art of collaborative piano: simple but creative hymn introductions and accompaniments.
13 *Lev Aronson Plays Cello Classics and Encores with Strings, Organ and Piano*, WORD Records, c. 1970.
14 Interview with this author and Joyce Jones, August 4, 2021.

5   A CHURCH MUSICIAN

1   Email to this author, dated July 22, 2022, First Baptist Church, Temple, Texas.
2   Kris Kaiser Olson interview, 2008–2009.
3   Kris Kaiser Olson interview, 2008–2009.
4   In fact, there were (and are) many Southern Baptist churches in Waco, Texas. First Baptist Church of Waco was also very much involved with Baylor and was the "church home" of many Baylor students and faculty. Baylor had enough Baptist students and faculty to share across the city.
5   For a clear and respectful account of William J. Reynolds' departure from the Church Music Department of the Baptist Sunday School Board, see David Music, *William J. Reynolds: Church Musician* (Macon, Ga.: Smyth & Helwys, 2013).
6   William J. Reynolds, *Songs of Glory: Stories of 300 Great Hymns and Gospel Songs* (Grand Rapids: Baker, 1990).
7   Even without Reynolds' vote, Elvis Presley was indeed voted into the Hall of Fame at this time.
8   Kris Kaiser Olson interview, 2008–2009.
9   "His Will Our Own," from *God's People* by Kurt Kaiser and Charles F. Brown, WORD, 1974.
10 "The Lord's Prayer," Albert Hay Malotte, G. Schirmer, 1935.
11 The CD case liner includes comments by Burt Burleson, former DaySpring pastor, and Eric Howell, current DaySpring pastor. This CD is not to be confused with the 2009 CD of similar title (both released by Kurt Kaiser Music) *Come*

Away: The Music of Kurt Kaiser, Jenni Till, Soprano. The shared title is from Burt Burleson's text "Come Away."

12 Interview with this author, August 2021.
13 Interview with this author, August 2021.
14 Interview with this author, August 2021. The hymn "Come Away" was recorded twice on the Kurt Kaiser Music label: in 2009 as the title song on a CD by soprano Jenni Till, and in 2017 as the title song on a CD of piano offertories by Kurt and Kathy Gladen Johnson (no lyrics). Both Burt Burleson and Eric Howell wrote short statements for the case liner of the second CD.
15 Kurt Kaiser and Charles F. Brown, *God's People*, WORD, 1974.
16 Eric Howell, from an interview with this author, and from his remarks at Kurt's memorial service, November 16, 2018.
17 Kris Kaiser Olson interview, 2008–2009.
18 Kurt Kaiser's personal copy of *Hymns Selected and Revised in 1928, Tunes Added in 1970*. The spacing reflects Kurt's father's writing.
19 Otto Kaiser, *Otto Kaiser: His Story*, compiled and printed by Richard "Dik" Kaiser, Chicago, Ill., July 2001, p. 132.
20 *Pass It On: Kurt Kaiser/Piano & Orchestra*, WORD Records, no date; *The Lord Is My Strength and My Song*, WORD Records, no date.
21 "An Evening of Worship and Celebration: Kennedy Center. Washington, D.C., July 22, 1986."

BIBLIOGRAPHY

Bishop, William Robert. *Christian Youth Musicals: 1967–1975*. Unpublished Doctor of Musical Arts dissertation, New Orleans Baptist Theological Seminary, 2015.

Bloch, Chana. *Spelling the Word: George Herbert and the Bible*. Berkeley: University of California Press, 1985.

Botts, Timothy R. *Windsongs*. Wheaton, Ill.: Tyndale House, 1989.

Bradley, Randall, ed. *A Distant Harmony: The Papers of the Hearn Symposium on Christian Music*. Waco, Tex.: Baylor University School of Music, 2003.

Carmichael, Ralph. *He's Everything to Me*. Waco, Tex.: WORD Books, 1986.

Horner, R. Bruce. *The Function of Music in the Youth for Christ Program*. Unpublished Master of Music Education thesis, Indiana University School of Music, 1970.

Kaiser, Helmuth Richard, and Nate Kaiser. *Kurt Kaiser: Sing All the Verses*. Unpublished. Produced via Shutterfly, 2020.

Kaiser, Otto. *Otto Kaiser: His Story*. Compiled and printed by Richard "Dik" Kaiser. Chicago, Ill., July 2001.

Liesch, Barry. *People in the Presence of God: Models and Directions for Worship*. Grand Rapids: Zondervan, 1988.

Lim, Swee Hong, and Lester Ruth. *Lovin' On Jesus: A Concise History of Contemporary Worship*. Nashville: Abingdon, 2017.

Moser, Stan. *We Will Stand: The Real Story behind the Songs, Artists and Executives that Built the Contemporary Christian Music Industry*. Brentwood, Tenn.: Christian Music United, 2015.

Music, David W., and Paul A. Richardson. *I Will Sing the Wondrous Story: A History of Baptist Hymnody in North America*. Macon, Ga.: Mercer University Press, 2008.

Peacock, Charlie. *At the Crossroads: An Insider's Look at the Past, Present, and Future of Contemporary Christian Music*. Nashville: Broadman & Holman, 1999.

Price, Deborah Evans. "History of Word Entertainment." In *WORD: The Story, the Songs: Celebrating Six Decades of Hits*. Songbook. Word Music, 2011.

Reynolds, William J. *Songs of Glory: Stories of 300 Great Hymns and Gospel Songs*. Grand Rapids: Baker, 1990.

Scallon, Rosemary, with Lucy Elphinstone. *Dana: An Autobiography*. London: Hodder and Stoughton, 1985.

Swedien, Bruce. *Make Mine Music*. New York: Hal Leonard Books, 2009.

HYMNALS AND SONGBOOKS (LISTED BY TITLE)

Everybody Sing 'n' Celebrate! Compiled by Cliff Barrows, Bruce Howe, Kurt Kaiser, and John Purifoy. Winona Lake, Ill.: The Rodeheaver Co.; Sole Selling Agent: WORD, 1979.

A Few Hymns and Some Spiritual Songs Selected 1856 for The Little Flock. Rev. 1881. Oak Park, Ill.: Bible Truth Publishers.

The Baptist Hymnal. Nashville, Tenn.: Convention Press, 1991.

The Hymnal for Worship & Celebration. Waco, Tex.: WORD Music, 1986.

Hymns Selected and Revised in 1928, Tunes Added in 1970. Sunbury, Pa.: Believers Bookshelf, 1970.

The New Church Hymnal. Edited by Ralph Carmichael et al. Lexicon Music, 1976.

Sing 'n' Celebrate! Compiled by Kurt Kaiser, Sonny Salsbury, and Billy Ray Hearn. Waco, Tex.: WORD, 1971.

Sing 'n' Celebrate! Volume 2. Compiled and edited by Kurt Kaiser, Sonny Salsbury, Billy Ray Hearn, Charles F. Brown, and Robert C. Black. Waco, Tex.: WORD, 1975.

CORRESPONDENCE

Anthony, Gary, to Terry York. July 22, 2022. Email describing Kurt's response to a fire at Gary's church.

Harelik, Harry I., to Mr. and Mrs. Kurt Kaiser. October 18, 2010. A thank you letter for an event held in the Kaiser home.

Hearn, Billy Ray, to Kurt Kaiser. January 26, 2006. Email regarding Billy Ray receiving an award.

Kaiser, Craig, to Kurt Kaiser. June 8, 1983. Handwritten Father's Day note.

Kaiser, Kurt, to Bethel Evangelical Free Church. Chicago, Ill. Letter. August 13, 1958.

Kaiser, Kurt, to Dr. and Mrs. L. S. Anderson. May 18, 1955. Letter. Kurt asks for Pat's parents' approval to give Pat an engagement ring for her birthday.

Kaiser, Kurt, to Kent Kaiser. July 31, 2007. Letter. Observations about their fishing trip to Alaska.

Kaiser, Kurt, to Pat Anderson. July 4 and 6, 1955. Letters. Kurt expresses his admiration for Ralph Carmichael.

Kaiser, Kurt, to Pat Anderson. July 27, 1953. Letter. Relates boating accident.

Kaiser, Kurt, to Pat Anderson. August 7, 1953. Letter. First time Kurt told Pat that he loved her.

Kaiser, Kurt, to Pat Anderson. November 11 and 28, 1953. Letters. Relate observing speaking in tongues and divine healing.

Kaiser, Otto, to Kurt Kaiser. July 31, 1975. Letter. Writing of pain in a positive sense, inspiring the song "I Am Willing, Lord."

McCracken, Jarrell F., to Bill Mann. September 14, 1957. Letter. Referencing Kurt's work as an arranger and a record producer for an upcoming recording session in Chicago.

McCracken, Jarrell F., to Kurt Kaiser. August 27, 1957. Letter. Referencing meeting Kurt and Pat. He also says that he is looking forward to many recording sessions in the future.

Name withheld by this author, to Kurt Kaiser. September 20, 1980. Letter commenting on Kurt's humble response to a standing ovation.

Prou, Xavier, to Craig Kaiser. March 5, 2019. Email response to an inquiry by Craig.

Reynolds, William J., to Kurt Kaiser. February 2, 1980. Letter responding to Kurt's recognition of Dr. Reynolds' forced retirement from the Church Music Department of the Baptist Sunday School Board.

Reynolds, William J., to Kurt Kaiser. September 5, 2001. Letter congratulating Kurt on his election to the Gospel Music Association's Hall of Fame.

WORD Entertainment to Kurt Kaiser. August 27, 1999. Letter explaining the rights to the master recording tape of *The Lost Art of Listening*.

RECORDINGS BY TITLE

The Addicts Sing: Nine Former Addicts. LP. Produced by Kurt Kaiser. WORD Records, no date.

Anita Bryant: Abide With Me. LP. WST-8532-LP. Arranged and conducted by Kurt Kaiser. WORD Records, no date.

Beautiful Savior. CD/cassette. Produced by Kurt Kaiser. Daughters of St. Paul, c. 1989.

Bill Carle: Songs from the Redemption Story. LP. Kurt Kaiser, pianist; Jim Brewer, organist. Carletone. Bill Carle Sacred Music Foundation. Hollywood, c. 1953.

Bill Carle: Songs from the Word with the Kurt Kaiser Orchestra. LP. WST-8039-LP. WORD Records, c. 1960.

Bill Carle's Favorite Gospel Songs. LP. Kurt Kaiser, pianist; Jim Brewer, organist. Carletone. Bill Carle Sacred Music Foundation. Hollywood, c. 1953.

Bill Mann. LP. Arranged, directed, and produced by Kurt Kaiser. WST-8047-LP. WORD Records, c. 1960.

Bill Mann: Music in the Air. LP. Earl Backus, guitarist. Musical arrangements by Kurt Kaiser. WST-8086-LP. WORD Records, 1961.

Bill Mann & Kurt Kaiser: On a Sunday Evening. LP. WST-8407-LP. WORD Records, no date.

Burl Ives: How Great Thou Art. Arranged and conducted by Kurt Kaiser. WST-8537-LP. WORD Records, no date.

Burl Ives: Shall We Gather at the River? LP. Arranged and conducted by Kurt Kaiser. WST-8339-LP. WORD Records, no date.
Burl Ives and the World Vision Korean Orphan Choir Sing of Faith and Joy. LP. Produced by Kurt Kaiser. W-3259-LP. WORD Records, no date.
The Cambridge Singers Directed by John Rutter: Volume II, The Heritage of English Church Music. LP. SPCN 7-01-893410-9. WORD Records, 1985.
Canticles for Brass: King's Brass. LP. Produced by Kurt Kaiser. 7-01-896510-1. WORD Records, 1985.
Carol Lawrence: New Friends. LP. Produced by Kurt Kaiser. WST-8689-LP. WORD Records, 1975.
Carol Lawrence: Tell All the World about Love. LP. Kurt Kaiser, Executive Producer. WORD Records, 1977.
Cliff Barrows and the Gang: Along the Trail. LP. WORD Records, 1967.
Cliff Barrows Now! With the Kurt Kaiser Singers. LP. WST-8500-LP. WORD Records, no date.
Come Away: The Music of Kurt Kaiser, Jenni Till, Soprano. CD. Kurt Kaiser Music, 2009.
Come Away: Offertories by Kurt Kaiser & Kathy Johnson. CD. Kurt Kaiser Music, 2017.
Dana: Let There Be Love. LP. SPCN 7-01-887910-8. WORD Records, 1984.
Dana: Totally Yours. LP. WSB-8850. WORD Records, 1981.
Dana Stephenson: In God's Time. CD. Kurt Kaiser Music, 2002.
A Decade of Dedication: 10th Anniversary Album. LP. WORD Records, 1961.
Emmanuel: Fantasia for Violin and Orchestra. CD. Michael W. Davis, violin; Kurt Kaiser, composer/conductor. City of Prague Philharmonic Orchestra. Kurt Kaiser Music, 2005.
Ethel Waters Reminisces: With Reginald Beane at the Piano. LP. Produced by Kurt Kaiser. WORD Records, no date.
Evie. LP. WST-8628-LP. WORD Records, 1974.
Evie: Gentle Moments. WST-8714. WORD, 1976.
Evie Again. LP. WST-8642-LP. WORD, 1975.
Fairest Lord Jesus: The Baylor University A Cappella Choir. LP. Produced by Kurt Kaiser. Conducted by Hugh Sanders. Piano: Stephen Nielson. Hymn settings: Fred Bock, Tom Fettke, Clare Fischer, Kurt Kaiser, and Neil Richardson. 7-01-900610-8. WORD Records, 1986.
George Beverly Shea: Angels Shall Keep Thee. LP. Title song by Kurt Kaiser. WORD Records, 1976.
George Beverly Shea: Amazing Grace How Sweet the Sound: Beloved Hymns and Gospel Songs. CD. Arranged by Kurt Kaiser. KNB Music, 2004.
George Beverly Shea: Moments, Volume 1. CD. Arranged by Kurt Kaiser. Star Song, 1996.
George Beverly Shea: Tender Moments, Volume 1: Echoes of My Soul. CD. Arranged by Kurt Kaiser. KNB Music, 1997.

George Beverly Shea: The Longer I Serve Him. LP. Coproduced by Arthur Smith and Kurt Kaiser. Arrangements by Kurt Kaiser and Bill Purcell. WORD Records, 1975.

God's People. LP. Kurt Kaiser and Charles F. Brown. WSB-8728. WORD Records, 1974.

Go Tell It On the Mountain: Bill Mann with the Concert Orchestra of Stockholm. LP. Kurt Kaiser arrangements. W-3321-LP. WORD Records, c. 1965. Includes Kurt Kaiser's setting of "Blessed Assurance."

Hale & Wilder: Shenandoah. LP. Conducted by Kurt Kaiser. WORD Records, 1978.

Hallelujah Jubilee: The London Emmanuel Choir. LP. Arranged and produced by Kurt Kaiser. WST 9576. WORD Records, 1977.

Handel's Messiah: Recorded by Eastman Chorale and Philharmonia. Multiple cassettes. Eastman School of Music, University of Rochester, Alfred Mann edition. Conducted by Donald Neuen. Executive Producer: Kurt Kaiser. SPCN 7-01-892950-4. WORD Records, 1984.

Handmaiden of the Lord: Songs of Mary. CD/cassette. Produced by Kurt Kaiser. Daughters of St. Paul, 1988.

Handmaiden of the Lord: Songs of Mary, Volume 2. CD/cassette. Produced by Kurt Kaiser. Daughters of St. Paul, 1991.

An Hour with Kurt Kaiser. LP. Word Radio Special. RSA 30. Produced and hosted by Rich Germaine. WORD Records, 1981.

How Sweet the Sound: The Baylor University Chamber Singers. LP. WSB 8868. WORD Records, 1981.

Hymns: Anita Kerr, Kurt Kaiser. LP. WST-8692. WORD Records, 1977.

Hymns: Christopher Adkins, Cello, Stephen Nielson, Piano. CD. Settings by Kurt Kaiser. Kurt Kaiser Music, 2006.

Hymns of Prayer: Inspiring Orchestral Arrangements by Kurt Kaiser. LP. W-3327-LP. WORD Records, c. 1961.

I'm Here, God's Here, Now We Can Start. Ralph Carmichael and Kurt Kaiser. LS-5624. Lexicon Music, 1973.

Improvisation on a Groove. Unpublished cassette. March 21, 1997.

In Heavenly Love Abiding. Hymn Settings and Producer: Kurt Kaiser. Cello: Anne Martindale Williams. Pianist: Stephen Nielson. LP. SPCN 7-01-897310-4. WORD Records, 1985 / CD. 5011CD. Kurt Kaiser Music, 1985.

In His Love: Robert Hale and Dean Wilder. LP. Produced by Kurt Kaiser. WSB-8888. WORD Records, 1982.

Jim Roberts: How Great Thou Art. LP. With the Stockholm Concert Orchestra. Conducted by Kurt Kaiser. WST-8426-LP. WORD Records, c. 1977.

Jim Roberts and Norma Zimmer: Whispering Hope. LP. Arrangements by Kurt Kaiser. Orchestra conducted by Kurt Kaiser. WST 8364-LP. WORD Records, no date.

Just for You: Song Stylings by Dick Baker. LP. Produced by Kurt Kaiser. W-3189-LP. WORD Records, no date.
Joni Eareckson: Joni's Song. LP. WSB-8856. WORD, 1981.
Joni Eareckson: Spirit Wings. LP. WSB-8878. WORD, 1982.
Just a Little Talk with Ethel. Ethel Waters. LP. Produced by Kurt Kaiser. WORD Records, 1977.
Just for You: A Loving Adventure with God . . . A Joyful Occasion with One Another. LP. Kurt Kaiser. Orchestrated by Bill Pursell. WSB-8728. WORD Records, 1979.
Kaiser, Otto, and Elisabeth Kaiser. Reading Scripture and singing hymns. Produced by Kurt Kaiser. Cassette, undated and untitled.
Ken Medema: Fork in the Road. LP. WST-8567-LP. WORD Records, 1972.
Keyboard Legends: Masterful Arrangements Performed by Four Renowned Pianists. CD and keyboard book. Pianists: Fred Bock, Kurt Kaiser, Max Lyall, and Don Wyrtzen. WORD Music, 1996.
The Korean Children's Choir: To the World with Love. LP. Arranged by Kurt Kaiser. WST-8523-LP STEREO. WORD Records, 1972.
Kurt Kaiser: The Lost Art of Listening. CD. Kurt Kaiser Music, 1995.
Kurt Kaiser: Oh, How He Loves You and Me. CD. Kurt Kaiser Music, 2005.
Kurt Kaiser Piano: A Part of Me. LP. WORD Records, 1981.
Kurt Kaiser, Piano. LP. WORD Records, 1960.
Kurt Kaiser: Psalms, Hymns, and Spiritual Songs. CD. The Sparrow Corporation, 1993.
Ladies of Song: The Soul of Gospel Music. Margaret Aikens, Celeste Scott, and Robbie Preston. Produced by Kurt Kaiser. Word Records, no date.
Legacy. CD. 5020/21. Kurt Kaiser Music, 2013.
Lev Aronson Plays Cello Classics and Encores with Strings, Organ and Piano. LP. Produced by Kurt Kaiser. WST-8528-LP. WORD Records, c. 1970.
Limited Edition, The Crusade of a Lifetime: A Musical Tribute to Billy Graham. LP/CD. Brentwood Music, 1996.
The Lord Is My Strength and My Song. LP. WORD Records, no date.
Love Is Born: Favorite Christmas Carols from Around the World. CD/cassette. Produced by Kurt Kaiser. Daughters of St. Paul, 1992.
Master Designer: Kurt Kaiser at the Piano with Orchestra. LP. WST-8322-LP. WORD Records, no date.
Moments for Meditation with Bill Mann, Lyric Tenor. LP. Arrangements by Kurt Kaiser. W3033-LP. WORD Records, no date.
Music for Brass and Organ: Diane Bish at the Ruffatti Organ. LP. Produced and conducted by Kurt Kaiser. 7018908108. WORD Records, 1983.
Music from a Royal Wedding: Diane Bish at the Ruffatti Organ. LP. WSB-8869. WORD Music, 1981.

A Musical Tribute to Kurt Kaiser. Cassette. Dana, Joni Eareckson Tada, Frank Boggs, Anita Kerr Singers, Robert Hale, Larnelle Harris, Anita Bryant, Dave Boyer, Bud Tutmarc, Evie. 7-01-894250-0. WORD, 1985.
Myrtle Hall, Thank You, Lord. LP. Conducted and produced by Kurt Kaiser. WORD Records, 1977.
Natural High: A Folk Musical about God's Son. Composed and conducted by Ralph Carmichael and Kurt Kaiser. Light Records, Lexicon Music, 1970.
Olde Carols Ever New. CD. Helen Ann Shanley, flute; Richard Shanley, clarinet; Kurt Kaiser, piano. KKM 5022. Kurt Kaiser Music, 2015.
Organ Solos from "Tell It Like It Is": Played by Clare Fischer. LP. LS-5596-LP. Light Records, Lexicon Music, 1972.
Parkening Plays Bach: Christopher Parkening. LP. 7-01-890410-2. WORD Records, 1984.
Pass It On: Kurt Kaiser/Piano & Orchestra. LP. WORD Records, no date.
Praise the Lord: 500 Mennonite Men. LP. WST-8602-LP. WORD Records, 1973.
Preludes to Faith: Kurt Kaiser, Pianist, with the Tokyo Symphony Orchestra. LP. Conducted by Ralph Carmichael. SS-2400-LP. Sword Records, Waco, Tex., c. 1961.
Ray Price: This Time Lord. LP. Myrrh/WORD Records, 1974. Includes Kurt Kaiser's "Bring Back the Springtime."
Robert Hale & Dean Wilder: Break Forth and Sing. LP. Produced by Kurt Kaiser. WORD Records, 1977.
Seasonings: Spring. CD. Kurt Kaiser and Brian Konzelman. KNB Music, 1993.
Sing and Be Not Silent: Psalms in Song. CD/cassette. Produced by Kurt Kaiser. Daughters of St. Paul, 1990.
Sing 'n' Celebrate: A Double Album Singalong. LP. Directed by Kurt Kaiser. WORD Records, 1972.
Sing 'n' Celebrate, Volume 2: A Double Album Singalong. LP. Directed by Kurt Kaiser. WORD Records, 1973.
Songs of Faith for Singing and for Listening. CD. Kurt Kaiser, accompanist. WoodSong, 2000.
Stephen Nielson: Music of the Masters. CD. Produced by Kurt Kaiser. Kurt Kaiser Music, 1986.
Strength for Today, Bright Hope for Tomorrow: Bill O'Brien with Kurt Kaiser at the Piano. CD. Engineer: Bruce Swedien. Kurt Kaiser Music, 1999.
Tell It Like It Is: A Folk Musical. LP. Ralph Carmichael and Kurt Kaiser. LS-5512. Lexicon Music; distributed by WORD, 1969.
Tennessee Ernie Ford and The Jordanaires: Swing Wide Your Golden Gate. LP. Produced by Kurt Kaiser. WORD Records, 1978.
Things That Endure: Kurt Kaiser & George Stokes. CD. Produced by Kurt Kaiser Music. Baylor Alumni Association, 2001.

Wayne Newton: Only Believe. LP. Arranged and conducted by Kurt Kaiser. WST-8586-LP. WORD Records. 1972.
Windsongs. VHS video. Musical arrangements by Kurt Kaiser. Tyndale House, 1989.
The Wonder of Christmas. CD/cassette. Produced by Kurt Kaiser. Daughters of St. Paul, 1988.
Word 1951–1976: Twenty-Five Years on the Growing Edge of Faith. LP. Records 1–3, SPL-127-129. WORD Records, 1976.
The World Vision Korean Orphan Choir in a Concert of Christmas Music. LP. Arranged and produced by Kurt Kaiser. W-3196-LP. WORD Records, no date.
World Vision Korean Children's Choir: Ring of Happiness. LP. Arranged by Kurt Kaiser. WST-8451-LP. WORD Records, no date.
You Are Special. Cassette. Lyrics by Bob Woolley. Music by Kurt Kaiser. 4196-84. Van Ness Press/Genevox Music Group, 1989.
Youth for Christ International Official Album. LP. Choir, brass band, and musicians directed by Paul Mickelson. Accompanists: Kurt Kaiser, organ; Donna Maines, piano. W-3055-LP. WORD Records, 1958.

CHORAL SCORES

Carmichael, Ralph, and Kurt Kaiser. *I'm Here, God's Here, Now We Can Start.* #37652. Lexicon Music; distributed by WORD, 1973.
Carmichael, Ralph, and Kurt Kaiser. *Natural High: A Folk Musical about God's Son for Youth Choir and Soloists.* #37507. Lexicon Music; distributed by WORD, 1970.
Carmichael, Ralph, and Kurt Kaiser. *Tell It Like It Is: A Folk Musical for Choir and Solos.* Sole Selling Agent: Sacred Songs. Lexicon Music, 1969.
Kaiser, Kurt. *The First Christmas.* Adult choir musical. Compiled and edited by James W. Brewer. Choral arrangements by Kurt Kaiser. Billings, Mont.: Accent Music, 1955.
———. *The First Christmas.* Revised edition. Compiled and edited by James W. Brewer. Choral arrangements by Kurt Kaiser. Production notes by Robert A. Dahlstrom. Minneapolis: Accent Music, no date.
———. *Just for You.* Adult choir musical. #37901. WORD, 1979.
Kaiser, Kurt, and Bryan Jeffery Leech. *The Pursuit of Excellence: The Way Out of Mediocrity.* Adult choir musical. #3010087012. Waco, Tex.: Chancel Music, a division of WORD, 1984.
Kaiser, Kurt, and Burt Burleson. "River Song." Anthem. Kurt Kaiser Music, 1997.
Kaiser, Kurt, and Charles F. Brown. *God's People.* Adult choir musical. #37684. WORD, 1974.
Kaiser, Kurt, and Wesley L. Forbis. "Passage." Anthem. AMP 0468. Houston, Tex.: Alliance Music Publications, 2002.

Malotte, Albert Hay. "The Lord's Prayer." Solo score. New York: G. Schirmer, 1935.
Purifoy, John, arranger. "Oh, How He Loves You and Me (with 'Jesus, Lover of My Soul')." Choral anthem. #00121725. Brookfield Press/Hal Leonard Press, 1975.
Red, Buryl, and Ragan Courtney. *Celebrate Life*. Youth/young adult musical. Broadman Press, 1972.
Woolley, Bob, and Kurt Kaiser. *You Are Special*. Senior adult musical. 4150-28. Van Ness Press/Genevox Music Group, 1989.

NEWSPAPERS AND PERIODICALS

Adams, Lucy. "Oh, How He Loves You and Me." *The Enterprise Mountaineer*, Waynesville, N.C. March 17, 2004.
Carle-Tones (promotional newspaper). Hollywood, Calif. Vol. 1, no. 1, October 1953.
Child Evangelism. Child Evangelism Fellowship. Vol. 22, no. 8, August 1963.
Christian Reflection: A Series in Faith and Ethics. The Center for Christian Ethics at Baylor University, 2009, 2015, 2016.
Cosper, Mike. "Defiant Joy: Shaped by Grief, Buoyed by Faith, Bono Discusses Four Decades of Art and Activism." *Christianity Today*, December 2022, p. 37.
Darden, Robert. "Tell It Like It Is: An Afternoon with Waco's Most Beloved Musician." *WACOAN: Waco's City Magazine*, July 2008, pp. 78, 88–90.
Greene, Richard S. "George Beverly Shea Sings Out at 69." *Chattanooga News-Free Press*, Chattanooga, Tenn. Photos by Alan Vandergriff. September 17, 1978. Page C3.
Hoover, Carl. "Art of the Rat." *Waco Tribune-Herald*, Waco, Tex. Photos by Rod Aydelotte. November 15, 2018. Page 1A.
———. "Composer's Work Helped Shape Worship Music." *Waco Tribune-Herald*, Waco, Tex. Photo by Rod Aydelotte. November 13, 2018. Page 1A.
———. Obituary of Kurt Frederic Kaiser. *Waco Tribune-Herald*, Waco, Tex. November 15, 2018. Page 4A.
Music, David W. "Turning Points in Baptist Church Music." *Baptist History & Heritage*. Vol. 52, no. 3, fall 2017, pp. 65–77.
Olson, Kay. "Letter from Sweden." *Waco Today*, January 2000, p. 84.
Sanchez, Aaron E. "Bob Dylan's Overlooked Christian Music." *Sojourners*, September 3, 2019. https://sojo.net/articles/bob-dylans-overlooked-christian-music.
Thiessen, Carol R. "Kurt Kaiser Reaches for the Higher Notes." *Christianity Today*, May 21, 1982, pp. 40–41.
"What Really Happened at Explo '72." CRU online, October 15, 2015. https://cru.org/us/en/about/what-we-do/what-really-happened-at-explo-72.html.

INDEX

Addicts, The, 48, 48n40, 63, 108
Adkins, Christopher, 38, 87, 91, 169
American Conservatory of Music, Hammond, Indiana, 7n3
Anderson, Andrew Lance "Andy," 5n2
Anderson, L. S., Dr., 4–6, 32
Anderson, Patricia: see Kaiser, Pat
Anderson, Sue (McGarvin), 4, 5
Anthony, Gary, 145

Bailey, Donald, 32, 140, 141n11
Baker, Dick, 53n47, 62, 118n22
Baptist Hymnal, The, 1991, 159
Baptist Sunday School Board, 101, 104–5, 133, 149, 150n5
Barrows, Cliff, 27, 45, 67, 72, 83n20, 132, 133n5
Bateman, Piers, xvi, 84
Baylor Religious Hour Choir (BRH), 45n38, 62, 124, 132–33, 141, 148, 154, 159
Baylor University, 1–3, 25, 27, 30–31, 32, 45, 45n38, 62, 75, 77, 78, 96, 97, 105, 106, 108–9, 113, 116, 124, 127–30, 131–42, 132n4, 135n6, 141n11, 148–49, 149n4, 154–56, 157, 159, 167
Baylor University, School of Music, xvi, 2, 106, 132, 136, 154
Bethel Community Church (Bethel Free Church), Chicago, 24, 43, 60–61, 146–47
Billy Graham Association, 45, 72
Billy Graham Crusade, 27, 44–45, 66, 109, 132, 139
Bish, Diane, 75–76
Blankenship, Mark, 68
Bledsoe, Tom, 44–45, 45n38
Blessed Assurance, 61–62
Blue Rock Artist Ranch & Studio, Wimberly, Texas, 97, 153
Bock, Fred, 42n34, 43, 77–78, 82
Bond, Fiona, 128
Boone, Pat, 64
Bradley, Randall, 136
Bratcher, Lydia, 135
Bring Back the Springtime, 39, 83, 161–62
Brown, Charles F. "Charlie," 17n8, 118, 118n21, 133n5, 134, 141, 148, 152n9, 157n15
Bryant, Anita, 64, 83n20, 84n21, 85, 161
Burleson, Burt, 32, 135–36, 138, 153, 153n11, 156–57, 157n14, 170

Campus Crusade for Christ, 51, 99–100
Carl, Anthony, 138
Carle, Bill, 5, 7, 22, 22n14, 23, 43, 46–48, 82
Carmichael, Ralph, 24, 26, 26n18, 27n19, 27n20, 45, 47–48, 49, 53, 71, 82, 83n20, 85, 89, 90, 103, 105, 107, 107n7, 113–14, 114n18, 116, 116n20, 121, 132, 136–37, 162
Cason, Don, 85–86, 177n23, 177n24
Celebrate Life, 80, 80n19
Christian Booksellers Association, 111, 167
Church of the Air, Billings, Montana, 5, 21, 46, 146
Clawson, Cynthia, 59

Colón, Carlos, 155, 156
Courtney, Ragan, 80, 115, 176n19
Creative Waco, 128, 128n1
Crockett, Billy, 68, 95, 97, 153

Damascus Christian Church, Bronx, New York, 63
Daughters of St. Paul, The, 166, 13n3
DaySpring Baptist Church, Waco, Texas, 9, 118, 127, 135, 151–58, 153n11, 162
Dove Award, 87, 89–90, 167
Dylan, Bob, 59, 59n4, 65

Elliot, Jim, 22, 70
Estes Park, Colorado, 86
Evans, Dale, 28, 64, 83n20
EXPLO '72, 51, 51n43

Fettke, Tom, 77–78
First Baptist Church, Waco, Texas, xvi, 44, 120, 132, 149n4, 169
Fischer, Clare, 53, 77–78
Forbis, Wesley L., 159
Ford, "Tennessee" Ernie, 13n2, 64, 85, 161
Fork in the Road, 70, 70n12

Gast, Paul, 15
Gast, Walter "Wally," 15, 15n6, 15n7
Glorieta Baptist Assembly, 32
God's People, 17, 17n8, 118, 118n21, 141, 152n9, 157, 157n15
Good News, 101, 104–6, 105n5, 108

Hale, Robert, 53, 53n47, 64, 75, 84n21, 119
Hall, Myrtle, 67–68
Halverson, Dick, 24
Hayes, Mark, 82
He Careth for You, 36, 64, 119, 120
Hearn, Billy Ray, 82, 89–90, 96, 105n5, 107, 121, 133, 133n5, 136, 137
Hearn Symposium, 136–37
Heyde, Stephen, 130
Hill, Dennis, xvi, 84
Hines, Jerome, 65, 83n20
His Will Our Own, 36, 68, 118, 152n9

Howe, Bruce, 84, 133n5
Horan, Dr. Leta, 134
Howell, Eric, 153n11, 157, 157n14, 158n16, 169–70
Hustad, Donald "Don," 44, 66, 83n20
Hymnal for Worship & Celebration, The, WORD Music, 1986, 39, 158–59
Hymns: Anita Kerr, Kurt Kaiser, 42, 42n33
Hymns of Prayer: Inspiring Orchestral Arrangements by Kurt Kaiser, 43

I Am Willing, Lord, 35–36
I'm Here, God's Here, Now We Can Start, 116–19, 116n20
In His Love, and In His Pity, 75, 91, 119, 169
Ives, Burl, 13n2, 64–65, 83n20, 85

Jackson, Cy, 57, 66
Johnson, Kathy Gladen, 153, 169–70, 157n14
Jones, Joyce, 141, 142n14
Just for You, Dick Baker, 62, 53n47, 118n22
Just for You, Kurt Kaiser, 53, 53n47, 75, 91, 118–19, 118n22

Kaiser, Craig, 24–31, 31n25, 169
Kaiser, Elisabeth, 11–14, 17, 23, 34
Kaiser, Helmuth Richard "Dik," 12, 13, 16, 19–21, 23, 161n19
Kaiser, Kent, 3, 24, 25, 27, 29–31, 30n22, 30n24, 169
Kaiser, Kurt: *A Part of Me*, 35, 35n28, 38, 51, 51n42
Kaiser, Martin Siegfried, 13, 15n4, 15n5, 16, 23
Kaiser, Otto, 11–13, 12n1, 13n2, 16, 20, 23, 33–35, 33n26, 159–62, 161n19
Kaiser, Pat (née Anderson), ix, xi, xv, 3–7, 3n1, 5n2, 22–29, 31–32, 35, 43, 46–48, 57n1, 62, 64, 71–73, 80, 85, 90, 109, 109n10, 127–30, 146, 147–48, 151, 155, 156, 166

Kaiser, Sigrid Friede, 12, 13, 16, 23, 91n29
Kaiser, Tim, 24, 25–28, 26n17, 31
Karlsson, Evie (Tornquist), 27, 35n27, 64, 71–72, 77, 83–85, 83n20, 84n21, 92–93
KDUR radio station, Durango, Colorado, xv, 54
Kerr, Anita, 42, 42n33, 64, 83n20, 84n21
Keyboard Legends, 42, 42n34
KGHL radio station, Billings, Montana, 22
KNB recording company, 96
Konzelman, Brian, 96, 97n34
Korean Children's Choir (Korean Orphan Choir), 63–65, 83n20
Kruschwitz, Robert, 137
Kurt Kaiser Music, Inc., 95, 171
Kurt Kaiser Singers, 45, 116
KWBU radio station, Waco, Texas, xv, 140

Ladies of Song: The Soul of Gospel Music, 62
Laity Lodge, 97
Lane Tech High School, Chicago, 13n3, 18, 21
Lawrence, Carol, 31, 64, 66, 83n20, 85
Lim, Swee Hong, 99, 99n2
Long Journey, 38, 91, 169
Lovelace, Wendell P., 19
Lyall, Max, 42n34, 43

Mann, Alfred, 76
Mann, Bill, 28, 57n1, 58, 60–62, 60n5, 60n6, 61n7, 82, 83n20
Master Designer, 44, 100
McCracken, Jarrell, 2, 57–60, 57n1, 62, 64, 70, 79, 82, 102, 116, 148
McGarvin, Jeff, xv, 54, 54n58
McLennan Community College (MCC), 96, 130–31
McPherson Grammar School, Chicago, 7n3, 17
Medallion Series, 74–75, 78, 85, 88

Medema, Ken, 53n47, 68, 70, 70n12, 71, 82, 83n20, 84, 85, 119, 138–39, 139n8, 170
Mickelson, Paul, 24n16, 44, 57, 59, 83n20
Moody Bible Institute, Chicago, 19, 52
Montana, Billings, 5, 20–22, 22n14, 46, 70, 146
Montana Gospel Crusade, 21
Moser, Stan, 84, 121, 121n23
Music, David, 106–7, 150n5

Natural High, A Folk Musical, 27, 27n20, 79n18, 114, 116–18
Neuen, Donald, 76
Newton, Wayne, 5n2, 65, 85, 161
Nielson, Stephen, 38, 75, 77–78, 87–89, 89n27, 91, 169
Nolte, Ewald, 7
Northwestern University, 3, 4, 7, 24, 47, 58, 60, 61, 135, 146, 173, 173n3

Oasis: A Gathering of Well-Seasoned Souls, 138
O'Brien, Bill, 52, 52n46
Oh, How He Loves You and Me, xv, 23, 36, 50, 51, 51n42, 71, 80, 83, 86, 91–94, 93n31, 100, 102, 109, 122, 136, 142, 150, 151, 152
Oldenburg, Bob, 105–6, 105n5
Olson, Kris (née Kaiser), ix, 3, 8n4, 12n1, 17n9, 18n10, 18n11, 24–25, 27–29, 28n21, 30n22, 39, 40n31, 40n32, 48n41, 58n3, 68, 68n11, 79n18, 87n26, 101n4, 107–9, 108n8, 108n9, 109n11, 110n12, 114n19, 127, 140, 141n10, 146, 148n2, 148n3, 152n8, 155, 160n17, 165
Owens, Ron and Patricia, 70

Palermo Brothers, the, 71
Palermo, Louie, 71
Palermo, Phil, 71
Parkening, Christopher, 76
Peacock, Charlie, 121, 122n24
Pearce, Bill, 82, 83n20
Pierce, Bob, 24, 26, 43, 47, 57, 146

Plymouth Brethren Church, 3, 17, 148, 152, 161
Porter, Euell, 148
Preston, Billy Lee, 62
Prou, Xavier "Blek le Rat," 128–30
Purcell, William "Bill," 49, 64
Purifoy, John, xvi, 82, 84, 133n5, 148

Raymer, Elwyn, 104, 121
Red, Buryl, 68, 80n19, 82
Reynolds, William J. "Bill," 150–51, 150n5, 159
Richardson, Neil, 77–78
Riversong, 32
Roberts, Jim, 28, 67, 83n20
Rocky Mountain College, 21
Rogers, Roy, 28, 65, 83n20
Ruth, Lester, 99–100, 99n2
Rutter, John, 77

Sacred Records, 71
Sanders, Hugh, 77
Savage Club, The, 73, 73n15, 73n16
Scallon, Rosemary Brown "Dana," 64, 64n9, 75, 84n21
Schultz, Chad, 38, 91
Seabough, Ed, 68
Seventh & James Baptist Church, Waco, 2, 3, 27, 28, 105, 108, 111, 118, 127, 132, 133–34, 147–49, 151, 154, 155, 156
Shea, George Beverly "Bev," xvi, 31, 45, 71, 83–84, 83n20, 85, 97, 161
Smoak, Merril, 136
Southern Baptist Convention, 2, 62, 101, 103, 132, 133, 149, 150
Spirit Wings, 72, 73n14
Stanton, Tom, 86
Stephenson, Dana, 95–96
Sterling, Robert, 44, 82, 90–91
Stokes, George, 31, 135, 135n6
Swedien, Bruce, 52–53, 52n45, 67, 68, 120, 171

Tada, Joni Eareckson, 72–73, 73n14, 77, 84n21, 86

Tell It Like It Is, 25, 27, 27n19, 45, 48, 49, 53, 79, 89, 100–105, 101n4, 107–14, 114n17, 116–18, 124, 128, 132–33, 141
That's for Me, 49, 100
Thrift, Susan, 157
Tokyo Crusade, 26
Traveling Mercies, 95–97

Vatican II, 3–4, 8, 106, 115

Waco Symphony Orchestra, 127, 130
Waco Tribune-Herald newspaper, 8, 127, 128, 128n1
Waters, Ethel, 49, 64, 66, 83n20
Wheaton College, 7, 22
Wilder, Dean, 53, 64, 75
Williams, Anne Martindale, 77, 88
Windsongs, 94, 94n32
Winona Lake, Indiana, 24, 45, 47–48, 73n16, 111
WMBI radio station, Chicago, xv, 19, 22, 35, 45, 52
Woolley, Bob, 120
WORD, Inc., 2, 8, 17n8, 24n16, 27, 30n23, 32, 35, 35n28, 39, 42–44, 42n33, 42n34, 43n36, 43n37, 47, 48n40, 51n42, 53n47, 57–91, 60n5, 60n6, 61n7, 70n12, 73n14, 85n22, 95–96, 101–4, 106, 107, 107n7, 111n14, 116, 116n20, 118, 118n21, 118n22, 121, 132, 133–34, 133n5, 136, 141, 141n13, 148–50, 152, 152n9, 157n15, 158–59, 161n20, 162, 165, 166
World Vision International, 24, 26, 43, 47, 57, 63, 65
Wyoming, Worland, 4, 5, 7, 22, 23, 24, 30, 32, 46
Wyrtzen, Don, xvi, 42n34, 43

Young, Robert H., 1–3, 75, 140–41
Youth For Christ, 5, 20, 24, 24n16, 47, 59, 71, 100, 111–12, 114n16, 159

Zimmer, Norma, 28, 67, 83n20

www.ingramcontent.com/pod-product-compliance
Lightning Source LLC
Chambersburg PA
CBHW061246230426
43662CB00021B/2447